THE POLITICAL SUBJECT

Essays on the Self from Art, Politics and Science

D1167179

Lawrence & Wishart Limited
99a Wallis Road
London E9 5LN

Website Address: www.l-w-bks.co.uk

First published 2000

Copyright © Lawrence & Wishart 2000
Individual articles copyright the author

The author has asserted her right under the
Copyright, Designs and Patents Act, 1988, to be
identified as author of this work.

All rights reserved. Apart from fair dealing for the
purpose of private study, research, criticism or review,
no part of this publication may be reproduced, stored
in a retrieval system, or transmitted, in any form or
by any means, electronic, electrical, chemical, mechanical, optical, photocopying, recording or otherwise,
without the prior permission of the copyright owner.

British Library Cataloguing in Publication data.
A catalogue record for this book is available from
the British Library.

ISBN 0 85315 914 9

Typeset in Liverpool by Derek Doyle & Associates,
Printed and bound in Great Britain by
Redwood Books, Trowbridge.

THE POLITICAL SUBJECT

Essays on the Self from Art, Politics and Science

Edited by
Wendy Wheeler

Lawrence & Wishart
LONDON

Contents

Introduction:
The technological dream of order?
Or politics otherwise?

Despite contemporary cries of 'modernise or die' from businesspeople, politicians and managers, the era of political modernity – with its relatively stable ideologies and dreams of order – is over. Modernity, having dissolved the original forms of the binding ties of tradition and religion, is now itself in crisis, leaving people struggling to find ways of organising their personal and communal lives in meaningful ways – though this is enacted in differing temporalities in different parts of the globe. The European Enlightenment took apart the older, integrated, world-view of tradition, and partitioned it into three spheres: science, morality and art.[1] Belatedly, we are now discovering that none of these partitioned-off spheres has ever wholly broken free from our older, perhaps evolutionarily ancient, selves. Recognising this, however, and seeing the ways in which our older needs and narratives inform our newer ones, may help us to practice a different modernity in more fruitful ways. As confidence in the project of modernity has seeped away, all the uncertainties imminent within Enlightenment itself have been unleashed. But this unbounded postmodernity does not necessarily presage the dystopian future often depicted within popular culture. With thought and, above all, creativity, we might find our way to an exciting, and much more human, new modernity in which the technological dream of order, which has so beset modern imaginings, is finally laid to rest.[2]

Central to any exploration of what that new modernity might look like is the question of the experience of selfhood which will inform and accompany it – particularly as this relates to questions of political agency. Jean-Francois Lyotard has said that the postmodern writer always 'comes too soon' and that he or she is always writing the 'what will have been done'.[3] My own understanding of this dilemma ('a crisis

1

in representation'), which is endemic in the life of a culture undergoing a period of rapid technological and social change, is that it means that writing the 'new' must often proceed in forms in which 'emergent' features may be invisible to eyes still focused on residual elements.[4] Under such conditions, politics does not always happen where you would expect it to. As it searches for a new and appropriate aesthetics, the life of the polity – politics – may well get done 'otherwise'. In fact, recognition of this may itself be one of the new ways of thinking about human lives and goods which are so desperately needed at the present time. It seems clear to me that the current notion of the world offered by mainstream politics, political economy and political science is – at least in Britain – terribly narrow. For all its claim to sound economic management and to a sort of ideology-free common sense, and for all its exhortations to everyone else to modernise, the first British government of the twenty-first century, under Tony Blair, maintains a world view – both in terms of political economy and general epistemology – which would be recognisable to, and endorsed by, any early nineteenth-century liberal. The complexity of the individual, the dynamics of groups, the relationship between individual and group and the interactions between them in the public sphere of politics and culture, seem entirely to have eluded the first twenty-first century government. The fact of this narrow vision, and the social and cultural impoverishment which it produces, is one theme which runs through many of the contributions here which, together, begin to instantiate 'politics otherwise'.

The idea for this book was first suggested by Steve Reicher on the Nexus email list initiated in the spring of 1998 to discuss Tony Blair's 'Third Way'. Several people involved in this discussion, including Sebastian Kraemer, Alan Finlayson and myself, raised concerns during the debates about the limited view of the nature of the self which informs much political debate and policy-making. This led to further discussions about the relationship of the self – the subject of politics – to modernity. The aim of this volume, then, has been to bring together a collection of essays that help illuminate this question of the nature of the self; and to seek work from writers representing an historical and disciplinary breadth of approach to the question. I hope that readers of this book will be people for whom politics and its practitioners are of great importance, and that this volume will contribute to widening the debate about the nature of the subject of any politics – human beings. We hope to explore some of the contingent histories and knowledges which have informed and moulded the complex and mysterious biology of human creatures into self-conscious selves.

2

In responding to Steve Reicher's challenge, I have tried to provide room for several different voices and disciplines to begin to do 'politics otherwise', through discussing 'the political subject' in order to discover what its new politics might be. The volume is divided into two parts. Part I (Early Modern and Modern Selves) contains six essays exploring historical formulations of selfhood. The much longer Part II (Contemporary Selves) contains eleven essays on contemporary subjectivities and their direct or indirect implications for the future of this century's political thought and practice.

PART 1: EARLY MODERN AND MODERN SELVES

This section includes essays that cast light on changes in thinking about the human self which have occurred at different times and in different places throughout the period of modernity. These changes have both reflected and affected the political context in which they took place. Each essay, in its own very particular way, shows that views about the human self have changed in response to other social, cultural and economic changes, and that these changes have affected society's views about the nature of politics.

In 'Bad Manners at the Anatomist's Table: Tyson's Pygmie and the Naturalisation of Truth', Erica Fudge provides a study of a ground-breaking piece of empirical science conducted during the early modern period, in the late seventeenth century. She shows how the uncomfort-able truths about animal and human similarities which Tyson's research exposed meshed with other anxieties of the time about the human condition and humanity's economic future. Being 'above the brutes', in terms of having the power to reason, was often horribly undermined by the ease with which men slipped, often drunkenly, into brutishness; and this produced considerable anxiety in an age increasingly commit-ted to the pursuit of reason and the development of a civil and scientific (as opposed to superstitious and martial) society. Fudge argues that the contemporary desire to establish reformed manners, through which the inner man could then be morally shaped, as well as economically directed, influenced Tyson's scientific (i.e. empirical) and undoubtedly ground-breaking observations. His work thus demonstrates that real scientific truth was, right from its beginnings, deeply immersed in the cultural and political concerns of its time (Tyson was later seen as part of the line of scientists whose insights ultimately enabled the work of Darwin). The separation of science and culture, which modernity constantly seeks to establish, was, right from the very beginning, a slip-pery task. And this of course has implications for theories about the rational nature of the subject of politics.

Tyson's attempt to determine the relationship between man and the animals (in this study the relationship between human and chimpanzee – Tyson's 'pygmie' – which we now know to be genetically close), in order to find out what is special about, or particular to, the human, charts a wandering course between physical and rational similarities and differences; it becomes increasingly difficult to disentangle what belongs to the truth of nature and what to the fables of men. Tyson's 'pygmie' stands as an opening character on the stage of modern science – whose end can perhaps be seen three hundred years later in the emergence of holism, complexity and ecological thought – which could be understood as an attempt to rediscover humankind's natural life.

Colin Counsell's essay, 'Navigating Selfhood: Geographical Space and the Early Modern Remapping of the Subject', compellingly argues that a significant change from medieval senses of the self was brought about during the period of early colonial exploration, with its maps and other navigational needs. The individual's possibilities for 'knowing his or her place' in the scheme of things came to be radically altered. Counsell then asks us to think in a similar way about the equally significant effects of changing contemporary experiences of space and locality, and to reflect on how these relate to the navigation and discovery of present (global and local) senses of the self; these changes, of course, affect the self's capacities as an actor (perhaps especially a political one).

Paul McSorley, in 'Local History: Property, Place and History in the English Country House Poem', meditates on the seventeenth-century equivalence between property and the landowner's moral and political properties, between place and propriety. This linkage, noted by Alisdair MacIntyre in *After Virtue*, leads to an understanding of morality as being rooted in deeds which are in conformity to one's place in the – still stably located – scheme of things. The implication is that physical dislocation will lead to social dislocation and that this aspect of modernity will cause morality to lose both its moorings and, strictly speaking, its meaning. McSorley argues that contemporary theories of '... grand narratives of identity formation in the seventeenth century – or what is often called "early modern subjectivity"' might in fact obscure some of the more complex local histories of identity that could be deduced from studies of contemporary texts. In his emphasis on locality and contingency, McSorley warns us against a too-easy sense of a determined 'development' in relation to an idea of selfhood; and in so doing he also warns of the ways in which readings of the past can be funnelled into 'grand narratives' which secretly serve present preoccupations. As McSorley implies, the exhortation to 'become modern' – as if to do otherwise would be to drag one's feet in the face of inevitable development – is to present a reading of history in which ideological choice disguises itself as implacable inevitability.

Mary Peace's essay, 'Prostitution and the Growth of Desire: The Rise and Fall of Sentimental Economics in the Eighteenth Century', looks at the links between eighteenth-century discourses of virtue and the rise of political economy. Focusing her discussion on the London Magdalen Hospital for the Reception of Penitent Prostitutes, Peace argues that its history can stand as an emblem of the history of economic discourses of virtue – in their rise and fall. Contemporary arguments about the meaning of virtue, whether it was innate ('inborn') or socially inculcated ('inbred'), paved the way for an economic language of 'instinct' or desire (and whether this was 'inborn' or 'inbred' hardly mattered in the end). With this, Peace suggests, the doctrine of 'self-interest', derived from (a perhaps partial reading of) Adam Smith's *The Wealth of Nations*, is finally able to uncouple the formerly fixed relationship between commercial and virtuous activities.

When, during the 1980s, prime minister Margaret Thatcher famously called for a 'return to Victorian values', she intended to invoke the century's spirit of earnest self-improvement and self-reliance, exemplified in governance by laissez faire, and also the spirit of those solid middle-class men, women and families whose weight, stability and domestic solidity stares out at us from both figures and domestic design in early photographs. But Jenny Bourne Taylor's essay, 'Fallacies of Memory in Nineteenth-Century Psychology: Subjectivity and Cultural Authority', which discusses nineteenth-century mental science, suggests otherwise: since it was a civilisation unhitched from both religious and traditional certainties, the aura of stability associated with the Victorians may be more accurately thought of as expressing a counterbalance to an unnerving lightness of being – especially in regard to the nature of consciousness, self-identity and memory. The implication of Bourne Taylor's essay is that, in the attempt to manage human beings, political discussions of 'how humans are' may involve a degree of both personal and historical forgetfulness.

In '"Here with the Karroo-bushes and the red sand": Olive Schreiner and Colonial Self-Reliance', Carolyn Burdett describes the late nineteenth-century conflict of ideas between scientific and rational utilitarianism on the one hand, and 'intuitive' romanticism on the other. Using the life and work of the South African writer Olive Schreiner – particularly the latter's *Story of An African Farm* – Burdett shows how the politically progressive 'new woman' Schreiner was able to deploy both her colonial roots and the philosophy of Ralph Waldo Emerson in order to mount a critique of the modernisation in which she so vitally believed. In Schreiner's attempt to recast the debate about abstract reason versus situated intuition, we can see the lineaments of a problem we still face. In being reminded once again that, as Schreiner saw, this conflict is immanent within historical European modernity, we may also understand – as do some of the other essays in this volume – that a true reviving of the project of modernity must also include, as science (which is to say knowledge), those mysterious and incalculable, but thoroughly enworlded, aspects of human experience which modern 'scientific' knowledge has been inclined to exclude.

PART II: CONTEMPORARY SELVES

In drawing upon and developing the work of Sigmund Freud, Sebastian Kraemer's essay on attachment theory forms a bridge between the nineteenth century and the twenty-first. In spite of the hostility sometimes directed against it, the persistence of psychoanalytically informed thought suggests that the basis of the Freudian insight remains relevant for thinkers today.

The great importance of our early attachments is an insight that spans the last two centuries. In the twenty-first century that insight remains as important as it was at the end of the nineteenth. Freud's early work on the biological basis of mind in the neurobiology of the brain, which led to his later emphasis on the 'literary' nature of the unconscious – as well as his 'faint damning' as being 'a great essayist but not a real scientist', finds resonances in contemporary evolutionary neurobiology.[5] In 'Politics in the Nursery', child psychiatrist and attachment theorist Sebastian Kraemer argues for the continuing importance of these modern theoretical insights, which remind us of the primitive sources of supposedly rational allegiances, identifications, antipathies and projects. Kraemer argues that the sources of a person's later political affiliations and beliefs are, much more than we like to think, strongly influenced by the quality and type of early social, emotional and physical care a child receives. Such affiliations, born of an infant's early attachments, Kraemer suggests, 'are already in place before they go to school'. Not only does this argument raise some uncomfortable questions about the ways in which the rhythms and quality of early infant care may be damaged by modern imperatives, it also raises questions (not for the first time) about the extent to which the future is damaged by a narrow and impoverished idea of 'rational' behaviour. Furthermore, the insistence of the importance of the instinctual in our lives (for example, all emotionally well adults respond instinctively to small infants in physically very similar ways in terms of voice modulation, facial distance, and so on) raises serious questions about the deleterious effects of any political management which fails to take sufficient account of our human-ness – a point which Kraemer drives home.

Steve Reicher's 'Mass Psychology and the (Re-) Analysis of the Self' continues the collection's general affirmation of the importance of affect, and of the self as always thoroughly (socially) enworlded and local. Reicher documents challenges that have been made to the idea that the enworlded social self of masses and the group represents an irrationality, and lack of contained selfhood, which imperils the sovereignty of the critical bourgeois monadic self. Arguing that the behaviour of crowds has its own order, coherence and logic, Reicher sets his face against the widely-held view of mass action as characterised by unreason: 'what has to give is not the notion that people in crowds act in interested, meaningful and controlled ways, but rather the notion that the individual self is the sole arbiter of interest and control'. Rejecting the dominant utilitarian model of the rational self-interest-pursuing individual, and noting that crowd behaviour presents us with the phenomenon of the 'social self', and thus the need to 'reconceptualise rationality', Reicher's arguments are politically very far-reaching.

In 'On the Subject of New Labour', Alan Finlayson argues that, in New Labour imaginings of the present and the future as modernisation – globalisation, the knowledge economy, education for life, flexibility – the source of agency is no longer the person of Enlightenment and modern political theory; instead, turning the subject/object relation on its head, it is the idea of modernisation itself which has become the source. As Finlayson maintains, the idea of modernisation 'has most of the key characteristics of a person in late capitalist society'. Sharing the inhumanity of all modern systems imperatives, 'modernisation' declares that selves, rather than conditions, must change – they must ceaselessly reinvent themselves as employable commodities for the market. With this rhetoric of 'modernise or die!', the traditional Enlightenment goods of, say, education are 'not seen primarily as an introduction into the moral or traditional culture of the nation, nor as a way of empowering individuals to think openly and freely' but, rather, 'as the mechanism by which individuals can equip themselves, and by which the national economy can feed itself, with the appropriate skills for the new economy'. With this peculiarly non-political view of the world in which There Is No Alternative to the present socio-economic organisation (real politics being, precisely, about choices), Finlayson suggests that a more timely slogan would be 'politicise or die!'.

What most of the essays here encourage the reader to think about are the ways in which a politics governed, as modern politics is, by systems imperatives, is unable to take into account the nuances of what it is to be a human being – and this applies equally to politicians, their advisers, and the public which is the final object of political acts. This is true of any modern bureaucracy, of course, if it operates under the direction of managers who must continually seek to prove their effectiveness, to the extent that the system becomes unable to respond to the actual life-world of humans; the system can then become inhuman in its demands, even though it is run by humans.

Ashok Bery's essay, ' "We have grown to look at the large world as part of us": Modernity and the Nation in Two Indian Novels of the 1930s', looks at the question of political identity as faced by Indian writers confronting the systems imperatives of the 'machine' of European modernity in the decade before Independence. In addition, the writers had to take on the many different affiliations of religion and caste within India itself. Their formulations, Bery suggests, may offer models for thinking through decentralised political identities elsewhere in the present.

Peter Middleton's essay, 'Getting Some Distance on the News: Simon Armitage, Douglas Oliver and the WTO', usefully reminds us that states of fragility, interruptedness, mixtures of mental and bodily distraction, and so on, are the normal condition of being human – it is the fantasy of the totally managed world that could be regarded as abnormal, insane. Citing Adorno's suggestion that we might be most intellectually engaged when we are able to find the distance to know this – to be 'aversive' – Middleton suggests that our empirical (and overwhelmed) engagement with the world of politics and news is perhaps best served by the 'foolish things' – in this case, poetry. Thus poetry can consciously transform, refine and clarify the world through mixing it up in a human way which mimics our real reception of national and world events. In other words, politicians and other supposedly worldly men pretend to an empirical immediacy and grasp of things, one that is unaffected by their own, all too human, participation in the life-world, in all its subtle disorder: in fact they disavow their involvement in a way in which art never does. Art, Middleton implies, may thus be more 'truthful' than the supposed realism of political and journalistic assertion and commentary. Newsman Douglas Oliver's poetry, which Middleton discusses, puts that true mixture and mess back into political responses; and this allows Middleton to ask how political activism and participation in public culture can work with the knowledge that, in the speed and immediacy of events, 'political subjects will read the news as events in their own worlds and narratives, coloured by their own mourning, elation, anxiety, fear and joy' – precisely as does Oliver's political poetry.

Stuart Murray's essay on representations of identities in postcolonial novels – 'Self, Community and History in the Postcolonial Novel Since 1945' – argues, in agreement with both Carolyn Burdett and Ashok Bery, that it remains the case that the fragmentation and social dysfunction of western societies are often seen more clearly from the 'speeded up' clarity of the postcolonial margins; in the centre disruption and social breakdown has crept in more slowly, and with greater stealth. Murray notes the ways in which writers of the postcolonial period in the Caribbean, Africa and South America show the tensions within the self which are the results of colonial rule. The lesson this might teach us – and this is often hidden when viewed from an autonomous and privileged centre – is to recognise the deep effects on the self-experience of individuals which is brought about by the manner in which a people is governed, the ways in which it is addressed and policed, and the aspects of the population which are demonised. In other words, the arrogant mentality of the coloniser – wherever s/he is found – is profoundly impoverishing to those it addresses.

One of the effects of what Lyotard has described as the postmodern 'incredulity towards metanarratives' – a widespread refusal to believe that the world and human life can be reduced to one all-encompassing 'story' – has been the rise of complexity science. Aided by the vastly increased powers of modern computer technology, complexity science has allowed us to understand that all living systems (brains, societies, languages, institutions, for example) are complex, non-linear, relational, evolving and in a state far from equilibrium. In such systems, analysis of the parts (the method associated with modern science) does not yield an accurate picture of the whole. This is largely because complex systems contain many feedback loops, which are capable of producing features and qualities not found in any of the constituent parts. (This is referred to as 'emergence'.) Nonetheless, we have also learned that, alongside the possibility of chaos, a feature of complexity is the tendency to produce new order and patterns. The implication of this is that understanding the initial conditions of any vital system is extremely important, and that interference which is ignorant both in regard to initial conditions and the subsequent specific history of a vital system is likely to produce unintended consequences.[6] As might be expected, one of the areas in which complexity theory has been most enthusiastically explored is management theory; in this regard, the message of complexity is to 'create the most appropriate and fertile "initial conditions", and then get the heck out of the way so that the system can act creatively in adapting its responses. The surprising fact of self-organisation (Ilya Prigogene's 'order out of chaos'[7]), when taken alongside an understanding of the importance of locatedness and contingency (which is also a feature of Paul McSorley's arguments about the self), suggests that the 'will to manage' associated with contemporary politics needs to be acted upon with caution.

In 'The Complex I', Paul Cilliers and Tanya de Villiers explore the implications of complexity for our understanding of subjectivity. Arguing that earlier accounts of the self fail to capture its complexity, and lead to 'an impoverished account of what it means to be human', their essay – in line with deconstructive thinking – shows that selves must be thought of as 'in process' and always shaped by their specific and contingent histories and culture: the 'self is constituted by its relationships to others and the world'. This means that there can be no hard and fast rules for successful political outcomes; each case must take account of particular circumstances, and be sensitive to both initial conditions and to history. Whether exercised in social science, economic science or political science, the 'command' view of the subject 'leads to a kind of "colonisation" of subjects' in which false determination and calculation replace sensitivity and receptivity to the evolution (whether morally right or wrong) of a system's values. To be a self, Cilliers and de Villiers say, is always to be constituted relationally, ethically and, thus, politically.

Linking the need for a complex understanding of human selves to the language of emotional literacy, James Park argues in his essay, 'The Feeling State and the Emotionally Literate Self', that the 'creativity' which educationalists and business leaders wish to promote, and the 'partnerships' which policy-makers propose as the way forward to successful organisations, can only be achieved by developing a deeper understanding of the psychological mechanisms which often cause those with participatory intentions to degenerate into behaviours aimed at control and mastery. Park calls for an approach to education, management and constitutional change which encourages the manifestation of the qualities associated with 'emotional literacy'.

Written in the contemporary cultural context of repeated claims that the working future is feminine, because women work more effectively in the 'people' economies which now constitute the major areas of production in western societies, Jonathan Rutherford's essay, 'The Life of Men: An Ethics of the Male Self', meditates upon what it is in a man which impedes his access to 'an ethics of the male self'. Searching for forms of being male which are not, in themselves, a form of violence to men, and yet which do not perpetuate the violences of patriarchy, Rutherford contrasts the masculine world of the 'law' and language as described by Freud with the non-violence of 'mere life'. Rutherford suggests that the philosopher Emmanuel Levinas's idea of the significance of existence – as consisting in an ethical demand to take responsibility for the existence of the 'other', rather than a violent assertion of self and mastery – offers an ethic of responsibility which might be appropriate to masculine identity. He goes on to offer an ethics of masculinity which might be described as 'attentive responsibility'.

Finally, Kevin Warwick's report on his extraordinary experiment with a computer chip temporarily implanted under his skin, 'The Chip and I', will provoke thought on the extent to which an embodied mind might be altered by the extension of its 'body' and consciousness via computers. The ego, Freud rightly reminds us, is a 'bodily ego'; Warwick suggests that computers may be the prosthetics of the future, and that the development, via them, of direct mind to mind contact may be a scientifically realisable possibility. If this is the case – and bearing in mind Douglas Oliver's reminders about our multi-faceted, often fantasmatic, engagement with the political realities of the world in mind – we may wonder about the ways in which technology itself might finally undo the technological dream of order.

KNOCKING ON THE DOOR OF FREEDOM

In concluding this introduction, and before the reader dives into the interesting and thoughtful essays which have been delivered to me for this volume, it is worth noting – as a sign of the times – the perhaps surprising degree of coherence and agreement across these essays from diverse disciplines. When I asked for contributions I neither expected nor necessarily wanted coherence or agreement – my main aim was to garner contributions from a wide range of interesting thinkers. And yet coherence and a sort of consensus appeared. The focus of it appears to form around two, related, ideas. The first, sometimes explicit, sometimes implicit, takes the form of a continued warning against too much rigidity in the attempt – political or bureaucratic – to manage human societies. The second focus for consensus is some sense that enduring human qualities of affect or instinct can be thwarted and damaged by the imposition of 'foreign' (supposedly rationalising) forms of governance. The 'colonial' mentality can, it turns out, and as some of the essays here remind us, just as easily work at 'home' as 'abroad'.

But what 'message' can be derived from this nascent consensus? Firstly, I think it must be that there is a growing sense, which must be a part of the continued growth of democracy, that trust, itself, must be democratised. It is no longer the case that we, the people, put our trust in God, or governments; instead secular democratic societies require governments to put their trust in the people who have granted them temporary power. Thus, several of the essays in this volume engage directly or indirectly with our conception of the public sphere of civil society in which an enlightened and ethically engaged political sense is to be played out by the social group. In fact, perhaps it would not be too much to suggest that every essay here, inasmuch as it questions the making of knowledge in the past and the present, seeks to explore the sphere of public debate – what it counts as knowledge and how, in the past, this has been constructed – in order to widen debate in and about civil society and its political effects in the present. In effect, each chapter seems, to me, to ask 'what if all these bits and pieces of history and interpretation were to be taken seriously in a contemporary polis?'. Another way of putting this would be to say that our contemporary understanding of politics (most especially by politicians) remains hopelessly narrow (and perhaps arrogantly so). The ideal Enlightenment aspiration, for an enlarged, educated and intellectually rich civil society, has never been achieved (although the United States of America, for all its flaws, has probably got closest); and we might surmise that this is so because the political class, led by modern scientific and systems imperatives, has never been able to acknowledge properly (or has been mightily frightened of acknowledging) the confusing multiplicity and affectedness of what Husserl, and Habermas after him, have called the 'life-world'. The promise of democracy is that the life-world of the masses (not just the life experiences of the privileged) will somehow get into the account. Mass democracy expresses itself as an endless knocking on the door of privilege in search of freedom. Perhaps one of its most central demands is the recognition that politics, if it is to be genuine and true, and not simply a matter of limited partisanship and power, must always be thought wider and, through the expanse of more generous minds, 'otherwise'.

NOTES

1. This partition is, of course, implicit in Kant's three great Critiques – as Jürgen Habermas argues in 'Modernity v. Postmodernity', *New German Critique*, 22 (Winter 1981).

2. See W. Wheeler, *A New Modernity? Change in Science, Literature and Politics*, Lawrence & Wishart, London 1999.

3. J-F. Lyotard, 'Answering the Question; What is postmodernism?', in J-F Lyotard, *The Postmodern Condition*, tr. G. Benington & B. Massumi, MUP, 1984.

4. The useful idea of cultures as containing 'residual' and 'emergent' forms comes, of course, from Raymond Williams. The invisibility of the new is sometimes described in the form of a story about Australian aborigines being unable to 'see' Captain Cook's ship when it first appeared. In this, probably apocryphal, tale, the Australians couldn't 'see' the sailors until they climbed into their (to aboriginal eyes more recognisably proportioned) long-boat to row ashore.

5. See, for example, G. Edelman, *Bright Air, Brilliant Fire: On the Matter of Mind*, Penguin, Harmondsworth, 1994; and M. Turner, *The Literary Mind: The Origins of Thought and Language*, OUP, Oxford, 1996.

6. For a discussion of this in relation to nineteenth-century pedagogy and the production of aberrant selves, see chapter 2, *A New Modernity? Change in Science, Literature and Politics*, *op.cit.*

7. I. Prigogene & I. Stengers, *Order Out of Chaos: Man's New Dialogue With Nature*, Bantam, 1986.

Bad manners at the anatomist's table: Tyson's pygmie and the naturalisation of truth

ERICA FUDGE

In the early modern period one of the most conventional vehicles for illustrating and teaching the cultural ideals of the human world was the animal.[1] In beast fables, legends and emblem books, the animal was used to exemplify moral 'truths'. As an illustration of the application of logic, what better story than that of Chrysippus's dog, who, by deduction, followed the correct path; or of true loyalty, what better exemplar than Odysseus's hound, Argus, who died on the reappearance of his loved and lost owner? From another point of view, what better way to depict the unnaturalness of cunning than through the story of the fox who feigned death to gain easy access to his prey; or to represent the dangers of parental over-protectiveness than through the narrative of the ape who loved her babe so much she hugged it to death?[2] Whether as emblems of good behaviour or of bad, the animal asked human readers to reassess their own actions.

But, of course, unlike the truth, which is fact, such fables are fictions: that is, they can be recognised as creations, cultural productions. The moral of the beast fable may be given credence, but its role as an absolute authority is always under question. Despite the assertion of the prophetic role of its original author – Homer, Aesop – the authority of the fable in some ways lays bare the process by which truths are achieved: it presents them as words voiced by creatures who cannot really speak. By doing this, by revealing the ventriloquism involved in the assertion of truth, the fable paradoxically undercuts the possibility of that truth as an inevitable and indisputable fact.

Science would seem to offer a counter to these equivocations of fiction. In his major scientific work, *The Great Instauration* (1620), Francis

Bacon complained that 'fables and superstitions and follies which nurses instil into children do serious injury to their minds'.[3] The mythical interpretation of nature contained in emblem books and animal fables must, he argued, be left behind if the scientific endeavour is to be truly successful. In place of the anthropomorphism of speaking beasts, Bacon and his followers advocated the anthropocentrism of human dominion. Through experimentation – the repeated experience of truth – 'facts' about the natural world could be learned by humans, and these facts could, in turn, be used to speak about life and morality and to enhance human power.

This assertion of the power of science was clearly voiced by Thomas Sprat in his *History of the Royal Society* of 1667, a study in which Bacon is seen as a Moses figure, leading the true believers away from the fabulous corruption of the heathens.[4] Sprat wrote that the individual scientist works on behalf of the whole Society – they '(as it were) carry the eyes and the imaginations of the whole company into the *Laboratory* with them'. Finally, in front of the 'whole *Company*', the experiments are repeated and tested, and it is then, and only then, that a true judgement and resolution of 'the matter of *Fact*' can be made. Sprat continues: 'This *critical* and *reiterated scrutiny* of those things, which are the plain object of their eyes, must needs pull out of all reasonable dispute, the reality of those operations, which the *Society* shall positively determine to have succeeded' (p99). The rhetoric is devoid of any notion of moral engagement: science is objectively, provably true.

Because of this emphasis on the indisputable nature of scientific truth it would seem that science could also be the ideal realm in which to voice moral truth. Sprat does not shy away from such an idea: in the dedication of his *History*, addressed to Charles II, he argues that the work of the Royal Society is 'An *Enterprise* equal to the most renoun'd Actions of the best *Princes*. For, to increase the Powers of all Mankind, and to free them from the bondage of Errors, is greater Glory than to enlarge *Empire*, or to put Chains on the necks of Conquer'd *Nations*'. More important than colonialism, scientific discovery reaches beyond politics and, at its heart, is apparently the promise of an absolute human freedom.

Following Sprat's and others' mythologising of the power of science, a popularly conceived faith in experiment arose which argues that what is scientific, what is carefully and objectively observed, is *true*. This essay traces a problem with this interpretation of science, and examines the way in which moral ideas were made to appear natural (that is to say *scientific*) in one late seventeenth–century anatomical study. Edward Tyson's *Orang-Outang, Sive Homo Sylvestris* is the first ever comparative anatomy of a human and a chimpanzee.[5]

Presented to the Royal Society in June 1698, and published the following year, *Orang-Outang* holds a particular place in the history of
science in its recognition of 'a new family of hominid apes intermedi-
ate between man and monkeys'.[6] Tyson's work was the first in which
the natural order was scientifically systematised to present the ape as
the highest of all non-human animals. Long before Darwin, this seems
truly modern, but, as well as redrawing the chain which links humans
and animals, Tyson's text also enters a contemporary *moral* debate.

At the time Tyson performed his anatomy, the campaigns by the
Societies for the Reformation of Manners were at their height, working
to promote moral rectitude. What was needed was a way of making
moral rectitude appear natural, that is, part of a scientific understanding.
Tyson felt he had found such a way in his anatomy of the chimpanzee;
in this scientific text, and apparently against Bacon's ideas, the animal is
once again used to represent 'natural' moral truth. The problem which
emerges from this conjunction of science and morality has implications
not only for our perception of science, but also for the problematic
nature of the separation of the species. The status of humanity – as part
of nature and also raised above it – is brought to the fore and some very
important problems emerge. A close reading of this one significant
anatomical text reveals that science (and here I am dealing with the
science of man – of what it is to be a person) is as full of fiction – wish,
metaphor, anthropomorphism, narrative – as any analogous fable.

REWRITING THE CHAIN

In *Orang-Outang* the Chain of Being which linked all of the natural
world, from the stone to the divine, is rewritten, via the emerging
method of comparative anatomy, to include the anthropoid ape at the
top of the animal kingdom, one link from the human. The 'pygmie', as
Tyson terms the creature,[7] is 'the Nexus of the Animal and the
Rational'.[8] It stands as the missing link between the human and the non-
human animal worlds. What distinguishes Tyson's model from Darwin's
later work is the question of evolution: for Tyson the chain of being is
static, there can be no movement of species. One hundred and sixty years
before the publication of *The Origin of Species*, Tyson's new claim for
the superiority of the pygmie does not alter the fact that it remains
firmly, and permanently, inferior to humanity: it remains an animal. This
is the model of the natural world which Tyson applies to his anatomy,
even as he catalogues the fact that the pygmie, when dissected and
compared in measurements, weights and structure to both a monkey and
a human, is like the human in more ways than it is like the monkey.[9]

Tyson, who in a previous work termed ephemeron flies 'these *Automata*', adopts the methodology of mechanical philosophy, and takes anatomy as the point of departure in constructing his chain.[10] Natural philosophy had once placed animals which were useful, and had what was perceived to be a cognitive similarity to man, at the top of the chain. The dog, the horse, the ape, and even the elephant were regarded as of the highest order. Philemon Holland's 1601 translation of Pliny's *Naturall Historie* makes this point clearly: '… the Elephant … commeth nearest in wit and capacitie, to men: for they understand the language of that country wherein they are bred, they do whatsoever they are commaunded, they remember what duties they be taught, and withall take pleasure and delight both in love and in glorie'.[11] This idea was reproduced in other works in the early modern period: in 1607 Edward Topsell wrote that: 'There is not any creature so capable of understanding as an Elephant'.[12] In 1647 the Neoplatonist Henry More reiterated the point: 'The Dog, the Horse, the Ape, the Elephant, / Will all … / sternly claim their share in use of right reason.'[13] Because of this – their perceived capacity to reason – these animals were placed at the top of the chain.

This mode of thinking was overturned in Tyson's work. The use of mechanical philosophy, the separation of mind from body, with the emphasis placed on the physical, apparently removed the problematic issue of animal cognition from the debate. Mary Midgley has recently written that 'dualism gradually collapses into a kind of "materialism" which means having nothing to say about mind at all',[14] but, following Descartes, the emphasis on speaking as the distinguishing feature of humanity is important for Tyson. Descartes argued that speech is proof of cognition, and that all humans – 'even madmen' – speak, whereas animals cannot, thus proving 'not merely that the beasts have less reason than men, but that they have no reason at all.'[15] Tyson takes this as his cue in his discussion of the pygmie's vocal chords. The fact that the pygmie has the organs for speech 'exactly as 'tis in *Man*' does not disturb Tyson: 'if there was any farther advantage for the forming of *Speech*, I can't think but our *Pygmie* had it. But upon the best Enquiry, I was never informed, that it attempted any thing that way.'[16] The fact that the organs are mechanically like those of the human is enough for the resemblance – in fact, is perfect. Tyson writes, 'The *Organs* in *Animal* Bodies are only a regular *Compages* of Pipes and Vessels, for the *Fluids* to pass through, and are passive. What actuates them, are the *Humours* and *Fluids* … if all depended on the *Organ*, not only our *Pygmie*, but other *Brutes* likewise, would be too near akin to us (p55).'

If, as mechanical philosophy proposed, the body and the mind were separable, so too were the anatomy and its potential actions. An action such as speech requires reason, and reason is the one thing which the pygmie does not have. The fact that it possesses the organs for speech is important in the representation of the chain of being. The chain is always gradual: for Aristotle the boundary between even the inanimate and the animate was 'indistinguishable'.[17] More poetically, in the early seventeenth century George Herbert wrote of the natural gradation of things: 'Frogs marry fish and flesh; bats, bird and beast; / Sponges, non-sense and sense; mines, th'earth & plants.'[18] The physical similarity of the pygmie to humans is what marks it out as the 'Nexus', the missing link, but it does not mean that the animal holds the same status on the chain as does humanity. In fact, as Robert Wokler has noted, Cartesian dualism, when mixed with the Aristotelean notion of the Chain of Being, offered Tyson the possibility that 'bodily organs which were anatomically the same might be functionally distinct.'[19] The pygmie, despite the physical similarities, remains a passive animal, an object of anatomical analysis, not a subject for human unease.

But the use of mechanical philosophy in *Orang-Outang* does not mean that Tyson abandons the emblematic character of the pygmie. Traditionally, the ape had been figured as an emblem of human actions: imitative, lustful, foolish.[20] Topsell wrote that 'the body of an ape is ridiculous, by reason of an indecent likeness and imitation of man'.[21] Claude Perrault, whose work in the Royal Society of Sciences in Paris in the 1680s was a massive influence on Tyson, still wrote of the ape and the bear – which he felt shared this characteristic – that their 'deformity' was based on 'the ill resemblance which they both have, with the handsomest of all Animals', man.[22] In these instances, the ape was like the human, but its resemblance placed it at a distance rather than close. It is a shadow human, a false and insubstantial likeness to be disregarded, treated with the contempt its failed imitation (aping) deserves.

Tyson abandons the idea of imitation in his analysis of the pygmie and, as noted, regards the physical similarities of animal and man as a necessity in the establishment of the gradual chain of being. But despite the anti-mythic stance of seventeenth-century science, the mixing of the modes of representation – of symbolic and mechanical – in Tyson's work reveals problems in the text which make the distinction between human – active subject – and animal – passive object – impossible to maintain. The ambivalent nature of the pygmie undercuts claims for the objectivity of *Orang-Outang*, and reminds us that at this crucial juncture in the history of science the line between human and animal is not made clear but rather is blurred, even totally erased.

THE RETURN OF ANTHROPOMORPHISM

The scientific rationale of Tyson's work is clearly stated: the aim of the book is 'improving the Natural History of Animals, and affording the Reader any Delightful and Useful Instructions'.[23] Following this declaration Tyson introduces the object of his analysis, the pygmie, and, in truly conventional fashion, moves through a list of writings about the animal from classical and contemporary writers. The anatomical sections of the text – the comparative measurement of the animal with the monkey and the human, the osteology and the myotomy (studies of the skeleton and musculature) – follow, but what interrupts the flow from the acknowledgement of the importance of classical learning to the empirical dissection is a sequence of anecdotes which upset both the objectification of the pygmie and the establishment of a clear distinction between the species.

The use of anecdotes and personal recollection is not itself problematic within the new science. Conrad Gesner, whose work in the mid-sixteenth century was a precursor to the establishment of empiricism in the seventeenth, wrote of the emerging new scientific methodology:

> I did not only sit still and turne ouer books, but gaue my selfe diligently to enquire of euery Country-man or trauailer, a perticular and exact obseruation of the nature of euery beast: and for this course I conferred with strangers of other nations, which by any occasion either were resident among vs, or passed accidently through our country, & made of their relation the most diligent notes that I could gather.[24]

This use of the personal anecdote was taken up a century later by the Royal Society where field workers were employed: 'sailors, military men, traders, and native and foreign observers' were used to gather 'appropriate matters of fact'.[25]

Tyson, following convention, makes frequent references to the sources of his information about the life of the pygmie: 'When I was dissecting it, some Sea-Captains and Merchants who came to my House to see it, assured me, that they had seen a great many of them in *Borneo, Sumatra*, and other Parts, tho' this was brought from *Angola* in *Africa*'. 'I was told by the Owners...'.[26] But the introduction of these anecdotes, while part of the scientific endeavour, also undermines Tyson's methodology. There is a constant, and jarring, anthropomorphism at work which Tyson both uses and denies.

For example, Tyson cites Samuel Purchas's description of the wild-man of Borneo and writes:

In this Character there are several things I could take notice of, and I may hereafter have occasion to refer to some of the Particulars; But what is mention'd of its *Cry*, like a Child's; and it's expressing the *Passions* of Joy and Grief, by making a Noise with it's Feet, is agreeable enough to the Relation I had of our *Pygmie*: For I heard it *Cry* my self like a *Child*; and he hath been often seen to kick with his Feet, as Children do, when either he was pleased or angered (p25).

The pygmie cries like a child. Where Tyson had argued that form and function – vocal chords and speech – are distinct, and that this was where the difference between pygmies and humans existed, he now proposes that the animal can vocalise like a human, albeit an immature one. It is as if the similarities of form cannot stand up to the anthropomorphism of the anecdote. What Tyson can theorise – the Aristotelean Chain of Being – and what he sees and hears, are at odds. In order to counter this, and despite the claims of mechanical philosophy to regard the body as the meaningful object of analysis in anatomical work, Tyson moves the boundary between human and animal further within.

John Locke's *An Essay Concerning Human Understanding* was published nine years before Tyson performed his anatomy of the pygmie, and some of the more conventional ideas voiced in this work find their way into Tyson's anatomy. For Locke children can learn and animals can experience. Learning requires abstract reasoning and an animal is capable only of simple reasoning. He writes, 'I think, *Beasts compare* not their *Ideas*, farther than some sensible Circumstances, annexed to the Objects themselves. The other power of Comparing, which may be observed in Men, belonging to general *Ideas*, and useful only to abstract Reasonings, we may probably conjecture Beasts have not.'[27] There can be a similarity, but it does not go any deeper than the surface. The possibility of an animal having the capacity for abstract reason is closed down, and this is where the distinction exists.

Tyson appears to concur with Locke's argument: he writes 'those *Nobler Faculties* in the *Mind* of *Man*, must certainly have a *higher Principle*'.[28] He abandons the tangible proofs of anatomy and experience, the body and the sight, and he resorts, instead, to the hypothesis of sagacity, because the pygmie is physically *too like* the human. In doing this he has moved outside of the repeatable proof of science. We can turn to Locke, once again, as he highlights something of the elusiveness of truth here. Attacking the idea that the human mind is constantly thinking, and citing (dreamless) sleep as an obvious instance where the existence of thought is impossible to prove, Locke writes, 'they must needs have a penetrating sight, who can certainly see, that I think, when I cannot perceive it my self, and when I declare, that I do not; and yet can see, that Dogs and Elephants do not think, when they give us all the demonstration of it imaginable, except only telling us, that they do not do so'.[29] Almost in passing Locke has recognised that if scientific proof can only be gained through the repeated exhibition of facts then animals would *appear* to think. To refuse to believe that animals possess reason (albeit of a simple kind), is to refuse, he seems to imply, empirical truth.[30]

As if this was not enough, the problem Tyson faces in his attempt to find a rationale for the chain of being goes further even than this. What follows the description of the pygmie crying in *Orang-Outang* is a description of the skin, the mammae, the musculus membrane, and an examination of some of the creature's internal organs. Tyson begins his analysis of the stomach and logically looks at the question of the pygmie's diet.

> What chiefly our *Pygmie* affected, when *Wild*, I was not informed of; after it was taken, and made tame, it would readily eat any thing that was brought to the Table; and very orderly bring its Plate thither, to receive what they would give him. Once it was made Drunk with *Punch*, (and they are fond enough of strong Liquors) But it was observed, that after that time, it would never drink above one Cup, and refused the offer of more than what he found agreed with him. Thus we see *Instinct* of *Nature* teaches Brutes *Temperance*; and *Intemperance* is a Crime not only against the *Laws* of *Morality*, but of *Nature* too.[31]

Here, scientific rhetoric gives way to a moral rhetoric of temperance, and the pygmie becomes the emblem of sobriety. Tyson has moved from mechanical philosophy, with its emphasis on the physical, to the cognitive possibilities of the animal.

The stress on the natural sobriety of the pygmie sets Tyson's work apart from earlier representations of anthropoid apes. Over ninety years earlier, Edward Topsell had argued that '[apes] will drinke wine till they be drunke'.[32] Tyson distances himself from this convention, and by doing this – by refusing one site of human difference from the beast – he also confuses his argument about the duality of form and function, vocal chords and speech, and ultimately, I suggest, animal and human. How can Tyson's ape learn sobriety when Tyson would seem to be reiterating ideas about the impossibility of an animal engaging in abstract reasoning?

The answer to this lies outside of the anatomical endeavour. Tyson's *Orang-Outang* needs to be placed within its cultural context to be fully understood: empirical science, like literature, is bound to the moment of its creation, and claims for the scientific text as neutral, unbiased and objective fail to recognise the cultural embeddedness of anatomical discovery.[33] There is nothing objective in Tyson's work on the pygmie; rather it can only be understood if it is read as a moral as well as an anatomical text.[34] When placed in context not only can we see one way in which the scientific text was used for a political purpose, we can also begin to think about the nature of human superiority.

REFORMING MANNERS

In the aftermath of the Glorious Revolution of 1688 the call for England to look to itself and to its place in the divine order gathered strength. According to one historian of the period, England 'had by Divine providence narrowly averted the disaster of a tyrannical Catholic monarchy, and in order to prevent actual Divine punishment for the country's sins a reformation of manners was necessary'.[35] In 1689 William III wrote:

> As our duty requires, we most earnestly desire, and shall endeavour a general reformation of the lives and manners of all our subjects, as being that which must establish our throne, and secure to our people their religion, happiness, and peace, all which seem to be in great danger at this time, by reason of that overflowing of vice, which is too notorious in this as well as other neighbouring nations.[36]

As a response to the sense of England's falling away from God's design, the Societies for the Reformation of Manners (SRMs) began to emerge, not only in London, but also in other English cities.[37] Writing in 1698, Josiah Woodward argued that the SRMs had only one real purpose: 'to put a stop to our overflowing Wickedness, remove our Plagues, and to dispose us into a Meetness for the Blessings and gracious presence of God'.[38] These Societies, made up of dissenting as well as more orthodox Anglican voices, took the moral campaign to the streets in the most practical way possible: the SRMs hired constables to go around noting and arresting offenders. In 1699 Ned Ward satirised this hiring of constables in *The London Spy*: the constable, he wrote, 'is a man most commonly of a very scandalous necessity who has no way left, but, pimp-like, to live upon other people's debaucheries'. He goes on, 'Of all people I know, I think their [the constables'] employement is most like the dog-whippers of a church, whose business it is to watch the tails of every proud bitch and lascivious puppy from committing an indecency'.[39] The work of the constable is to train the animal out of man, even though the animal would seem always to be there. Despite criticisms such as Ward's, however, the main focus of attention of the SRMs remained 'those, that for the time to come, shall impudently dare, in Rebellion against the Laws of God and Man, to Swear and Curse, to profane the Lord's day, or be guilty of the loathsom Sin of Drunkenness'.[40] At the base of this desire for purity was the place of England as a power in Europe.

Shelley Burtt has called the constables hired by the SRMs 'a sort of citizens' vice squad'.[41] They encapsulate one method used by the Societies which was, she argues, 'coercive' rather than 'persuasive/regulatory': that is, they aimed to *punish* individuals for breaking laws meant to establish behavioural norms' rather than to persuade 'through preaching, charity, and private moral instruction' (p155-6). But, of course, coercion can only work so far: ideas truly gain power, as Stuart Hall has argued, 'from winning a substantial degree of popular consent'.[42] Not dissimilarly, Bruce Grelle argues that, in order to achieve a 'degree of universality', ideas must have an 'ability to go beyond the expression of the narrow sectional interests of particular social-economic classes'.[43] In other words, what is enforced will never be true. Both Hall and Grelle are invoking the ideas of Antonio Gramsci, but a similar understanding of the power of consent was undoubtedly also recognised by those who supported the need for a reformation of manners in the late seventeenth century. Between 1698 and 1711 the role of education (as opposed to coercion) in this hegemonic drive was made visible in the establishment of Corporations of the Poor in fifteen cities in England.[44] In Bristol the Corporation established a hospital and a workhouse, both institutions emphasising the role of work in the re-establishment of England as a Godly nation.[45] What is recognised here is that morality cannot be instilled through force alone, that education is needed to spread ideas and to create a 'collective will'. From this period on, science too has an increasingly powerful role to play, and moral education and scientific truth meet in Edward Tyson.

A direct link between Tyson and the Corporation of the Poor in Bristol can be traced in the Corporation's *Transactions* where it is recorded that in 1698, the year he performed the anatomy of the pygmie, Tyson donated £100, a very sizeable sum, 'to be distributed among the poor'.[46] Also recorded is 'Dr Tyson's Sermon Gift' to the parish church of St Stephen's in Bristol. This was a financial gift which had been instigated by Tyson's grandfather and which was paid to relieve the financial strain on the treasury of St Peter's Hospital, another institution established by the Corporation of the Poor, which had been supporting the lecture.[47]

As well as this financial link, Tyson's work as physician to Bedlam Hospital in London between 1684 and 1703 is also testament to his commitment to some of the ideals which were promoted by the Corporations of the Poor. In John Strype's rewrite of Stow's *Survey of London*, published in 1720, Strype records Tyson's 'brief Relation' about Bedlam. This relation is important, not just because of the links which can be made to the ideas of the Corporations of the Poor (I return to these), but because of the sense of the fragility of human status which it voices.

In his discussion of the Hospital, Strype reproduces an extract from a contemporary sermon by one Dr Ibbot: 'These are sad objects indeed', says Ibbot of the Bedlam inmates, 'They shew us to our selves in the worst Disguise, by turning us to the weak and dark side of Human Nature; and serve to convince us what little Reason we have to glory in our Wisdom, or in any intellectual Attainments; since the strongest Brain may so suddenly, and by so many Accidents be disordered'.[48] Once again, the cognitive capacity of the human comes under scrutiny here: the distinction from the animal – reason – can be easily lost. Because of this the mad become a kind of *memento insani*: a reminder of how close we all are to unreason.

But Strype also notes that during Tyson's time as physician to the hospital two out of every three patients had been cured and discharged (the figure was supplied by Tyson himself). The discharge of the patient was not the end of the hospital's involvement, however: 'where [the patients] are destitute of Friends, and unprovided with common Necessaries, a Charity was given by a Person unknown, at the Physician's Discretion, to give what he shall think convenient for their present Subsistence, or to provide them with Cloaths for the present *till they shall fall into Business*'.[49] The intention of Bedlam under Tyson, like the hospitals and workhouses established by the Corporation of the Poor in Bristol, is to reintroduce the lost soul to work, to usefulness. 'Ideots', that is, the incurable insane, were not taken into Bedlam under Tyson: 'those are judged the fittest Objects for this Hospital that are raving and furious, and capable of Cure'.[50] Tyson's work was not to shelter the lost, but to educate those who were out of step, in order that they might be able to return to fully human status. The irony here, of course, is that while the pygmie cannot evolve into a human, the human can dissolve into an animal-like status. Tyson's work at Bedlam is, in this sense, the other side of the coin of his anatomical work: in the former he attempts to replace humans in their position at the top of the chain, in the latter he attempts to prove that the pygmie can never rise above its status as an animal.

But Tyson's assertion of ideals which can be traced to the campaign for the reformation of manners are most problematically traced in his scientific work. Gramsci argued that those who function as intellectuals within society play an important role in the state: they are 'the dominant group's "deputies" exercising the subaltern functions of social hegemony and political government.' Among these 'subaltern functions' he includes 'The "spontaneous" consent given by the great masses of the population to the general direction imposed on social life by the dominant fundamental group'.[51] To achieve spontaneous consent an idea must come to be regarded as inevitable, unquestionable, and this is where we return to the seventeenth century and the claims for the power of science. If science is (or rather, poses as) objective, then the information which it presents to its audience is also objective. It does not belong to any one political or religious group, it belongs, rather to humanity as a whole. It is this power of science which Tyson draws upon to support his moral ideas on the proper nature of the human subject.

In the image of the sober pygmie, scientific support is offered for the moral proposals of the SRMs. The pygmie's refusal of punch makes natural what is, in fact, moral and social. The coercive strategy of the SRMs and the persuasive strategy of the Corporations of the Poor are overlaid with scientific proof: '*Intemperance* is a Crime not only against the *Laws of Morality*, but of *Nature* too'. Put simply, if the pygmie can learn sobriety Tyson has not only underlined the naturalness (and therefore truth) of temperance, he has also revealed the pygmie to be as capable as any member of the Royal Society of abstract reasoning, of moving outwards from the individual proven case to the general statement as the inductive method proposed. The pygmie's drunkenness is enough to teach him that punch is disagreeable: he becomes an empiricist, trying by experience the world of strong liquors and learning through the trial the facts about alcohol. In order to promote his moral ideals Tyson undercuts his own findings. The pygmie becomes not so much 'the Nexus of the Animal and the Rational' as the epitome of the human: the scientist himself.

CONCLUSION: THIS IS NOT THE END

Tyson notes that when the pygmie 'goes erect, as a *Biped*, it appears [in front] less hairy, and more like a *Man*'.[52] This anatomical detail is not, of course, left on its own. As if to prove his point Tyson adds an anecdote. And once again, the anecdote does not serve so much to illustrate the anatomical point, as to offer up an illustration of the problem at stake in the text:

> After our *Pygmie* was taken and a little used to wear Cloaths, it was fond enough of them; and what it could not put on himself, it would bring in his Hands to some of the Company to help him to put on. It would lie in a Bed, place his Head on the Pillow, and pull the Cloaths over him, as a Man would do; but was so careless, and so very a Brute, as to do all Nature's Occasions there (p8).

There is a slippage here from the impersonal pronoun 'it' to the more personal, and human, 'him'. But there is also a more general problem: the ape lies in a bed. But, it wets that bed. Children, of course, learn not to do this; and the logic of Tyson's work is that an ape can also learn, otherwise an ape would be a useless image of sobriety. But if an ape can learn, and its anatomy is virtually indistinguishable from a human's, what is there to separate the human from the pygmie in this empirical world where experience, sight, is all?

In Tyson's work, the pygmie is an emblem of humanity at the dinner table, but a danger to humanity on the anatomist's table. Through Tyson's links with mechanical philosophy and the Societies for the Reformation of Manners we can watch human dominion undoing itself in a text which presents itself as supporting the superiority of humanity. Tyson's pygmie completes the chain of being, is the nexus; *Orang-Outang* is the first time this is recognised anatomically. But a contextual reading of the text reveals links with moral arguments which make it difficult, if not impossible, to read the pygmie as totally different from man. By the end of *Orang-Outang* the boundary between human and animal has not been strengthened, it has been confused. The anecdotes which pepper the anatomy reveal the pygmie to be a creature not only physically, but also cognitively more like a human than a monkey. Difference in both body and mind has been undone.

The classic studies of Tyson's work by Cole and Montagu do not recognise this anthropomorphic turn of the text. Even as Montagu's biography reveals Tyson's link with the campaign for the reformation of manners, he does not regard this as relevant to an understanding of his scientific work. For him, science and morality exist in separate spheres, and Tyson is 'on a par with such figures as Copernicus, Vesalius, Newton, and Darwin'.[53] The two – the separation of science from morality and the writing of great scientific works – seem to co-exist. My reading of *Orang-Outang* as a problematic work in the history of humanity as a species does not mean, though, that the text should be ignored, disregarded as 'poor science'. Indeed, *Orang-Outang* might offer us an important starting point for a reassessment of the human relation with the animal. Perhaps Tyson's work, as it reveals the close connections between science and morality, should be reclaimed as a text that also reveals how difficult it is to separate definitively human from animal. In Tyson's anatomical work we can see one of the most natural 'truths' we possess – that of the absolute otherness of animals – being at once reinforced through the performance of the anatomy, and itself anatomised, taken apart. The question is, I suppose, how long can we continue to have a belief in both the absolute difference of human and animal and a recognition of this unsettling contiguity? In the context of this discussion the emphasis on the dynamic nature of ideology might be something worth celebrating. As Stuart Hall has argued: 'hegemony is never forever'.[54]

I would like to thank Sue Wiseman and Alan Marshall for their helpful comments and suggestions on this paper.

NOTES

1. For a discussion of the role of the animal fable in education see Erica Fudge, *Perceiving Animals: Humans and Beasts in Early Modern English Culture*, Macmillan, Basingstoke 1999, pp69-73.
2. These stories are related in: Luciano Floridi, 'Scepticism and Animal Rationality: the Fortune of Chrysippus' Dog in the History of Western Thought', *Archiv Fur Geschichte der Philosophie* 79:1 (1997), 27-57; Homer, *The Odyssey*, Penguin, London 1946, pp266-267; *The Book of Beasts*, T.H. White (trans), (1954), reprinted, Alan Sutton, Stroud 1992, pp53-54; Geffrey Whitney, *A Choice of Emblemes and Other Devices* (1586), p188.
3. Francis Bacon, 'The Plan' of *The Great Instauration* (1620), in Spedding, Ellis and Heath (eds), *The Works of Francis Bacon* (1859), reprinted, Friedrich Fromann, Stuttgart 1963, Volume VI, p30.
4. See Abraham Cowley's prefatory verse, 'To the *Royal Society*,' in Thomas Sprat, *The History of the Royal Society* (1667), sig.Bv.
5. The full title of Tyson's work is *Orang-Outang, sive Homo Sylvestris. Or the Anatomy of a Pygmie Compared with that of a Monkey, and Ape and a Man* (1699).
6. F.J. Cole, *A History of Comparative Anatomy: From Aristotle to the Eighteenth Century*, Macmillan, London 1944, p219.
7. The term Chimpanzee was not introduced into English until 1738. See

Londa Schiebinger, *Nature's Body: Gender in the Making of Modern Science*, Beacon, Boston 1993, p78.

8. Tyson, *op.cit.*, Dedication to Lord Somers, np.

9. At the end of *Orang-Outang* Tyson lists the ways in which the pygmie is more like a human than a monkey, and more like a monkey than a human. It resembles man in 48 places, and the monkey in 34 (pp92-95).

10. Edward Tyson, 'To the Reader' in Jo. Swammerdam, *Ephemeri Vita: Or the Natural History and Anatomy of the Ephemeron, A Fly that Lives but FIVE HOURS* (1681), sig.A2v.

11. Philemon Holland, *The Historie of the World, Commonly called, The Naturall Historie of C. Plinius Secundus. Translated into English by Philemon Holland Doctor in Physicke* (1601), p192.

12. Edward Topsell, *The Historie of Fovre-Footed Beastes* (1607), p196.

13. Henry More, 'Psychathanasia, or The Second Part of the Song of the Soul' in *Philosophical Poems*, Cambridge 1647, p84.

14. Mary Midgley, 'Descartes' Prisoners', *New Statesman*, 24.5.1999, p50.

15. René Descartes, *Discourse on the Method* (1637), in *The Philosophical Writings of Descartes*, Cambridge University Press, Cambridge 1985, Volume I, p140.

16. Tyson, *op.cit*, p51.

17. Aristotle, *De animalibus historia* VIII, I, 588b, cited in Arthur O. Lovejoy, *The Great Chain of Being: A Study of the History of an Idea* (1933), Harper Torchbooks, New York 1960, p56.

18. George Herbert, 'Providence' (1633), in C.A. Patrides (ed), *The English Poems of George Herbert*, Dent, London 1974, p133.

19. Robert Wokler, 'Tyson and Buffon on the Orang-utan', *Studies on Voltaire and the Eighteenth Century* 155:5 (1976), 2306.

20. On this see H.W. Jansen, *Apes and Ape Lore in the Middle Ages and the Renaissance*, Warburg Institute, London 1952; Joyce E. Salisbury, *The Beast Within: Animals in the Middle Ages*, Routledge, London 1994.

21. Topsell, *op.cit.*, p4.

22. Claude Perrault, *The Natural History of Animals* (1702), first printed in French in 1687, p43. Tyson relies heavily on 'The Anatomical Description of Two Sapajous and two other Monkeys', in *Memoirs For A Natural History of Animals, Containing the Anatomical Descriptions of Several Creatures Dissected By The Royal Academy of Sciences At Paris, Englished by Alexander Pitfeild, Fellow of the Royal Society* (1688), from the French original of 1676.

23. Tyson, *op.cit.*, 'Dedication to Lord Somers', np.

24. Conrad Gesner, 'The First Epistle of Doct. Conradvs Gesnervs' in Topsell, *op.cit.*, sig. 1v.

25. Barbara J. Shapiro, *Probability and Certainty in Seventeenth-Century England: A Study of the Relationships between Natural Science, Religion, History, Law and Literature*, Princeton University Press, Princeton 1983, p22.

26. Tyson, *op.cit.*, pp2 and 8.

27. John Locke, *An Essay Concerning Human Understanding* (1689), Peter H. Nidditch (ed), Oxford University Press, Oxford 1975, pp157-158. Locke is following a conventional distinction between humans and animals here: in the thirteenth century Albertus Magnus argued that the pygmie may seem to 'have something imitating reason, but it lacks reason', in, *De Animalibus*, I.1.3, cited in Resnick and Kitchell, 'Albert the Great on the "Language" of Animals', *American Catholic Philosophical Quarterly* 70:1 (1996), p58.

28. Tyson, *op.cit.*, p55.

29. Locke, *op.cit.*, pp115-116.

30. As W.M. Spellman notes there is a difference in Locke's thought between the figure man 'the biological organism who shares a host of traits with plants and animals' and person: personhood being 'something each one of us acquires over the course of our education into rationality from childhood, and God is interested solely in the moral component at judgement, not in the biological unit which provides but a temporary vehicle for the person.' Spellman, *John Locke*, Macmillan, Basingstoke 1997, pp63-64. Following this, Locke's refusal to deny animals cognition would make the status of the beasts even more like that of men.

31. Tyson, *op.cit.*, p30.

32. Topsell, *op.cit.*, p4.

33. See John Henry, 'The Scientific Revolution in England', in Roy Porter and Mikulas Teich (ed), *The Scientific Revolution in National Context*, Cambridge University Press, Cambridge 1992, p199.

34. In a recent article Susan Wiseman similarly argues that 'in Tyson's anatomy ... the relationship between the empirical and the social, even political, continues to be intimate'. See her 'Monstrous Perfectibility: Ape-Human Transformation in Hobbes, Bulwer, Rousseau', in Fudge *et al* (eds), *At the Borders of the Human: Beasts, Bodies and Natural Philosophy in the Early Modern Period*, Macmillan, Basingstoke 1999.

35. R.B. Shoemaker, 'Reforming the City: The Reformation of Manners Campaign in London, 1690-1738', in Davison, *et al* (eds), *Stilling the Grumbling Hive: The Response to Social and Economic Problems in England 1689-1750*, Alan Sutton, Stroud 1992, p99.

36. William III, *His Majesty's Letter to the Lord Bishop of London* (1689), cited in Tina Isaacs, 'The Anglican Hierarchy and the Reformation of Manners 1688-1738', *Journal of Ecclesiastical History*, 33:3 (1982), pp392-393.

37. For an overview of the SRMs see T.C. Curtis and W.A. Speck, 'The Societies for the Reformation of Manners: A Case Study in the Theory and Practice of Moral Reform', *Literature and History*, 3 (1976), pp45-64.

38. Josiah Woodward, *An Account of the Rise and Progress of the Religious Societies in the City of London &. of the Endeavours for Reformation of Manners which have been made therein*, second edition (1698), p63.

39. Ned Ward, *The London Spy* (1698-9), fourth edition, 1709, Paul Hyland (ed), Colleagues Press, East Lansing 1993, pp275, 276.

40. Anon., *Proposals for a National Reformation of Manners, Humbly offered to the Consideration of our Magistrates and Clergy* (1694), p25.

41. Shelley Burtt, 'The Societies for the Reformation of Manners: Between John Locke and the devil in Augustan England', in Roger D. Lund (ed), *The Margins of Orthodoxy: Heterodox Writing and Cultural Response, 1660-1750*, Cambridge University Press, Cambridge 1995, p152.

42. Stuart Hall, 'Gramsci's relevance for a study of race and ethnicity', in David Morley and Kuan-Hsing Chen (eds), *Stuart Hall: Critical Dialogues in Cultural Studies*, Routledge, London and New York 1996, p424.

43. Bruce Grelle, 'Hegemony and the "Universalization" of Moral Ideas: Gramsci's Importance for Comparative Religious Ethics', *Soundings* 78:3-4 (1995), 526.

44. Figure cited in Tim Hitchcock, 'Paupers and Preachers: The SPCK and the Parochial Workhouse Movement', in Davison et al (eds), *op. cit.*, p148.

45. See Mary E. Fissell, 'Charity Universal? Institutions and Moral Reform in Eighteenth-century England', in Davison et al (eds), *op.cit.*, pp124-5.

46. James Johnston, *Transactions of the Corporation of the Poor, in the City of Bristol*, Bristol 1826, cited in Montagu, *op.cit.*, p224. Tyson's father had been Mayor of Bristol from 1659-1660.

47. T.J. Manchee, *The Bristol Charities*, Bristol 1831, vol. 2, p.327, cited in Montagu, *op. cit.*, p328.

48. 'Spittal Sermon at St *Brides* by Dr. *Ibbot*', cited in John Strype, *A Survey of the Cities of London and Westminster* (1720), Volume I, p197.

49. Srype, *op. cit.*, p196, Italics added.

50. *Ibid.*

51. Antonio Gramsci, *Selections from the Prison Notebooks of Antonio Gramsci*, Lawrence and Wishart, London 1971, p12.

52. Tyson, *op. cit.*, p8.

53. M.F. Ashley Montagu, 'Tyson's *Orang-Outang, Sive Homo Sylvestris* and Swift's *Gulliver's Travels*', *PMLA*, LIX (1944), p84.

54. Stuart Hall, 'Interview: Culture and Power', *Radical Philosophy* 86 (Nov/Dec 1997), p30.

Navigating selfhood: Geographical space and the early modern remapping of the subject

COLIN COUNSELL

An assumption central to the work of a range of contemporary spatial theorists is that space is socially constructed. For such as Lefebvre, Soja and de Certeau, space and society exist in a symbiotic relationship: social relations presuppose complementary spaces for their functioning, while those spaces are themselves enacted into being solely by the practice of such relations.[1] But this formulation fails to acknowledge the full role of a third term in the process, that of subjectivity. For if spaces are demarcated in social, material practice, this assumes a self for whom those spaces already exist conceptually, an agent in whose gaze the spatial continuum is already mapped out for action.

This is nowhere more evident than in periods of major epistemological change, for it is then that conflicting spatial models collide, revealing their constructedness. In *The Production of Space* (1991) Lefebvre notes:

> The passage from one mode of production to another is of the highest theoretical importance for our purposes, for it results from contradictions in the social relations of production which cannot fail to leave their mark on space and indeed to revolutionise it. Since, *ex hypothesi,* each mode of production has its own particular space, the shift from one mode to another must entail the production of a new space ... examination of the transitions between modes of production will reveal that a fresh space is indeed generated during such changes, a space which is planned and organised subsequently.[2]

If changes in the relations of production cause a shift in space, then the subject perceiving/enacting it must undergo a comparable 'revolution'. In this essay I will examine the redrawing of social space as it occurred at a moment of epochal change in Europe: the Renaissance. In particular I will explore the role of what Lefebvre terms 'representations of space' in the formation of the social subject, the ways in which shifts in spatial models effect corresponding changes in the modes of subjectivity they posit.

We can begin by exploring premodern notions of space; the founding logic of which is best illustrated in reference to that most evocative of medieval spatial representations, the *mappa mundi*. *Mappi mundi* are of course geographically inaccurate, not least because they were designed less as tools for practical navigation than as symbolic models of the Creation. Some early examples, the so-called 'T-O' maps, consist of no more than simple geometrical diagrams (a circle divided by a T shape) showing the relative positions of Europe, Asia and Africa. Indeed, while later versions offer greater

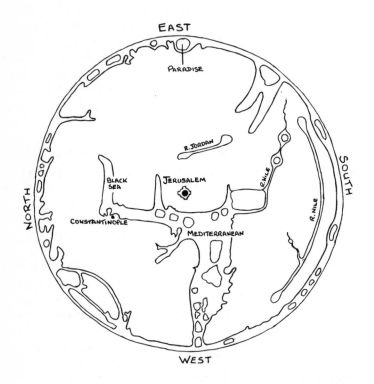

Figure 1

cartographic detail, the same basic geometry is evident in their arrangement, which comprises a disc with Jerusalem at its centre and, radiating out from it to form a symmetrical pattern, the three continents of the known world. Figure 1 shows a simplified version of the later form, based on a representative example, the Hereford *mappa mundi*.[3]

Viewed as a semiotic arrangement, one generating meaning, the first key feature of this model is the theological character of its hub. The city at the map's centre performs a general ontological function as a kind of spatial *point de capiton*,[4] for in anchoring the entire structure in the otherwise undifferentiated continuum of space, it provides a fixed point from which the map's quantification of that space can proceed. But the *mappa mundi* goes further, for with this function performed by Jerusalem – with all other sites located in reference to Christ's Holy City – space enters representation as part of the Christian paradigm. This is augmented by its directional orientation: the East, the location of Paradise and the direction from which Christ, reborn, will return, is 'highest', at the top. The map does not merely grant existing geographical contours a religious significance, it makes space meaningful, knowable, only within a discourse of Christianity. The terrain of the known world is thereby rendered a part of God's design; viewed semiotically, it is made to signify His divine plan.

If the hub that is Jerusalem pins the model in space, however, equally important is the patterning, the spatio-conceptual ordering, which this makes possible. The *mappa mundi* shows the three continents of the known world separated by seas; the map is, it appears, based an actual geography, its landmasses being distinguished by concrete barriers, which take up real space. But as we have noted, the cartographic accuracy of such maps is secondary to their symbolic loading, and in this sense one of the key qualities even of the later forms is their general symmetry. With the continents deployed in a pattern, the significance of the position of each, its site, shape and boundary, is derived from the whole. It is therefore the relations of the overall structure, the relations between its parts, which make them distinct, able to function oppositionally; that is, it is the pattern in its entirety which enables each of its components to bear symbolic freight, allowing Europe to stand for certain values, Asia for others.[5] Despite the waters which literally separate them, Africa, Asia and Europe are able to operate semically due to their conceptual, typological distinction from each other, a distinction expressed by their separation in space.[6]

This mobilisation of tangible reality as a sign of an intangible order illustrates the essentially sacramental character of the *mappa mundi*. Partly as a result of a neoplatonic dimension to early Christian theology, mediated by such as Augustine, the realm of the profane was viewed by the medieval church as less 'real' than that of the sacred, merely an imperfect reflection of the latter's divine and eternal forms.[7] Epistemologically subordinate to the immaterial, the meaning granted the material world was therefore a function of its place in the theological schema, the parts of the Creation being valued and understood in reference to the Creator's plan.

Sacramental paradigms accordingly foster a representational logic in which the qualities of the concrete are semically subservient to those of the conceptual, and this logic is nowhere more evident than in representation's uses of space. In medieval religious painting, for example, space was customarily depicted as without quantity *per se*, rendered as merely the visual expression of greater, conceptual distinctions between objects: Christ would typically be placed on a level above mere saints (commensurate with his divinity) according to the spatial code of elevation, while the saints' distance from His divine body, and the quantity of space they occupied, was a measure of their relative theological status.[8] The same general aesthetic – of space dematerialised, symbolic of metaphysical values – governs the symmetrical deployment of continents in the *mappa mundi*, for, in its pattern, the space occupied by each land mass defines and is defined by the spaces occupied by the others, the watery zones between working primarily to render them distinct, able to express those theological distinctions by which the world was made knowable.

If such spatial divisions marked a theologisation of geography, however, most significant for this essay is that their founding logic posited a particular role for the viewing subject. This subject-positioning figured an investment of power, one which we can explore via the work of a more oblique theorist of spatiality, Michel Foucault. Writing in *Discipline and Punish* (1977) of the 'micro-physics of power' which order the modern penal system, Foucault notes how such power is characteristically 'exercised rather than possessed ... manifested and sometimes extended by the position of those who are dominated.' He continues:

> These 'power-relations' are to be analysed, therefore, not on the basis of a subject of knowledge who is or is not free in relation to the power system, but, on the contrary, the subject who knows, the objects to be

known and the modalities of knowledge must be regarded as so many effects of these fundamental implications of power-knowledge and their historical transformations. In short, it is not the activity of the subject of knowledge that produces a corpus of knowledge, useful or resistant to power, but power-knowledge, the processes and struggles that traverse it and of which it is made up, that determines the forms and possible domains of knowledge.[9]

For Foucault, then, hegemonic systems of 'knowing' position the subject within matrices of power. The objects of the world, the subject who views them, and the modality of knowledge which constitutes the subject/object relation – these are all facets of a single political mechanism, one in which the *kind* of knowledge mobilised works to position – effectively, to *construct* – a complementary subject. This Foucauldian gaze thus constitutes a three-part (visual) geometry in which power is encoded not simply in knowledge but in the perspective such knowledge offers the viewer and, most importantly, the epistemological practices it requires him or her to undertake.

Foucault of course focuses on 'surveillance' and the subject of modernity, but the equation of knowledge with power that he posits can be applied to other cultural and historical sites. On this basis we can begin to describe a political subject evident in premodern Europe, central to the construction of which is the relation between the viewer and meaning itself. Reading a painting of the kind described above entails decoding the material distance between objects – spatial quantity – for its immaterial, symbolic freight. It requires the reader to recognise that the real, material space s/he sees and occupies is subordinate to the *meaningful* space s/he *cannot* see. The *act* of interpretation, then, effectively places the viewer in a position of perceptual disempowerment; in order to know, you must first understand how little you *can* know, and perform that understanding in what you *do*.

Interpreting the *mappa mundi* demands the same recognition, for it too entails an act of symbolic transposition, the translation of the map's material distances, its 'profane' signifiers, into the conceptual signifieds of Christian theology. It presumes a similar acceptance that the mutable world – the merely material realm one necessarily inhabits *as* interpreter – is shaped by, and secondary to, the higher realm of the immaterial. To understand the *mappa mundi*, to be successfully 'hailed' by its discourse in an Althusserian sense,[10] is therefore to adopt the subject-position of this Christian self; and once again, this subject-positioning is effected less by a moment of 'identification' than by the hermeneutic work that must be undertaken, a cognitive role to be lived as part of a given mode of interpretative activity. It is not simply that the individual is denied access to the absolute of meaning. Rather, the process of reading requires the individual to *enact*, to performatively *be* a cognitively disadvantaged subject.

Mappi mundi thus illustrate a 'technology of power' particular to the world of premodern Europe, one which is evident in a range of practices drawn into Renaissance culture from the preceding period: the practice of syllogistic logic wherein truth was not determined empirically, via the observations of individual viewers, but by reference to the premises of acknowledged authorities and prayer in the Catholic church where communication with God was deemed possible only via mediating agencies, either the figures of the Church hierarchy itself or its pantheon of saints. These and other practices evidence a common Foucauldian 'modality' wherein knowledge resides in a realm distant from that occupied by the subject, one which s/he cannot access directly. This knowledge, moreover, is embedded not merely in the representation to be decoded but also in the experience of decoding it, a function of the interpretative process one must undertake in order to derive the proffered meanings.

This epistemological modality is fundamentally deterministic, for it disempowers its subject by defining him/her in reference to an immutable pattern which is by definition beyond any mortal's capacity to access. Positioned within a transcendent schema, the subject's knowledge is contingent upon epistemological insufficiency: one is 'known', but cannot oneself 'know'.[11] Just as the doctrine of original sin denied the Christian even a notional self-determination – being born into a state of sin, you *are* your place in the schema – so the meaning of geographical contours finally resides in a dimension beyond the material geography we experience.

This subject position was not the only one available in Renaissance Europe, however, for if it was rooted in a residual epistemology, newly emergent were cultural components which would soon be deployed as bases of a new one. The 'discovery' and subsequent colonisation of the New World not only provided one of the economic foundations of nascent modernity, it also prompted a redraughting of geographical space. If the known world was traditionally conceived as a pattern symbolic of a divine order, then, with the progressive colonisation of the Americas, that spatial model lost its epistemological foundation. Not only could 'Christian European' cultures be founded outside Christian Europe, the entire spatio-conceptual structure began to be undermined when the pattern was shown to have an outside – when this 'knowledge' was revealed to be incomplete. With subjects sailing beyond the limits of the old cartography, geography and the sacramental model of the self were no longer complementary.

I have so far focused upon maps: artefacts of the sort Lefebvre terms 'representations of space'; but equally illustrative are changes in the kinds of doxic knowledge which underpin social productive practice generally.[12] Significant in this respect are the practical means by which early modern travellers negotiated real space. Medieval and early Renaissance navigation was conducted using principles best exemplified by Mediterranean *portolani*.[13] Used to find a route from one coast to another, the typical *portolano* detailed the shorelines and the expanse of sea between. Superimposed on this was a compass rose, a fan of lines or 'rhumbs' indicating degrees of direction. To journey from one coast to another, the navigator found the rhumb which most exactly paralleled the line between his points of embarkation and destination, and sailed in that heading.

As early modern science developed, however, such practices were superseded. Latitude, which already played a role in voyages along longer and unfamiliar routes, was joined with longitude to offer a way of understanding position in space mathematically. As one best-seller has pointed out, it was not until the eighteenth century, with John Harrison's development of the chronometer, that it became possible to determine longitude accurately.[14] However, this invention is from our perspective less significant than the existence of longitude as a concept. This emerged much earlier, as the serious search for a reliable means of measuring longitude was begun at least as early as 1514 with the work of Johannes Werner. The impact of Galileo's reflections on the moons of Jupiter in 1610 demonstrates the firm place it already had on the European cultural agenda in the early seventeenth century: from the 1650s Galileo's system was actually used to redraw land maps.[15] In fact, Mercator's world map attempted to depict longitude in 'plain chart' form in 1569, albeit not entirely successfully, and relatively serviceable marine charts based on Mercator's model were available by the 1590s.[16] Thus longitude not only played a practical, if uncertain role in real navigation, it was culturally important as an idea, being sought, thought about and discussed, central to the way geographical space was conceived long before it could be precisely measured.

Although ostensibly purely practical, these navigational procedures in fact embody some of the founding structures of medieval
and modern thought respectively. We noted that the subject of sacra-
mentalism is disempowered; placed in a transcendant schema to
which you by definition do not have access, you *are* your place in the
system, and consequently can 'know' only by referring to acknowledged authorities. *Portolani* operate a similar logic. The charts do not
tell the navigator his (for it was always a man) position in space, or
that of his destination, so that he might plot a line between them.
Indeed, although some included marginal measuring grids, the charts
themselves do not measure space at all, they measure direction. The
difference is substantial, for direction is a form of knowledge which
is inherently relative, describing the relationship between two given
points – neither of which, in this case, is the position of the navigator.
The knowledge they supply therefore comprises not a location but a
relationship to other locations; knowledge is centred not on the navi-
gating-subject but in a schema in which that subject, lacking
knowledge, is placed. The subject-position he is required to adopt is
therefore a disempowered one, for the navigator is located in a structure inaccessible to the perspective which he, as operator of the
system, is required to take – he *is* his position in the logic of the chart.
Just as the viewer of the *mappa mundi* is sited relative to a pattern that
cannot fully be known, so with *portolani* the navigator's *geographical*
location is a function of a mapping whose knowledge transcends the
very vantage it offers him.

With the advent of the concept of longitude a quite different mode
of spatial knowledge becomes evident. Latitude and longitude are
first an abstract and mathematical way of conceptualising space, a
shift to the kind of rationalistic formulation characteristic of modernity. Moreover they grant space itself quantity. In the *mappa mundi*,
as in medieval religious painting, real spatial extent is secondary to
space's symbolic value; with latitude and longitude it is space itself,
which is measured, 'known'. Objects in Albertian perspective painting take up areas of a general, equalised space,[17] and similarly latitude
and longitude first calibrate space in the abstract to then determine an
object's position within it.

But of greater significance for this essay is that the practice itself
implicitly posited a new kind of subject. Although they locate the
traveller in real physical space, longitude and latitude position him
conceptually 'above' it, at a site of knowledge superior to it. The
mathematical computation itself requires that the navigator adopt a

vantage *upon* his own location, offering him that perspective as a way of understanding his geographical 'identity'. The vantage of the new navigator in this sense mirrors that of the subject of modernity. Descartes' model, which would provide the foundation for the modern Individual, posited an inner self distinct from the body, so that the latter was reduced to an 'automaton' and identity was made a function exclusively of the psyche.[18] This informs Descartes's own theory of scientific method and the modality of reason which developed from it. The modern rationalist or scientist presumes to view and interrogate material phenomena objectively; it is only by observing the world from a position of non-involvement that phenomena can, it is assumed, be explained by disinterested reason. Such objective 'distance' requires the absolute separation of the viewer from the world of objects he views, and which his own body occupies: precisely that separation on which the modern dualistic self is constructed.

Modern selfhood is thus founded in a realm quite distinct from the physical, and it is this form of subject that we see echoed in the new navigation. If the modern scientist will take an objective stance towards phenomena, will guarantee disinterestedness by conceptually removing himself from the world of objects he seeks to explain, then the navigator similarly assumes a rational distance from his own, real position: just as the Cartesian subject, founded in its interiority, stands aloof from its physical form, so the practitioner of longitude and latitude stands apart from the location of his material body. Whereas the old navigator is defined by his place in space, *is* his position in the structure, the new, self-reflective navigator is a product of his *knowledge of* that position.

This modern, dualistic arrangement – of self and knowable other, viewing subject and the world of objects it empirically views – found echoes in a variety of discourses. The Protestantism that blossomed in those countries most advanced along the path towards the new mode and relations of production insisted that the Christian's communication with God was unmediated, a direct link between conscience and the divine; just as, later, the Lockean citizen would enter the social contract from the reasoned vantage of his own volition. Resonating through a variety of key discursive formations, the new symbiotic conceptions of space and the self, enacted in the traversal of real terrain, would constitute the perspective at the centre of modern thought.

Such developments are representative of profound cultural

changes, for in all these modern practices and discourses the subject is no longer defined relative to a symbology of exterior structures, such as geographical borders; rather, in an epistemological reversal, its conception of geographical space is determined by a border which is *interior*, lying between the mind and the body. This made for a new relationship between geography and its viewer. Writing in *The Advancement of Learning* (1605) of the 'voyagers, to whom it hath been often granted to wheel and roll about the whole compass of the earth', Bacon states:

> ... this excellent felicity in nautical art, and environing the world, may plant also an expectation of further proficiencies and augmentations of sciences; especially seeing it seems to be decreed by the divine counsel, that these two should be coaevals ... as if the through passage or perlustration of the world, and the various propagation of knowledge were appointed to be in the same ages.[19]

Bacon draws a clear parallel between geographical discoveries and those of a scientific kind such as are proper to the agent of an emerging modernity. Both entail an act of illumination, the crossing of a border of ignorance, so that a rational, civilised and implicitly *European* knowledge is posed against a barbarous and benighted geographical other. By the time of his writing such dichotomies were by no means novel. Writing in his essay 'On Cannibals' in 1580 of the peoples encountered in what would become Brazil,[20] Montaigne appears to take a quite different view; their supposed barbarism, he argues, is in reality a greater nobility, for while old Europe is stale and decayed, over-civilised, the tribesmen retain an innocence which brings them closer to humankind's ideal, prelapsarian state. Although Bacon and Montaigne take opposite positions, each uses the semic potential of the new model of spatiality to construct the same defining axis, posing a rational and sophisticated Europe against an innocent and/or ignorant New World. More than a purely geographical space, Europe is made a continent of the mind, the home of a self-reflective subject who transcends mere physical location to be defined instead by qualities of reason.

In conclusion, the matters raised in this essay must prompt interesting questions about contemporary, modern and/or postmodern space and its navigations, and about the ways in which these might eventually come to be seen as influencing the formation of selves at the end of the twentieth century and the beginning of the new millennium. David

Harvey and Doreen Massey have written of the significance of the late modern 'time/space compression' in the context of globalisation, and both Edward Soja and Fredric Jameson understand contemporary time and space as effecting the possibility of a frightening (in Jameson's thesis, 'schizophrenic') ahistoricisation of the late modern or postmodern subject.[21] But however we are to understand these arguments, a study of a much earlier relationship between self and space should indicate the profound importance of giving political consideration to the experiences of the 'navigator' of our own times.

NOTES

1. Key texts from these authors include H. Lefebvre, *The Production of Space*, Donald Nicholson-Smith (trans), Oxford 1991; E. Soja, *Postmodern Geographies: The Reassertion of Space in Critical Social Theory*, London 1989; M. de Certeau, *The Practice of Everyday Life*, Berkeley 1984.

2. H.Lefebvre, *The Production of Space*, op. cit., pp45-46.

3. See P.D.A. Harvey, *Mappa Mundi: The Hereford World Map*, London 1996 for full reproductions of the map.

4. The term ultimately derives from Jacques Lacan, 'The agency of the letter in the unconscious or reason since Freud', in *Ecrits: A Selection*, Alan Sheridan (trans), London 1977. Although it is used somewhat promiscuously here, it still retains its Lacanian sense of an instrument of ontological anchoring.

5. For a discussion of the historical meanings traditionally ascribed the continents, see K. Wilson & J. van der Dussen (eds), *The History of the Idea of Europe*, London 1993.

6. Although the *Mappa Mundi* derives from Roman cartography, in which form it was originally disseminated about the Mediterranean rim, by the medieval period this model of geographical representation was particular to Europe. In the Middle and Near East, for example, continental divisions did not form the basis of geographical formulations (and hence of identity) until the principle was introduced from Western culture in the eighteenth century. See Wilson & Van der Dustan, *The History of the Idea of Europe*, and B. Lewis, *Cultures in Conflict: Christians, Muslims and Jews in the Age of Discovery*, Oxford 1995.

7. See for example W.T. Jones, *The Medieval Mind*, San Diego 1969.

8. See Samuel Y. Edgerton Jnr., *The Renaissance Rediscovery of Linear Perspective*, New York 1975.

9. M. Foucault, *Discipline and Punish: The Birth of the Prison*, Alan Sheridan (trans), London 1984.

10. L. Althusser, 'Ideology and the Ideological State Apparatuses', in *Essays on Ideology*, London 1984.

11. For a discussion of the epistemological consequences of the medieval viewer's literal positioning in space, see my own article 'Traversing the Known: Spatiality and the Gaze in Pre- and Post-Renaissance Theatre', *Journal of Dramatic Theory and Criticism*, 11, 1996, pp19-33.

12. The term is used here in the sociological sense established by Bourdieu, designating the kind of taken-for-granted knowledge underpinning ordinary social practice. See P. Bourdieu, *Outline of a Theory of Practice*, Richard Nice (trans), Cambridge 1977.

13. The term was originally used to designate *written* descriptions of sea routes (known in Northern Europe as 'routiers' or 'rutters') but is now generally extended to include pictorial charts of the kind discussed here. See J. H. Parry, *The Age of Reconnaissance: Discovery, Exploration and Settlement 1450-1650*, Los Angeles 1963.

14. Dava Sobel, *Longitude*, London 1996.

15. *Ibid.*, p24.

16. See Parry, *The Age of Reconnaissance,* p146.

17. See Edgerton, *The Renaissance Rediscovery of Linear Perspective;* John Berger, *Ways of Seeing,* Harmondsworth 1972; Martin Jay, 'Scopic Regimes of Modernity', in Hal Foster (ed), *Vision and Visuality*, Seattle 1988; John White, *The Birth and Rebirth of Pictorial Space*, Cambridge 1988.

18. For an interesting discussion of the Cartesian remodelling of corporeality, see Bryan S. Turner, *The Body and Society*, London 1996.

19. F. Bacon, *The Advancement of Learning,* Michael Selbourne (ed), Oxford 1966, p51.

20. M. de Montaigne, *Essays*, J. M. Cohen (trans), Harmondsworth 1958.

21. See D. Harvey, *The Condition of Postmodernity: An Enquiry into the Origins of Social Change*, Oxford 1989; D. Massey, *High-Tech Fantasies: Science Parks in Society, Science and Space*, London 1992; F. Jameson, *Postmodernism: or, The Cultural Logic of Late Capitalism*, London 1991; E. Soja, *Postmodern Geographies.*

Local History: Property, Place and History in the English Country House Poem

PAUL McSORLEY

The country house poem of the seventeenth century flourished during one of the most turbulent periods of English political history.[1] This period is, as well, often identified as that within which a decisive transition from a pre-modern to a modern world took place. Between Ben Jonson's 'To Penshurst' (1612), which inaugurated the genre, and Andrew Marvell's 'Upon Appleton House' (c.1652), generally reckoned the last major example, England witnessed four decades of increasing conflict between the crown and key elements of the political estates (and some hitherto excluded from politics), culminating in Civil War, regicide and the establishment of a republic.[2] To many historians, these events constituted nothing less than a revolution in which a new social order – bourgeois and capitalist – triumphed over the residual elements of a feudal-aristocratic order held together by the anachronistic principle of the divine right of kings. This interpretation has been the one most widely accepted by politically radical literary critics writing on the literature of the seventeenth century, though it has been the subject of fierce debate among historians themselves, many of whom would see it as contentious, if not thoroughly discredited.

In this essay I will attempt to describe some of the ways in which, in seventeenth-century poetry, the country house (or country estate) became the focus of attempts to negotiate political identities in a period of turmoil. The identities in question are those of the poet, usually as client, dependent or friend of the owner of the house; of the owner, his family and other dependants; and sometimes that of the nation, since in some of the major examples of this poetry, consideration of the situation of the house and its inhabitants leads on to consideration of the nature and the state of the nation. A certain political identification is already implied by this extrapolation, since it implies the centrality of the country gentry, one of the social groups whose actions did so much to determine the direction of political events, to the destiny of the nation. The axes along which identities are established in the poems will be analysed as those of property, place and history.

James Turner has pointed out in *The Politics of Landscape* that in the seventeenth century property, specifically landed property, confers political identity in the wider commonwealth: 'Ownership of land becomes the sole condition for membership of the common-wealth'.[3] Those who do not own land are not, strictly, political subjects, do not possess agency and a voice in the political affairs of the kingdom. In the country house poem, the house and the surrounding estate function as metonyms for the moral and social values of the family or the person who owns them. One's property is an indication of one's properties, one's essential characteristics. 'Property' is also intimately connected with the idea of place. As Turner writes: '"Land" and "place" are equivalent to "propriety" – meaning in seventeenth-century England both *property* and *knowing one's* place'.[4] The order of the universe, like the structure of society, was supposed to depend on a hierarchy of places from lowest to high-est. Place is identity. However, 'place' is also to be understood here in the sense of specific 'location' or 'locality', of great importance to the identity of the country gentry, for many of whom, as recent revision-ist histories of the seventeenth century have tended to emphasise, the local often took precedence over the national, the 'county' over the 'country', and the affairs of the shire over affairs of state.[5] I make this point here because one of the main arguments of this essay will concern the ways in which grand narratives of identity formation in the seventeenth century – or what is often called 'early modern subjectivity'[6] – might in fact obscure some of the more complex *local* histories of identity that can be deduced from studies of seventeenth century texts, and I will argue for a focus on the historically, geographically and generically local understanding of political subjectivity.

I will also discuss the ways in which the country house poem imagines identities in relation to the past (of houses, families, persons, communities and nations) and in relation to the processes which sustain, transform or threaten them. The seventeenth century itself was one in which competing versions of history struggled for dominance, for example in disputes over the origins of the law, the 'ancient constitution', national origins, religious history and dynastic history. It has ever since been the subject of intense, often bitter debate among historians concerning historical narrative, explanation and method, and indeed conceptions of 'history'. I will go on to suggest that literary studies of the seventeenth century, especially those inspired by post-structuralist and postmodernist theories that have attempted to contribute to a 'history of the subject', have much to learn from these debates, and particularly from some of the participants whose premises and sympathies might seem furthest from their own.

In reading the country house poem in relation to questions of political subjectivity, it is useful to recall that twentieth-century historiography has circled endlessly around the significance of 'the country' and the role of the country gentry in seventeenth-century history.[7] Were they a class in ascent or decline? Were they a class at all? Were they the agents of constitutional reform, of revolutionary change, of conservative resistance to royal encroachment and innovation? Were they engaged with, or oblivious to, questions of national politics and of political principle? Were they united or divided? What were their religious sympathies? Were their loyalties and actions primarily determined by considerations of party, principle, religion, ideology, office, kinship, or 'county community'? These questions concern precisely the nature of the country gentry as political subjects.

Poetry does not pose questions of political subjectivity in the same way as historical writing, but it poses them nonetheless. In Jonson's 'To Penshurst',[8] (Penshurst was the home of the Sidney family) a kind of ideal commonwealth is imagined, one which we would now call 'feudal' in character, and which is quite different from the commonwealth imagined in Jonson's comedies, with their competing urban types (dissolute gentry, naïve or mercenary citizens, con men, thieves and prostitutes) caught up in restless competition for money and status; and is equally different from the state as imagined in his tragedies, of a Hobbesian, predatory struggle for supremacy within a powerful élite. The country is a repository of positive values, presented in a highly idealised form.

The copse that yields 'seasoned deer', the lower land with its sheep, bullocks, kine and calves, the middle ground where 'thy mares and horses breed', the banks stocked with coneys and the woods with pheasant and partridge, the well-stocked ponds and the orchards thick with seasonal fruits, all signify one of the central values of the country gentleman: good husbandry. The poem offers an idealised account of the social relations on the estate, which are simultaneously hierarchical and free from all conflict and resentment:

> And though thy walls be of the country stone,
> They are reared with no man's ruin, no man's groan,
> There's none, that dwell about them, wish them down;
> But all come in, the farmer, and the clown:
> And no one empty-handed, to salute
> Thy lord, and lady, though they have no suit.
> Some bring a capon, some a rural cake,
> Some nuts, some apples; some that think they make
> The better cheeses, bring them...
>
> But what can this (more than express their love)
> Add to thy free provisions, far above
> The need of such? Whose liberal board doth flow,
> With all, that hospitality doth know!
> ('To Penshurst', ll. 45-60)

Just as nature offers itself freely to the delight of the landed family, so their neighbours and tenants freely offer their produce: expropriated goods and labour become a loving gift. Further, these goods are superfluous. They merely add to an existing plenty. In fact, the household's 'liberal board' feeds all, and in a reversal of the real pattern of dependence, it is the family who provide for their workers and tenants, rather than the other way round.

The poet himself is placed in this ideal community where he feels he rightly belongs, in pointed contrast to the social division practised at other 'great men's tables':

> Where the same beer, and bread, and self-same wine,
> That is his lordship's, shall be also mine.
> And I not fain to sit (as some, this day,
> At great men's tables) and yet dine away.
> (ll. 63-6)

Social place is here signified by place at table. The medieval practice whereby all alike would dine together in the great hall in country houses had already practically disappeared, the family and most honoured guests withdrawing to a private room upstairs.[9] Jonson refers to a further refinement of social division, whereby even in the 'honoured' company not all dine equally from the same dish. In drawing attention to this, Jonson stresses the antiquity of the manners of Penshurst's owners, as they adhere to a tradition of hospitality elsewhere in decline. Commenting on Jonson and other seventeenth-century sources, Felicity Heal remarks that they share '... the definition of customary hospitality as 'other', as belonging to some time, space or social group that was not part of the centralist modern paradigm from which most observers operated'.[10]

The most important act of hospitality described in the poem is that offered to King James I, on an unexpected visit to the house:

> What (great, I will not say, but) sudden cheer
> Did'st thou, then, make them! And what praise was heaped
> On thy good lady, then! Who, therein, reap'd
> The just reward of her high huswifery;
> To have her linen, plate, and all things nigh,
> When she was farre: and not a room, but dressed,
> As if it had expected such a guest!
> (ll. 82-88)

Inside the house, in a traditional gendering of duties, it is the 'good lady' who is responsible for maintaining the gentry ideal, high huswifery indoors complementing high husbandry outdoors. These lines incorporate into the poem an account of the owner's place in the network of power leading up to the king, and the intimate relationship between the king and the country gentry. Penshurst is not like one of the extravagant prodigy houses (a Burghley or a Theobalds) built in the sixteenth century 'specifically as places to receive the queen'.[11] It is contrasted with such houses in the opening lines ('Thou art not, Penshurst, built to envious show/ Of touch, or marble ...'). Still it is worthy of a royal guest. The house and family are at the disposal of the king, for hospitable entertainment as they would be for the political, legal and fiscal duties expected of the country gentry as the king's deputies in their localities. It is significant that the union of monarchy and gentry is expressed in terms of the king's residence in the country house, rather than the gentleman's presence at court, implying that royal power, if not sovereignty, resides with, and in, this alliance.

The positive meanings which coalesce around the country estate in

'To Penshurst' are the praise of antiquity, in architecture and manners; of good husbandry and good 'huswifery'; of an ordered society free from envy and tension, underpinned by Nature and divine providence; the practice of hospitality; a proper appreciation of the role of poetry and letters, exemplified by the treatment of the poet and the humanist credentials of the Sidney family's history; and, finally, of an intimate alliance between the monarchy and the country gentleman. All this has seemed to some commentators to be too good to be true. Raymond Williams, in *The Country and City* describes the poem as '... a magical recreation of a natural bounty and then a willing charity, both serving to ratify and bless the country landowner, and, by a characteristic reification, his house'. It is an idealisation achieved, Williams writes, 'by the simple extraction of the existence of labourers'.[12] The idealisation serves a more positive function in Isabel Rivers' account of the poem: ' "To Penshurst" illustrates, embodied in the country house and its uses, the ideal function of the aristocracy, their position in relation to the king above them and the people below, their social responsibility in country life'.[13] It is a poem more deeply engaged with a problematic present, a time when dangerous rifts were already beginning to appear between monarchy and aristocracy, than with the feudal past: 'Jonson is not appealing to the feudal past but trying to provide an alternative pattern for the dangerous tendencies of the present' (p50).

Williams's point is important in drawing attention to what would need to be *forgotten* in order for us to become the kinds of subject imagined in the poem: the whole apparatus of oppression and exploitation involved in this kind of 'estate' (using the term in both its topographical and political senses) and the mystifications which represent rapacity as generosity. However, Rivers's account seems to be closer at least to the political intention of the poem as it might be conceived by anyone who doesn't simply wish that a seventeenth-century royalist had been a twentieth-century Marxist instead.

A more sympathetic account might invoke recollection rather than forgetting, and explain the idealisation as a deliberate strategy of Platonic anamnesia, a recalling of the Ideal (and truly real) form of society, parallel to Jonson's idealisations of the court in his masques, despite his awareness of the discrepancy between this ideal and the actual court. The act of anamnesia recalls the ideal form of society for the court and the country alike, and at the same time calls them back to the ideal. This ideal involves a certain imaginary de-centring of Stuart political life, which was becoming increasingly centred around the absolutist demands of James I, to the detriment of other members of the commonwealth. The poem replaces the court with the country (one of its potential antagonists) as a potential centre of the political. This can be interpreted as a deliberate strategy, an intervention, rather than a mystification: nobody could accuse the author of *Sejanus* and *Catiline*, after all, of naivety about the realities of political life in Stuart England, or of timidity when it came to exploring the Machiavellian realities of court life.

The form of Jonson's intervention is contingent on certain localised conditions. It is a matter of the poet speaking of politics from one of the places where speech was, for him, possible. Though in his element in public life, he was not a member of the political classes. He was dependent on the patronage of both the country gentry and the king, never having made a sufficient living from the professional theatre.[14] The poem envisages a situation in which the poet lives as an honoured guest in a country house itself honoured by the royal presence. There is also a conjunction of possibilities, some of them 'actual' (the fact that there was a tradition of patronage in the Sidney family, and that the Sidneys had begun to receive renewed royal favour under James, after a period of neglect under Elizabeth), some of them strictly literary: the existence of a tradition of Latin poetry in praise of country life, and of the Georgic, which he draws on extensively and which provides the discursive basis for his re-inscription of the English estate;[15] and the tradition of the *locus amoenus*, the 'delightful place' which provides a refuge from care.[16] From these necessities and these materials Jonson constructs, as Rivers says, 'an alternative pattern for the dangerous tendencies of the present'. Penshurst becomes the delightful place that offers refuge from the risks of social exclusion (for the poet) and social conflict in the wider world. If it is apparently a refuge in the past (the 'ancient pile' of line 5) it is worth noting that this is a version of the past (the ordered 'feudal' world, as a later age would call it) which was beginning to be put together in the sixteenth and seventeenth centuries as an imaginary alternative to threatening developments of the present.[17] If 'To Penshurst' is in any way a celebration of an older feudal world, it is an older world which was in the process of being invented when Jonson was writing.

By the time Marvell wrote 'Upon Appleton House' he had other notable examples of country house or estate poems to draw upon, including Thomas Carew's 'To My Friend G.N. from Wrest' and 'To Saxham'; Robert Herrick's 'A Panegyric to Sir Lewis Pemberton'; and Sir John Denham's politicised topography 'Cooper's Hill', at

least in its early versions. Some of these reiterate in different propor-
tions the features which were established in 'To Penshurst': praise of
the bounty of the estate; of antique hospitality; the praise of 'ancient
honesty' (Herrick, l. 42); the denigration of showy, especially classical, new styles in architecture; the 'definition by negatives' which
describes the house by saying what it is not. 'Upon Appleton House'
largely follows the pattern of 'To Penshurst', though with greater
elaboration, right from the opening stanzas, which can be seen as an
expansion of Jonson's opening lines, establishing the antique and
indigenous style of the house, in contrast with the newly adopted
classical principles being applied to English buildings.[18]

However, while taking Jonson and his successors as models, Marvell's
poem confronts a very different political situation. By 1652, the potential for conflict between crown and gentry, or court and country (or
between sections of one and sections of the other, as some historians
would have it), had become actual and reached its climax in the execution of Charles I. This forms part of the immediate context of the poem,
since it celebrates the home, at Nun Appleton, of Lord Fairfax, leader of
the Parliamentary forces in the Civil War from 1645-50. Marvell worked
as tutor to Fairfax's daughter Mary at Appleton House between 1650
and 1652. The poem is one of ambiguous celebration of retirement – a
common theme of the country house poem – but a retirement that in this
case was weighted with specific political content, since Fairfax left public
life because of his disgust with the execution of Charles, and with
Cromwell's policy of waging war on his former allies, the Scots. Fairfax's
retirement represents the recognition of a kind of limit, therefore: the
line beyond which even some committed parliamentarians, prepared to
risk much and to shed blood in the cause, were not prepared to go. The
nation, however, had already crossed this line.

The poem is full of images of encroachment and overturning, for
instance in the stanzas on the flood (stanzas 59-61):

> The river in itself is drowned
> And isles the astonished cattle round.
>
> Let others tell the paradox,
> How eels now bellow in the ox;
> How horses at their tails do kick,
> Turned as they hang to leeches quick;
> How boats can over bridges sail;
> And fishes do the stables scale.

How salmons trespassing are found;
And pikes are taken in the pound.
('Upon Appleton House', ll.473-480)[19]

These lines take Jonson's conceit of the 'Bright eels which ... leap
on land/ Before the fisher, or into his hand' ('To Penshurst', ll. 37-8)
and transform it into something more 'natural' (such things could
happen in a severe flood), but also more sinister: this invasion of the
land by creatures of the water, this overturning of the order of nature,
could actually happen. The line 'The river in itself is drowned' (l. 471)
suggests an even deeper confusion of categories, of subject and object,
of active and passive, which is repeated elsewhere in the poem.

The place of retirement is constantly invaded by the world that has
supposedly been left behind. The descriptions of the gardens and the
fields are saturated by military and political metaphors, for instance
in stanza 37:

When in the east the morning ray
Hangs out the colours of the day,
The bee through these known alleys hums,
Beating the *dian* with its drums.
Then flowers their drowsy eyelids raise,
Their silken ensigns each displays,
And dries its pan yet dank with dew,
And fills its flasks with odours new.
(ll. 289-296)

One could again multiply examples.[20] The *locus amoenus* has
become an armed camp. R.I.V. Hodge comments on the continual
intrusion of the world of war and politics, noting that the idea of
retirement is 'subverted by a mnemonic that instead of reminding
poet and patron of matters they want to remember, gives images for
thoughts they cannot forget'.[21]

As with many of Marvell's political poems, the chief example being
'An Horatian Ode Upon Cromwell's Return from Ireland', it is
almost impossible to discern a definite political 'position' within the
poem. This can easily be dismissed as an effect of urbane wit (the
poem is certainly witty). However, the wit itself is often a matter of a
veering away from, or withdrawal from, a position we expect the
poem to be moving towards, and it is tied in with a feature of the
poem which has been discussed by a number of critics, which is its

mimesis of disorienting optical effects, its playing around with scale, perspective and position, making it difficult for the reader to know where the poet is or where he/she is in relation to the objects described: the kind of optical conundrum represented, for instance, in Marvell's description of the cattle grazing on the newly-mown fields:

> They seem, within the polished grass
> A landskip drawn in looking-glass,
> And shrunk in the huge pasture show
> As spots, so shaped, on faces do –
> Such fleas, ere they approach the eye,
> In multiplying glasses lie.
> They feed so wide, so slowly move,
> As constellations do above.
> ('Upon Appleton House', ll. 457-464)

The complex of references to mirrors, landscapes, perspectives, magnifying glasses and telescopes is tied in with the period's general fascination with problems of optics, but whereas scientific optics sought to clarify the visual field, the effect here is deeply confusing. Robert Wilcher writes that the poem's '... disorientating shifts of style and of visual and mental perspective render uncertain the distinctions between subject and object'.[22]

The poem's problematising of visual perspective is matched by its problematising of historical perspective. The poem deals simultaneously with multiple histories: the history of the Fairfax family; the history of the Reformation (William Fairfax's 'rescue' of Isabel from some morally suspect nuns – stanzas 11-34 – is an allegory of the Reformation; and the allegory is tied in with the history of property in that the house came into the Fairfax family 'at the demolishing' – that is at the dissolution of the monasteries); the history of the civil war (the references noted earlier to Levellers); and also cosmic/ biblical history, with references to the Fall, the Tower of Babel, Exodus, the Flood and the serpent in the garden. Some of the positions in which poet and patron are situated in these different histories are flatly contradictory. For example, stanza 41 invokes the biblical history of the fall, national history, the immediate history of the war that has laid waste to England, and the puritans' own history of themselves as the Elect:

> Oh thou, that dear and happy isle
> The garden of the world ere while,

Thou paradise of foúr seas,
Which heaven guarded us to please,
But to exclude the world, did guard
With watery if not flaming sword.
 What luckless apple did we taste
To make us mortal and thee waste.
(ll.321-328)

These lines are reminiscent of John of Gaunt's invocation of England as a lost Eden in Shakespeare's *Richard II* as well as of the close of Milton's epic.[23] The flaming sword guarding Eden is replaced by a watery sword, but instead of excluding 'the world' (the ungodly, the un-English) it now excludes 'us'. As Englishman, the poet is inside; as Fallen man and as someone who has lived through the desolation of the civil war he and his countrymen are outside.

When Marvell writes of the country house it is clear that he cannot imagine it as the locus of a stable, settled identity as Jonson could forty years earlier. Property, place and history are unsettled and there is no one place (even an imaginary one) from which the poet may speak: instead, a restless and ingenious 'wit' veers from one position to another.

The contrast I have tried to describe between the sense of identity in two poems closely related in genre and structure might seem to some to be symmetrical with certain influential attempts to describe a 'history of subjectivity' in the early modern period.[24] I wish to conclude by saying why I am reluctant to describe this contrast in terms of such phenomena as 'the emergence of the modern subject'. My misgivings concern attempts to describe *long-term* or epochal or epistemic shifts in subjectivity. I've tended to use 'identities' rather than 'subjectivity' (except when qualified by 'political') so far because the latter term tends to imply something like the deep structural conditions of identity, and I don't think that the case has been made for historic shifts at this level. It is not just that I believe that the accounts of the emergence of the early modern subject given so far are inadequate: rather, any attempt to discuss subjectivity in this kind of duration is *bound* to be distorting, and clarifications hoped for by epochal generalisation are not worth the distortions they introduce.

The seventeenth century is seen by certain critics as crucial to an understanding of the emergence of 'modern' forms of subjectivity. It is in this period that a number of factors are said to come together to form the conditions within which a modern type of subjectivity can develop, if only in 'emergent' or 'incipient' form. Different critics stress different combinations of these conditions. One of the conditions is that an emergent capitalism forces massive social changes that bring about the demise of the feudal economic/social order. These social-economic developments are accompanied by major ideological shifts: the Reformation brings about a new stress on the individual's relationship with God; developments in scientific thinking associated with Bacon, for example, as well as Copernicus and Galileo, challenge the appeal to authority in matters of knowledge; Descartes ushers in 'modern' philosophy and inaugurates the period of Enlightenment rationality which remains the dominant paradigm until the late twentieth century. Accompanying these changes are said to be changes in the ways in which human beings experience themselves and their relationship with each other and the world: changes in subjectivity.

In *The Tremulous Private Body*, Barker's Foucauldian account of such changes describes a movement from a 'pre-bourgeois subjection', which 'does not properly involve subjectivity at all' to the (bourgeois) construction of 'subjectivity as the imaginary property of inner selfhood' (p31). The 'newly interiorated subject' (p52) has as its corollary a new 'subjugation' or 'de-realisation' of the body (pp94-5), associated particularly with Descartes' philosophy. Certain seventeenth-century texts, notably *Hamlet* and Marvell's 'To His Coy Mistress', are given as evidence of a transitional state between pre-bourgeois and bourgeois subjectivity. The section on Marvell (pp88-94) indicates clearly, though not explicitly, that this transition is to be understood in relation to a number of the developments mentioned above: a new attitude to love and to the body is bound up with a new emphasis on 'goods', 'effort' and a 'commitment to labour', with militant puritanism (the conjunction implying the 'Protestant work ethic'), and with the transition from an 'old empire' to a 'new republic' (the terms are used metaphorically, but also clearly gesture towards the English Revolution as a key event). Christopher Hill is mentioned at this point, a signal that the formation of this new subjectivity is understood as bound up with one of the 'high road' descriptions of the English Revolution (p88).

Belsey's account in *The Subject of Tragedy*, based on a study of dramatic representation from the fifteenth century to the Restoration, traces the movement from a medieval non-subject which can achieve at most a 'precarious unity',[25] to a post-Restoration subject characterised by a 'stable, transcendent unity' (however illusory) and a new 'interiority' that 'defines the humanist subject' (pp26,

35). In between, in the drama of the first half of the seventeenth century, we can detect a subjectivity that is more plural and problematic than humanist critics have allowed. Belsey is dealing here with representations of subjectivity, but the logic of her underlying premise that 'subjectivity is discursively produced' (p5) commits her to the view that these representations contribute to the production of ways of experiencing the self and the world. The change she describes from a medieval subjectivity (or non-subjectivity) to a 'liberal humanist' subject is explicitly linked with the political revolution of the seventeenth century:

> The implication of the argument from staging is that the unified subject of liberal humanism is a product of the second half of the seventeenth century, *an effect of the revolution* (my emphasis). Broadly this seems to me to be so. Liberal humanism, locating agency and meaning in the unified human subject, becomes an orthodoxy at the moment when the bourgeoisie is installed as the ruling class.[26]

Various objections have been voiced to these and similar narratives of great epochal shifts in subjectivity: for example, the ignoring of evidence from medieval texts which would suggest that 'interiority' is by no means a new phenomenon in the early modern period,[27] or the fact that the representation of the transition from a feudal to a modern subjectivity essentially replicates Burckhardt's nineteenth-century account, while disagreeing as to the reasons for the changes described.[28] Apart from other doubts concerning method, and the kind and quantity of evidence that would be required to persuade a sceptical reader of the validity of the claims being made, I would like to suggest further reasons why we should avoid appeals to epochal or epistemic categories such as 'the early modern subject'.

One reason for avoidance is the problem of teleology and its distorting effect on historical explanation. The term 'early modern', which has widely displaced the term 'Renaissance', has its own effect in mobilising our thinking about the past in a certain way. It inclines us to think about the seventeenth century as a kind of preparation for, or anticipation of, 'the modern', and to direct attention to those features which seem 'emergent', 'incipient' or 'promissory'. In his discussion of 'To His Coy Mistress' as a transitional text, Barker says: 'As the poem tends towards the future it reaches after objectives which will have to be wrested from life and from time, from history itself'.[29] The retrospective construction of texts and events as 'tending towards the future' means that we will read them, and their 'subjects' as unfulfilled precisely because they haven't reached their destination, which is 'the modern'. This is rather like an account of 'Third World' countries describing them in terms of how far they have progressed towards the 'developed' form of modern society. It becomes especially problematic if we see the (feudal) past, from which the early modern is 'emerging', as itself a construction of the early modern (as I briefly suggest above). Rather than posing the issue in terms of 'emergence', it might be fruitful to ask about the conditions in which it became possible to construct this 'past' to which one might 'return'.

The idea of the past as directed towards a certain goal (it 'reaches after objectives') is related to another objection to these histories of the subject. Recent historicisms have tended to differentiate themselves from older historicisms by, among other things, 'a shift from History to histories',[30] implying both a postmodernist 'incredulity towards grand narratives' and a shift of attention from the traditional topics of history towards some that have not been seen as suitable for historical enquiry (the Foucauldian histories of sexuality, of madness, of the body, of subjectivity). Yet the story of 'the history of the subject' as described by the critics discussed above constitutes one of the grandest of grand narratives ('this book is offered ... as more than a history of ideas', Belsey says). It concerns nothing less than a history of how we come to feel, think and act as we do, together with an account of all the possible determinants of those processes. And this narrative, at least in relation to English history, tends to be tied in with another grand narrative, what historians call the 'high road' approach to the English Revolution, which interprets events in the early seventeenth century as 'tending towards' or 'reaching after' an inevitable historical fulfilment in the 'English Revolution' (whatever happens before 1649 is to be explained as part of an historical process tending towards revolutionary transformation).

Within the discipline of history itself, the 'high road' approach (whether Whig or Marxist) has been challenged over the past few decades by various tendencies emphasising the importance of local, contingent and accidental causes contributing to the crisis of the 1640s and 1650s. Some of these studies have belonged to 'local history' in the traditional sense (detailed studies of counties, parishes and towns which have found a bewildering variety of local allegiances and identifications complicating the customary oppositions of royalist/parliamentarian, Anglican/Puritan, court/country). They have shown people negotiating their political identities with their family, their near neighbours, their county locale, and how these negotiations shaped responses to events which they often did not comprehend in terms of ideology or principle. Some of the challenges to the 'high road' approach have been grouped together, despite differences of approach, as 'revisionist' and though many of these have been concerned with issues of national politics,[31] many have also been 'localist' in the sense that they have stressed the short-term, the contingent and the chance conjunction of events (mistakes, for example, or misjudgements) in order to challenge the idea that deep-rooted social forces were pushing inexorably towards a 'revolutionary' upheaval, or any particular future.[32] The strength of revisionist history has been that it is not tied to teleology: it can acknowledge that a crisis occurred (though many revisionists play down its seriousness, describing what Marxists have called a 'revolution' as a 'revolt' or a 'rebellion'), but it does not feel compelled to explain all that goes before as a pre-history of, or a preamble to, a revolution that ushers in the modern.

Many of the revisionist historians perhaps take an approach which is at odds, both theoretically and politically, with literary Cultural Materialism and New Historicism. They are resolutely empiricist (a term of abuse to many literary theorists) and their political sympathies (or at least, the implications of their work) tend to be conservative, bound up with a disciplinary assault on Marxist and liberal explanation. However, many historians who do not share a conservative political orientation have acknowledged the contribution made by the localists and the revisionists to an understanding of the complexity of seventeenth-century history, and to forcing the realisation that the 'revolutionary' interpretation is one that cannot be taken for granted.[33] My contention is that literary historicism could learn from an approach that shuns teleology, and that approaches the subject not in terms of grand historical tendencies but in terms of tactical shifts, contingency, and with more attention to what Stephen Greenblatt calls 'improvisation' (unfortunately, Greenblatt restricts the scope of this useful concept by tying it in to one of the historical narratives of emergence that I criticise above: improvising identities is seen as a characteristic mode of *Western* and *Renaissance* behaviour).[34]

Those who have attempted histories of the subject have generally started with the aim (with which I sympathise) of showing that subjectivity is not unchangeable,[35] and that appeals to 'human nature' as the basis of the social order can be challenged by illustrations of historical difference. This does not, I believe, require the positing of a 'modern' subject against a 'feudal' or pre-bourgeois subject, even when accompanied by the usual caveats about the 'precariousness' and 'instability' of forms of subjectivity in a given age. The task of establishing historical difference could be accomplished at a much more local level, and could release a richer sense of improvisatory possibilities if it were *not* tied to the need to demonstrate the relevance of particular tactical choices to massive epochal shifts. Belsey herself notes the danger of 'collapsing the historical specificities and the ideological differences of three centuries into a single term' (p7), but then says that '... there are alternative dangers in a specificity which never risks generalisation. We may point to large differences, as well as to small ones, woods as well as trees, epochs as well as decades' (p7). It is not clear what the danger is in failing to generalise, other than that of spoiling a good story. Generalisation can become necessary in the face of overwhelming evidence (failing to note that winters are generally colder than summers would risk gardeners wasting a great deal of time, for instance), but the evidence in this case is hardly overwhelming. Further, the implication, which runs counter to Belsey's arguments about history elsewhere in the book, is that we are 'pointing to' large differences that simply exist. Woods are often planted where it is in someone's interest to do so, as the logic of her own argument reminds us, and as the history of the English landscape amply demonstrates.

It might seem in the interest of theorists of the left to posit historical differences in subjectivity, as a means of challenging conservative appeals to 'human nature' as the basis of social order. However, when the modern form of conservatism increasingly takes the form of demands that we 'be' modern – that is, identify ourselves with a political project which justifies itself by an appeal to historical necessity – it is perhaps time for the left itself to begin to question the story it has constructed of the emergence of the modern subject. This need not entail a return to a notion of the human essence, nor an appeal to the rich diversity of individual selves, though that too might be a useful improvisation in certain circumstances. It involves removing from our accounts of subjectivity any element of inevitability, and of insisting, as the revisionist historians of the seventeenth century have demonstrated, that things and people could easily be otherwise.

NOTES

1. Alastair Fowler's *The Country House Poem: A Cabinet of Seventeenth-*

Century Estate Poems and Related Items, Edinburgh University Press, Edinburgh 1994, is the most comprehensive collection of the genre, containing 77 'items'.

2. Alastair Fowler, *Conceitful Thought: The Interpretation of English Renaissance Poems*, Edinburgh University Press, Edinburgh, 1975, p116. Ben Jonson, *Ben Jonson: The Complete Poems*, George Parfitt (ed), Penguin, 1975; Andrew Marvell, *The Complete Poems*, Elizabeth Story Donno (ed), Penguin, 1972.

3. James Turner, *The Politics of Landscape: Rural Scenery and Society in English Poetry 1630-1660*, Basil Blackwell, Oxford 1979, p85.

4. *Ibid.*, p5.

5. Alan Everitt's *The Community of Kent and the Great Rebellion, 1640-1660*, Leicester University Press, Leicester 1966, is often cited as one of the earliest explorations of the ways in which 'localism' helped shape the English 'rebellion' (note, not 'revolution'). J.S. Morrill's *The Revolt of the Provinces*, Allen and Unwin, London 1986, is another example.

6. On the whole, I wish to avoid using the term 'early modern', since in discussions of the relationship between the seventeenth century and the modern, it seems to me already to beg the question.

7. See Perez Zagorin, *The Court and the Country: the Beginnings of the English Revolution*, Routledge and Kegan Paul, London 1969.

8. References are to the poem in George Parfitt (ed), *Ben Jonson: The Complete Poems*, Penguin, Harmondsworth 1975.

9. Mark Girouard discusses the resentments caused by the development in the sixteenth century of the system of 'two-tier' dining, with the family and close guests dining in an upper room rather than the great hall, Girouard, *Life in the English Country House*, Yale University Press, 1978, p88.

10. Felicity Heal, *Hospitality in Early Modern England*, Clarendon Press, Oxford 1990.

11. John Summerson, *Architecture in Britain, 1530-1830*, Penguin, Harmondsworth 1993, p58.

12. Raymond Williams, *The Country and the City*, Hogarth Press, London 1985, p32.

13. Isabel Rivers, *The Poetry of Conservatism 1600-1745: A study of Poets and Public Affairs from Jonson to Pope*, Rivers Press, Cambridge 1975, p40.

14. See Rivers, *op. cit.*, pp33-35 on Jonson and the system of patronage.

15. See Fowler, *The Country House Poem, op. cit.*, pp11-18, 'Sources and Genres'.

16. On the tradition of the *locus amoenus* in classical poetry, see Ernst Curtius, *European Literature and the Latin Middle Ages*, Willard R. Trask (trans), Routledge and Kegan Paul, London 1979.

17. Arguments put forward by common lawyers and antiquarians concerning the 'ancient constitution' and the 'feudal law', for instance, were put forward as part of the resistance to what were seen as dangerously innovative absolutist ideas held by the Stuarts. See J.G.A. Pocock, *The Ancient Constitution and the Feudal Law: A study of English historical thought in the seventeenth century*, University Press, Cambridge 1957; and Roberta Florence Brinkley, *Arthurian Legend in the Seventeenth Century*, Johns Hopkins, Baltimore 1937 on the political import of debates on the Saxon, Norman or 'British' origins of English law. What has been called the 'feudal revival' of the Elizabethan age might also be seen as a contribution to the *construction* of the feudal as we now understand it.

18. On the architectural aesthetics implied in these stanzas, see Lucy Gent, '"The Rash Gazer": Economies of Vision in Britain, 1550-1660' in *Albion's Classicism: The Visual Arts in Britain, 1550-1660*, Lucy Gent (ed), Yale University Press, London 1995, pp377-393.

19. 'Upon Appleton House' in Elizabeth Story Donno (ed), *Andrew Marvell: The Complete Poems*, Harmondsworth 1972.

20. See for example stanzas 37-49, 50-54, or 57, in which villagers grazing cattle are compared to Levellers, in a complex image that incorporates many issues involving common land, enclosure and political equality over which the Civil War was fought.

21. R.I.V. Hodge, *Foreshortened Time: Andrew Marvell and Seventeenth-century Revolutions*, D.S. Brewer, Cambridge 1978, p63.

22. Robert Wilcher, *Andrew Marvell*, Cambridge University Press, Cambridge 1985; James Turner, in *The Politics of Landscape* discusses the relationship between terms such as 'landscape', 'mirror', 'glass', 'prospect', 'prospective' and 'perspective', and their political uses, *op. cit.*, see pp42-48 especially.

23. Appleton House is described as 'paradise's only map' (l.769) in the penultimate stanza: the poem reads however like a map of paradise lost.

24. Especially those associated with either Cultural Materialism or New Historicism. The works concerned are, particularly, Francis Barker, *The Tremulous Private Body: Essays on Subjection*, Methuen, London 1984; Catherine Belsey, *The Subject of Tragedy: Identity and difference in Renaissance Drama*, Methuen, London 1985; Jonathan Dollimore, *Radical Tragedy: Religion, Ideology and Power in the Drama of Shakespeare and his Contemporaries*, The Harvester Press, Brighton 1984; Stephen Greenblatt, *Renaissance Self-Fashioning: From More to Shakespeare*, University of Chicago Press, Chicago 1980, and 'Psychoanalysis and Renaissance Culture' in, *Learning to Curse*, Routledge, London 1992, pp131-145.

25. 'Disunited, discontinuous, the hero of the moralities is not the origin of action; he has no single subjectivity which could constitute such an origin; he is not a subject', Belsey, *op. cit.*, p18.

26. *Ibid.*, pp33-34.

27. See David Aers, 'A Whisper in the Ear of Early Modernists; or, Reflections on Literary Critics Writing the "History of the Subject"' in David Aers (ed), *Culture and History 1350-1600: Essays on English Communities, Identities and Writing*, Harvester Wheatsheaf 1992.

28. In the middle ages, according to Burckhardt, man was 'conscious of himself only as a member of a race, people, party, family or corporation – only through some general category. In Italy this veil first melted into air; an *objective* treatment and consideration of the state and of all the things of this world became possible. The *subjective* side at the same time asserted itself with corresponding emphasis; man became an *individual*, and recognised himself as such', *The Civilisation of the Renaissance in Italy*, S.G.C. Middlemore (trans), p98. As Aers says (p195), this account would 'fit cosily into' many discussions of 'the emergence of the modern subject'.

29. Barker, *The Tremulous Private Body, op. cit.*, p88.

30. Louis Montrose, 'Professing the Renaissance: The Poetics and Politics of Culture' in H. Aram Veeser (ed), *The New Historicism*, Routledge, London 1989, p20.

31. Conrad Russell's *Parliaments and English Politics, 1621-1629*, Oxford University Press, Oxford 1979 is an influential example of this tendency.

32. The revisionists have 'concentrated on the short-term factors and have shunned the teleologies of both Marxists and Whigs', R.C. Richardson, *The Debate on the English Revolution Revisited*, Second Edition, Routledge, London 1988. For an overview of the impact of local history studies and 'revisionism' on seventeenth-century historiography, see Richardson, chs. 8 and 9.

33. See for example Ann Hughes, 'Local History and the Origins of the Civil War' in Cust and Hughes, *Conflict in Early Stuart England, op. cit.*, pp224-253.

34. Stephen Greenblatt, 'The Improvisation of Power' in H. Aram Veeser (ed), *The New Historicism Reader*, Routledge, London 1994, pp46-87.

35. Subjectivity as defined by liberal humanism 'is not natural, inevitable, or eternal; on the contrary, it is produced and re-produced in and by a specific social order', Belsey, *The Subject of Tragedy, op. cit.*, p223.

Prostitution and the growth of desire: The rise and fall of sentimental economics in the eighteenth century

MARY PEACE

In January 1796 the *Gentleman's Magazine* notes that a young artist called George Quinton is in the process of producing an engraving from a Thomas Duché painting of the London Magdalen Hospital executed in 1788-9. According to the *Gentleman's Magazine* the original painting, which no longer exists, depicts 'Charity, presenting an emaciated prostitute, in a state of despair, to three reclaimed females at the door of the Magdalen Hospital'.[1] Quinton's engraving appears to be a faithful reproduction of the painting (*Fig. 1*).

The supplicant prostitute is certainly in a state of despair: she is filthy; her hair is matted and standing on end; she is dressed in tattered finery; and she crouches like an animal on the floor. Sometime in the following year, however, Quinton revised the engraving. This wretched figure was replaced by a supplicant whose 'expression ... [is] a generalised depiction of sweetness', and whose wild hair has been ordered into 'neat, becoming curls'.[2] *(Fig. 2)* The originally despairing figure was exchanged for one who, in terms of the aesthetic logic of the engraving, was already reformed – apart from her clothing she now bore a much greater resemblance to the 'reclaimed females' than to her wretched predecessor.

The London Magdalen Hospital for the Reception of Penitent Prostitutes was established in 1758 – not quite forty years before the episode of the engravings – and was, in both conception and execution, unmistakably a product of the contemporary ascendancy of sentimental ideas.[3] I am using sentimental in a specifically eighteenth-century sense which I will explore below. In this essay I will argue that the identity and

Fig 1 George Quinton, after Thomas Spence Duché, *The Magdalen Hospital*, first state (1797). Reproduced courtesy David Alexander

Fig 2 *The Magdalen Hospital*, second state (1797) Courtesy Yale Center for British Art, Paul Mellon Collection.

history of the Magdalen Hospital were inextricably bound up, from its inception, with that of eighteenth-century sentimental discourse and that, in some ways, the establishment of the institution marks the limit of sentimental ideas. Quinton's revision of the engraving, I will suggest, registers a significant change not only in the values and attitudes of those associated with the Magdalen Hospital charity, but in the fortunes of sentimental discourse more generally. The episode of the revised engraving, I will argue, provides a peculiarly illuminating perspective from which to look at the politics of sentimental discourse in the latter half of the eighteenth century. It provides, moreover, a particularly useful historical background against which to think about modern attempts to marry social justice with the liberal economic theories which have now achieved a near global monopoly on truth. Specifically I am thinking of the theory put forward by Adam Smith in *Inquiry into the Nature and Causes of the Wealth of Nations* (1780), that the pursuit of enlightened self-interest by individuals and companies can benefit society as a whole. The paper will begin, however, with a brief discussion of Smith's earlier work – *The Theory of Moral Sentiments* (1759) – which ostensibly offers a very different theory of society.

A BRIEF HISTORY OF SENTIMENTAL DISCOURSE

The year after the establishment of the London Magdalen Hospital, Adam Smith famously opened his treatise, *The Theory of Moral Sentiments* (1759), with the following words:

> How selfish soever man may be supposed, there are evidently some prin-
> ciples in his nature, which interest him in the fortunes of others, and
> render their happiness necessary to him, though he derives nothing from
> it except the pleasure of seeing it. Of this kind is pity or compassion, the
> emotion which we feel for the misery of others, when we either see it, or
> are made to conceive it in a very lively manner.[4]

Like Hume, Hutcheson and Shaftesbury earlier in the century, Smith counters the Hobbesian assertion that humans are naturally self-ish and anti-social with the idea that, along with the five conventional physical senses, we are born with a moral sense: a sense which leads us spontaneously to feel for the plight of others.[5]

It is clear from other writings of the period that this moral sense, though usually represented as innate, and therefore implicitly trans-historical, is also held to be particularly associated with modernity. Measured in terms of the growth of charity, this moral sense is widely seen to be a predominant characteristic of the modern age and specifically of modern Britain. The novelist and magistrate Henry Fielding expresses a commonplace in 1749 when he declares that 'Charity, is the very characteristic virture [sic] at this time. I believe we may challenge the whole world to parallel the examples which we have of late given of this sensible, this noble, this Christian virtue'.[6] The paradox of the innate, but peculiarly modern moral sense – a sense frequently referred to in contemporary writings as sensibility – is explained by the belief that the moral sense is cultivated and refined by social and economic commerce. For Addison and Shaftesbury, writing at the beginning of the century, through to Hutcheson, Hume and a host of pamphlet and conduct-book authors active at the middle of the century, commerce, in its broadest sense, heightens and refines the individual's sensibility, making him/her more benevolent and humane. As both social and, particularly, economic commerce were expanding at an unprecedented rate in Britain in the first part of the eighteenth century, the association of increased sensibility and charity with modernity is hardly surprising.

Indeed, even John Brown – a vociferous and controversial mid-century critic of the increasing expansion of commerce – numbers the spirit of 'Humanity' among the virtues of the age.[7] Certainly, in his *An Estimate of the Manners and the Principles of the Times* (1758), he works hard to distinguish his idea of humanity from the charity which characterises the modernity described by his pro-commercial contemporaries.[8] Moreover, he is keen to assert that his humanity is a residual, ancient virtue which will counter the dire effects of commerce and not a modern phenomenon associated with increased commerce. Brown describes his spirit of humanity as '... that Pity for Distress, that Moderation in limiting Punishments by their proper Ends and Measures, by which this Nation hath always been distinguished' (p21). Yet as Brown enlarges upon his description of this ancient humanity, he finds it more and more difficult to maintain distinctions. He finds himself, at one point, fleetingly wondering whether the 'Humanity' he describes is not after all a product of 'effeminacy': a trait which is for him indissociable from the expansion of commerce. But this train of argument is then abruptly curtailed on the grounds that it is a '... [q]uestion more *curious* in its Progress, than *agreeable* in its Solution' (pp63-4). By the mid century, it seems, even the most severe critics of the expansion of commerce are at a loss to account for the increased incidence of charity without recourse to the sentimental argument which identifies it with a parallel increase in commerce.

The ascendancy of this sentimental argument marks the start of an era of supreme and unprecedented confidence and optimism about the sustainability of commercial growth. From the mid-seventeenth century until the mid-eighteenth century, responses to commercial growth had largely been dominated by the pessimistic paradigms of classical economic thought – from Plato's description of the rise of luxury and subsequent descent into anarchy in the *Republic*, to Livy's history of the fall of Rome. These classical-republican paradigms, which still so conspicuously informed the writings of John Brown, broadly argue that although the growth of commerce initially benefits a state – by freeing at least some of its population from a constant preoccupation with physical necessity, and allowing for the emergence of arts and philosophy – such growth must eventually lead to decay and dissolution. The constant stimulation and refinement of desires which necessarily accompany commercial growth would ultimately, it was argued, 'effeminate' a population, rendering it too delicate either to reproduce or to defend itself, and eventually the state would fall.

The sentimental argument, as Brown so tellingly discovers, is not entirely independent of the classical-republican trajectory. It too imagines the growth of commerce to result in the increased delicacy, or 'effeminacy' of the population. But in the sentimental argument this 'feminisation' of culture is, almost entirely, a positive phenomenon: it is what has stimulated the innate moral sense to greater acts of charity and humanity than were found in the ancient world.[9] Indeed, it is a phenomenon which, at their most optimistic, the sentimental writers believe will bind together and consolidate a commercial society, rather than a vice which will ultimately destroy its very fabric. It is, Adam Smith argues, effeminate beings: 'Persons of delicate fibres and a weak constitution of body, that in looking on the sores and ulcers which are exposed by beggars in the streets ... are [most] apt to feel an itching or uneasy sensation in the correspondent part of their own bodies'.[10] Other sentimental writers, including David Hume, are at times prepared to associate a more refined moral sense not just with effeminacy, but explicitly with women.[11] It is in the context of these arguments that we can best understand how, in Richardson's notorious sentimental novel *Pamela* (1740), a scarcely educated servant girl is empowered to convert not only her aristocratic lover, Mr B., to the paths of 'bourgeois' and Christian morality, but his entire family and most of his neighbours.[12]

It is also in the context of these arguments, I suggest, that one can understand the establishment of the Magdalen Hospital for the

Reception of Penitent Prostitutes as a crowning moment of confidence in the future of economic expansion.

THE MAGDALEN HOSPITAL AND SENTIMENTAL DISCOURSE

At its most stark my argument reads the establishment of the Magdalen Hospital as a supreme expression of confidence in the essentially beneficent nature of even the most apparently destructive version of femininity. The Magdalen project offered to prove that even the prostitute – traditionally a most potent symbol of the corruption associated with luxurious commerce – could be recuperated; that she could become a useful and productive member of society.

The Magdalen Hospital for Penitent Prostitutes was established in London in August 1758 according to a plan drawn up by Robert Dingley, a merchant associated with the Moscow Trading Company. It was funded in the manner of a contemporary commercial enterprise – by subscription – and, of the committee of eight original governors, five were, or had previously been merchants. They were, in the words of Samuel Richardson, men 'noble, if not by blood or descent, [then] intrinsically so from the generous benevolence of their worthy hearts'.[13]

The hospital offered to provide a refuge for, but also ultimately to reform and rehabilitate, avowedly penitent prostitutes – a category in which both recently fallen women and hardened streetwalkers were explicitly included. It proved simultaneously popular with the public and extremely controversial. The idea that the prostitute should generally be treated as a victim of society, and not solely as a perpetrator of social unrest, was certainly novel, particularly in terms of social policy. However, the polite public had been warmed to the position over the previous decade by the appearance and immense success of sentimental narratives of fallen women such as Richardson's vastly popular novel *Clarissa* (1748-9) and Smollett's portrait of the pathetic Miss Williams in *Roderick Random* (1748). Indeed Richardson's eponymous sentimental hero Sir Charles Grandison actually advocates the establishment of an institution such as the Magdalen Hospital in the novel of 1754.

There were, however, vocal detractors. The author of *Considerations on the Fatal Effects to a Trading Nation of the Present Excess of Public Charities* goes so far as to describe the Magdalen as 'That most infamous Institution, that degrades the very name of charity'.[14] And William Dodd, the first chaplain to the Magdalen Hospital, describes in his inaugural sermon of 1759 how the charity has met with ridicule from some quarters on the grounds that it is a 'scheme to wash Aethiopians white'.[15] Dodd, in this inaugural sermon, establishes beyond doubt the sentimental rationale for the institution. He confidently counters the last criticism with the assertion that it is entirely misguided, as 'every man that reflects on the true condition of humanity must know, that the life of a common prostitute, is as contrary to the nature and condition of the female sex, as darkness to light ... ' Later in the sermon Dodd explicitly invokes the idea of the prostitute's native female 'delicacy of sentiment' to justify the institution's commitment to rehabilitation. He states that in these women:

> ... the nobleness of virtue, and the delicacy of sentiment, have been rather canker'd over, than blotted out: and upon the first remove of the filth, have shewn themselves in particulars, which would do honour to the most exalted state and ideas.

THE 1790S, THE REVISED ENGRAVINGS, AND THE VICISSITUDES OF SENTIMENT

In the light of the imagery and argument of Dodd's inaugural sermon, the wretched and filthy supplicant of George Quinton's first and only faithful engraving of Duché's painting of the London Magdalen Hospital seems to indicate the persistence of an association between sentimental beliefs and the institution at the end of the century. The engraving provides an apt expression of Dodd's sentimental vision: Charity interceding to restore a seduced victim of corruption to her native state of innocence. But what are we then to make of its revision in 1797 – the following year? How should we understand the substitution of the abject, wretched figure with the much sweeter and neater supplicant? Does it perhaps indicate that since the late 1780s, when the original painting had been executed, this sentimental vision of charity had become an anachronism – that, by the mid-1790s, those associated with the Magdalen Hospital had turned their backs on the sentimental ideas that had provided the inspiration for the original institution?

A general comparison between the sermons delivered in the Magdalen Hospital Chapel in the 1790s and those from the late 1750s and 1760s certainly does seem to suggest the ascendancy in the institution of a very different ideological tone at the end of the century. When, for example, the Reverend H.E. Holder delivered the anniversary sermon at the Magdalen Hospital Chapel in 1792, he reminded the sinners in the congregation that if they did not look to God they would be damned, and damnation, he said, means

Hell within you!
Hell above you!
Hell below you!
The face of God turned from you!
Conscience accusing you!
Angels lamenting over you!
Devils triumphing at your fall![16]

This kind of apocalyptic rhetoric typifies the Evangelical preaching which became commonplace in the Magdalen Chapel in the 1790s, but which had no place in the sentimental sermons of the mid-century chaplain William Dodd. It typifies, according to historian Donna Andrew:

> that variety of Anglicanism that both acknowledged the utter depravity of man and the ubiquity of palpable evil and misery, and the necessity for individual moral reform and conversion before social improvement could take place.[17]

Holder's sermon, moreover, goes on implicitly to contradict Dodd's vision of the sinner as essentially virtuous but temporarily 'canker'd o'er', and in so doing offers a potential explanation as to why Quinton's engraving might have undergone revision in 1797.

> Picture to yourselves [he says] the effect on your own minds, the *disgusting* effect, I would say, of ugliness and deformity, in their greatest aggravations; and you will have the faintest idea of the detestation which must exist in the Divine Intelligence, upon the contemplation of sin.

Unlike the 'Persons of delicate fibres and a weak constitution of body' who populate the pages of Adam Smith's *Theory of Moral Sentiments*, Holder imagines that his congregation, and indeed that God himself, will experience detestation and disgust rather than sympathy at the sight of 'ugliness and deformity'. The assertion that detestation and disgust will be felt at the sight of ugliness and deformity seems to amount to a refutation of the existence of an innate moral, and socially binding, sense both in the subject and object of contemplation. If Holder's Evangelical sermon typifies the new ideological orthodoxy of the Magdalen Institution in the 1790s, then the revision of the engraving is easily explained: the new engraving represents 'the necessity for individual moral reform and conversion before social improvement could take place'. In the earlier engraving the prostitute looks degraded and unclean, but it is assumed that her 'inner' sensibilities remain innately good and ready to shine forth again at the touch of a largely secular Charity. In the later engraving, the prostitute must be taken at face value – her crime is such as must make her a detestable sight, yet, as her appearance is pleasant, we must be reassured that she is spiritually repentant and has become a worthy object of charity. Yet secular charity here has few powers of transformation or rehabilitation, its function is now rather to provide a refuge for the prostitute away from society. The charity that one should offer to the prostitute, according to Evangelical writer, Hannah More, should be the opportunity of religious redemption and not of a social rehabilitation. More declares that her readers should:

> ... be not anxious to restore the forlorn penitent to that society against whose laws she has so grievously offended; and remember, that her soliciting such a restoration, furnishes but too plain a proof that she is not the penitent your partiality would believe; since penitence is more anxious to make its peace with heaven than with the world.[18]

As Donna Andrew has pointed out, although the Magdalen was still theoretically concerned to send its inmates back out into society, there is plenty of evidence to suggest that in practice the charity had abandoned the ideal of rehabilitation, and that it considered its true function to be that of a house of quarantine. For Andrew this evidence lies primarily in two important changes. Firstly, by the end of the century the Magdalen had decided to stop teaching vocational skills to the women and had employed them instead in laundry-work. Secondly, the proportion of inmates who were released either to employment or to friends declined during this period, despite the fact that the Magdalen was taking in fewer women than at the mid-century, and that many of these were recently seduced, rather than hardened streetwalkers – factors which should have been favourable to their rehabilitation.

In short, by the 1790s, it seems, the Magdalen had become a very different institution to the one which had been set up in the mid century. It had abandoned its assertions of innate virtue in favour of the biblical doctrine of the fall, and abandoned its belief in the possibility, or even perhaps the desirability of social rehabilitation, in favour of a commitment to the containment of sinners. By the 1790s, the historian Edward J. Bristow suggests, the Magdalen Hospital had become a 'sanctimonious sweatshop,' and it is in this form that the institution was widely copied throughout the British Isles.[19]

The second-state, revised engraving might then be seen to give a much more appropriate expression to the predominantly Evangelical culture of the institution in 1796 – the now decorous supplicant can be seen to reflect both the recent decision to admit fewer hardened street-walkers into the institution and the sense that on the whole the project of rehabilitation had been abandoned in favour of the project of containment. Girls applying to the institution, the revision suggests, should have returned already to the path of religion. They should be already reformed, and not in need of conversion.

ROUSSEAU, BURKE AND THE POLITICS OF SENTIMENT IN THE REVOLUTIONARY DEBATES

There is some evidence to suggest that the culture of the Magdalen Hospital had been turning against the sentimental convictions of its founders as early as the 1770s.[20] The sea change, however, only really becomes conspicuous after 1789 when, as various commentators have recently argued, sentimentality became a highly contested cultural language in the politics surrounding the French revolution.[21] Indeed, as far as the Magdalen is concerned, it might be argued that the sea change can be traced specifically to 1791 when Edmund Burke published his 'Letter to a Member of the National Assembly'. In this influential letter, Burke laid the burden of the evils of the current situation in France at the gate of the arch-sentimentalist Rousseau, and more specifically on the doorstep of his mid-century novel of seduction and transformation, *La Nouvelle Heloïse*. Burke argues, somewhat melo-dramatically, that the National Assembly – the new governing body of revolutionary France – has effectively canonised Rousseau for the sentiments he expresses in this novel. In particular, Burke suggests, the assembly praises the novel for encouraging its readers to sympathise with the tutor who, by seducing the daughter he has been employed to teach, 'subvert[s] those principles of domestic trust and fidelity which form the discipline of social life'.[22] In promoting such sympathy for the tutor, Burke argues, 'every servant may think it, if not his duty, at least his privilege, to betray his master', and the betrayal of one's master, in Burke's view, is always only a short step from the betrayal of one's king. In the light of Burke's well-known 'Letter', sympathy for and a belief in the native virtue of a woman who allows herself to be seduced in her father's house is tantamount to treason, and it is not at all surprising that much of the sentimental rhetoric of sympathy had been abandoned by a such high profile charity as the Magdalen Hospital in the increasingly anti-revolutionary atmosphere of the mid-1790s.

In *A Sermon Preached in the Chapel of the Magdalen Hospital*, in 1807, Thomas Lewis O'Beirne distinctly echoes Burke's 'Letter' when he denounces Rousseau's writing – and specifically *La Nouvelle Heloïse* – for its pernicious influence on female morality and its incitement to radical politics. Rousseau, or as he calls him with reference to Burke's 'Letter', 'The canonised philosopher of Geneva',

> ... leads his pupil through all the blandishments of voluptuousness, all the violence of unrestrained desires, all the wild fancies of an over heated imagination; and by every insidious attack on all the venerable prejudices and sacred institutions that hath hitherto preserved the sanctity and purity of the union of sexes, raises her to the sublime character of a female philosopher, and of that monster of Christian days, a female Deist.[23]

Rousseau's *La Nouvelle Heloïse* was first published in England in April 1761, only three years after the establishment of the Magdalen Hospital, yet at the time of its publication it created no particular outrage in the periodicals of polite society, nor seemed to merit even a passing reference in the Magdalen-Hospital sermons.[24] Indeed a reviewer in the vastly respectable *Gentleman's Magazine*, writing in 1770, seems utterly oblivious of subversive implications when he says of Rousseau's novel that it '... inspires every virtue; the human soul is there seen in all its shapes. For my part I wish, that as soon as the heart is formed, it might be filled with this moral work'.[25] The novel seemed to pass as yet another sentimental work in the style of Richardson.

But Burke was, I think, right to distinguish between Rousseau's writings and those of the mid-century British sentimentalists. Like the British sentimental tradition, Rousseau does posit the existence of an innate sensibility, but, unlike his British counterparts, he does not suggest that this sensibility can be refined and cultivated by commerce. Indeed, for Rousseau, whose writing is explicitly informed by the classical-republican tradition I described above, all contact with the world, and particularly the world of commerce, corrupts.[26] The innate moral sense, in Rousseau, is not the force which binds together society as it is currently constituted, but a force which empowers individuals to question and subvert the validity of 'things as they are'. In *La Nouvelle Heloïse*, the heroine's sensibility encourages her not, as in Richardson, to resist and contain the advances of idle and luxurious aristocrats, but to enter into an affair with one of her father's servants.

It is perhaps Rousseau's simultaneous appropriation and subversion of the British sentimental tradition which explains why Burke, rather than attacking Rousseau for his sentimentality (as one might, perhaps, expect), attacks him instead for his 'false sympathies', and, in place, sets himself up as a true bearer of the sentimental flame.

Burke argues, for example, that Rousseau exhausts the

> stores of his powerful rhetoric in the expression of universal benevolence, whilst his heart was incapable of harbouring one spark of common parental affection. Benevolence to the whole species, and want of feeling for every individual … form the character of the new philosophy … He melts with tenderness for those only who touch him by the remotest relation, and then without one natural pang, casts away, as a sort of offal, an excrement, the spawn of his disgustful amours, and sends his children to the hospital for foundlings.[27]

Rousseau is painted here as the brutal and hard-hearted seducer who, far from being a sentimental hero, is himself a villain whose vile habits necessitate the existence of sentimental charities such as the foundling hospital – and by implication the Magdalen. True sentiment for Burke, as he had famously elaborated in his *Reflections on the Revolution in France*, 1790, is not a subversive force, but a force which binds society together.

One might surmise that what divides Burke and Rousseau are what each counts as 'society'. Burke certainly makes great play in his *Reflections* on the importance of listening to one's senses – to the voice of nature. But, for Burke, nature is always invariably on the side of society as it is currently constituted. He, for example, explicitly uses metaphors of nature to authorise the religious and civil laws which maintain the *status quo*.[28] Throughout the *Reflections* Burke appeals to nature to counter the ideas of the revolution. In response to the rhetorical question of why he should feel differently about the revolution to Dr Price (the pro-revolutionary clergyman whose sermon, *A Discourse on the Love of Our Country*, delivered in December 1789, had originally provided the inspiration for Burke's *Reflections*), he answers simply 'because it is *natural* that I should', and, when explaining why the English would never give themselves up to revolutionary atheism, he insists it is because:

> In England we have not yet been completely embowelled of our natural entrails; we still feel within us, and we cherish and cultivate, those inbred

sentiments which are the faithful guardians, the active monitors of our duty, the true supporters of all liberal and manly morals ... We preserve the whole of our feelings still native and entire, unsophisticated by pedantry and infidelity.[24]

Natural instinct in Burke's *Reflections* apparently acts as the ultimate arbitrator of right and wrong and yet, when probed, these instincts always turn out to be highly refined and cultivated. For Burke, nature unrefined amounts to savagery – a state characterised by the anti-social (because unregulated) desires of the individual. Burke's criticism of the unnatural subtleties of Rousseau's arguments, for example, turns out to mask a criticism of the Rousseauvian idea that virtue exists in a state of nature (p181). In other words, Burke's 'nature' is actually 'moral culture', and is decidedly *not* the innate and sufficient moral sensibility of Rousseau's writings, nor even the innate but ideally cultivated moral sense found in the writings of the earlier sentimental philosophers – Shaftesbury, Hutcheson, Hume and Smith. There is, in fact, absolutely no manner in which Burke believes in the idea of an innate moral sense which can alone be trusted to regulate the desires of the individual: it is, he says, 'necessary to cover the defects of our naked shivering nature' with the 'decent drapery of life'. We should embrace 'All the super-added ideas, furnished from the wardrobe of a moral imagination' (p171).

By the 1790s, sentimentality has finally split over the twin rocks of the French Revolution and the inherent paradox of an innate, but peculiarly modern, moral sense. Rousseau, it seems, has wrested free the idea of an innate sensibility – a sense which he then imagines to be corrupted rather than refined by modern society, but which authorises the individual to question the validity of things as they are. Burke, on the other hand, has abandoned 'inborn' sentiments for 'inbred' sentiments: he clings to the importance of 'manners' as promoted by modern commerce in countering the threat of revolution and maintaining the status quo.[30]

CONCLUSION

I have argued above that, for mid-century sentimental writers, the idea that each individual is in possession of an innate moral sense, which is cultivated and refined by commerce, had become a powerful argument for optimism about the sustainability of economic growth. I have also suggested that this argument depended to a great extent on the *redefinition* of the effeminacy which was associated with commerce in classical-republican discourse. In sentimental writing 'effeminacy' is redefined as 'femininity' – a positive force for social cohesion, rather than as a debilitating and corrupting one. Indeed effeminacy is rewritten not just as femininity, but often even as the native sensibility of women. It is in this context that I have read the establishment of the Magdalen Hospital as a crowning moment of confidence in the future of economic expansion. But must we then read the Magdalen's apparent abandonment of a belief in an innate moral sense as indicative of a wave of anxiety and pessimism amongst the polite and mercantile classes of Britain about the sustainability of economic growth?

On the whole I would suggest not. Certainly the sentimental attempt to reconcile virtue and commerce had largely failed: the native moral sense had proved itself potentially subversive; it had wandered off without commerce and modernity and was to provide the intellectual foundation for a wealth of future oppositional positions to capitalism – from Marxism to modern-day eco-activism. Burkean sentiment, on the other hand, having ultimately rejected the foundation of a native moral sense, could no longer trust the individual to restrain and limit his or her desires for the benefit of social cohesion. Yet by the 1790s, none of this really mattered. For effectively the first time in the history of western thought, a future had been envisaged in which the pursuit of self-interest by individuals and collectivities could benefit society as a whole, rather than lead to its ultimate downfall. The argument of Adam Smith's *Wealth of Nations* (1780) had begun to bite.

Over sixty years earlier, when the maverick Bernard Mandeville had starkly proposed in his satiric poem *The Fable of the Bees*, that 'private vice' was 'public benefit,' there had been almost universal outcry.[31] But it might perhaps be argued that sentimentality had paradoxically furnished the way for the acceptability of this argument through its promotion of the idea that by simply following our commercially stimulated instincts everything will turn out for the best.

The eighteenth-century sentimental ideas I have been discussing in this essay can be seen to represent the last point at which it was unthinkable to envisage sustained economic progress without also envisaging a sustainable restraint on human desires. In imagining this restraint to come from commerce itself, sentimental thought effected the transition between classical republican and modern liberal economic thought.

NOTES

1. 'George Quinton', *Gentleman's Magazine*, January, 1796, p9.
2. Ellen D'Oench, 'Prodigal Sons and Fair Penitents: Eighteenth-Century

Popular Prints', *Art History* 13 (1990), p337.

3. See Markman Ellis, *The Politics of Sensibility: Race, Gender and Commerce in the Sentimental Novel,* Cambridge UP, Cambridge 1996.

4. Adam Smith, *The Theory of Moral Sentiments,* A. Millar, London 1759, p9.

5. See David Hume, *Essays Moral, Political and Literary*, Eugene F. Miller (ed), Liberty Classics, Indianapolis, Indiana 1987; Francis Hutcheson, *An Inquiry into the Original of our Ideas of Beauty and Virtue,* 2nd ed. 1726, Garland, New York 1971; and Anthony Ashley Cooper Shaftesbury, *Characteristicks [of Men, Manners, Opinions, Times],* 3 Vols. ([London]: n.p., 1743-5.

6. David Owen, *English Philanthropy 1660-1960,* Belknap-Harvard, Cambridge, Massachusetts 1965, p11.

7. John Brown, *An Estimate of the Manners and Principles of the Times,* 7th ed., Vol. 1, L. Davis and C. Reymers, London 1765, p28.

8. Brown says that he does not mean '... that Smoothness and refined Polish of external Manners, by which the present Age affects to be distinguished', *Ibid.,* pp20-21.

9. The idea that the mid-eighteenth century witnessed a 'feminisation' of culture can be found in Terry Eagleton, *The Rape of Clarissa: Writing, Sexuality and Class Struggle in Samuel Richardson*, Basil Blackwell, Oxford 1982, p14. For a fuller discussion of gender and economic discourses in the eighteenth century see Mary Peace, *The Figure Of The Prostitute In Eighteenth-Century Sentimental Discourse: Charity, Politeness And The Novel,* unpublished DPhil., University of York, 1996.

10. Smith, *Theory, op. cit.,* p10.

11. Hume, 'Of the Delicacy,' *Essays, op. cit.,* p603. Note added to text in 1758.

12. See Eagleton, *The Rape, op. cit.*

13. Samuel Richardson, 'Preface,' in [Barbara Montagu], *The Histories of Some of the Penitents in the Magdalen-House, as Supposed to be Related by Themselves,* Vol. 1, John Rivington and J. Dodsley, London 1760, p3.

14. *Considerations on the Fatal Effects to a Trading Nation of the Present Excess of Public Charities,* S. Hooper, London 1763, p11.

15. William Dodd, *A Sermon on St. Matthew, Chap. IX. Ver. 12, 13. Preach'd at the Parish Church of St Laurence, near Guild-Hall, April the 26th, 1759, before the President, Vice-Presidents, Treasurer and Governors of the Magdalen House for the Reception of Penitent Prostitutes,* Davis and C. Reymers, London, [1759?]) pii.

16. Henry Evans Holder, *A Sermon Written for the Magdalen Chapel,* J. Debrett, London 1792, pp10-11.

17. Donna T. Andrew, *Philanthropy and Police: Charity in the Eighteenth*

Century, Princeton UP, Princeton NJ, 1989, p165.

18. Hannah More, *Strictures on the Modern System of Female Education*, Vol. 1, T. Cadell jun. and W. Davies, London 1799, pp47-48.

19. Edward J. Bristow, *Vice and Vigilance: Purity Movements in Britain Since 1700*, Rowman and Littlefield, Totowa, New Jersey 1977, p66.

20. See Marilyn Butler, *Jane Austen and the War of Ideas,* Clarendon Press, Oxford 1987, p21.

21. For example, Butler, *op. cit.*; Cathy N. Davidson, *Revolution and the Word: The Rise of the Novel in America*, Oxford UP, New York 1986; Claudia L. Johnson, *Equivocal Beings: Politics, Gender, and Sentimentality in the 1790s: Wollstonecraft, Radcliffe, Burney, Austen,* University of Chicago Press, Chicago 1995; and Nicola Watson, *Revolution and the Form of the British Novel, 1790-1825, Intercepted Letters, Interrupted Seductions*, Clarendon Press, Oxford 1994.

22. Edmund Burke, 'Letter to a Member of the National Assembly', *The Works of the Right Honourable Edmund Burke*, 12 Vols., Vol. iv, John C. Nimmo, London 1899, p33.

23. Thomas Lewis O'Beirne, DD, *A Sermon Preached in the Chapel of the Magdalen Hospital*, Hatchard, London 1807, pp17-18.

24. Judith H. Macdowell, introduction, *La Nouvelle Heloïse: Julie, or the New Eloise*, by Jean-Jacques Rousseau, translated and abridged by Judith H. Macdowell, Pennsylvania State UP, University Park, Pennsylvania 1968, p2.

25. 'The Characters ... ' *Gentleman's Magazine, and Historical Chronicle*, Vol. XI., D. Henry, London 1770, pp444-456.

26. See Jean-Jacques Rousseau, 'Discourse on the Sciences and Arts', *The First and Second Discourses*, Roger D. Masters (ed), Roger D. and Judith R. Masters (trans), St Martin's Press, New York 1964.

27. Burke, 'Letter', *op. cit.*, pp27-28.

28. Burke describes the ideal process of making changes in the government as that of taking 'care not to inoculate any cyon alien to the nature of the original plant.' Edmund Burke, *Reflections on the Revolution in France: And on the Proceedings in Certain Societies in London Relative to that Event,* Conor Cruise O'Brien (ed), Pelican-Penguin, Harmondsworth 1968, p117.

29. Burke, *Reflections, op. cit.*, p182.

30. See J. G. A. Pocock, 'Introduction,' Edmund Burke, *Reflections on the Revolution in France,* Hackett, Indianapolis 1987, for a full discussion of Burke's commitment to an Enlightenment discourse of manners.

31. Bernard Mandeville, *The Fable of the Bees*, Phillip Harth (ed), Penguin, London 1970.

Fallacies of memory in nineteenth-century psychology: subjectivity and cultural authority

JENNY BOURNE TAYLOR

The Present, in our lives, is ever closely bound up with the Past, and the cord that unites them is all woven of strands of memory. When we know that on the soundness of that cord we often hang honour, love, faith, justice, things more precious than life itself, our reluctance to test its strength would be as senseless as that of Alpine travellers who should refuse to try that rope which is to support them over the abyss, lest perchance, in sooth, it might prove to be insecure.[1]

Frances Power Cobbe tested that cord in 'The fallacies of memory'; a lengthy piece published in the American magazine *The Galaxy* in 1866 and reprinted the following year in *Hours of Work and Play*. She found it extremely frayed. Cobbe begins her discussion self-reflexively. 'The aberrations of memory have in them this peculiarity: we never remember that our remembrance is not merely habitual, but faulty', she argues. 'We treat all mistakes as exceptional, rather than instantial' (p87). The act of recollection can never be separated from its representation, and the cultural and institutional contexts in which that remembering takes place. Even the most articulate and well-educated people lack the verbal resources to describe a particular remembrance; historical writing is selective, generating its particular mythologies and legends, while (she writes), '… in our Courts of Justice it is notorious how continually the most honest witnesses contradict one another on the simplest matter of fact, and thereby prove the inaccuracy of memory, even when acting under the pressure of conscience, alarmed by judicial oaths and the tremendous result of a trial for a capital offence' (p96). Cobbe describes how specific scenes are transformed in the 'screen memories' of visual recollection, such as in the case of a 'most scrupulously conscientious friend' who, describing a performance of table turning, distinctly remembered that no one was anywhere near the table, but who later, when consulting her notes of the event, saw that she had described six people with their hands actually resting on it.

'Whenever we bring memory to test it is habitually found to be defective', Cobbe concludes, 'and it is this that must serve for the basis of scientific analysis of the faculty' (p102). She modestly admits that she has no pretensions to develop such a science, 'nor to the remotest suggestion, helping to throw more light than has already been shed by psychological writers upon the nature and laws of this department of our mental organisation'. But one thing she can do, she asserts, is to debunk the memorial metaphor so beloved by poets and rhetoricians – that of writing itself:

> Memory is neither an impression made, once for all, like an engraving on a tablet, nor yet safe for an hour from obliteration and modification, after being formed. Rather is memory like a finger-mark traced on shifting sand, ever exposed to obliteration when left unrenewed; and if renewed, then modified and made, not the same, but a fresh and different mark ... We remember, not the things themselves, but the first recollection of them and then the second and then the third, always the latest recollection of them. A proof that this may be so will be found by anybody who will carefully study the processes of his own mind, after he has once detailed at length, in words, any scene he has previously witnessed. He will find himself constantly going over *precisely what he has narrated* and no more ... Thus, in accordance with various laws of mind, each fresh trace varies a little from the trace beneath ... (pp103-4)

Cobbe's remarks seem sharply to anticipate late twentieth-century debates about the transmutation and displacement of memory, although they take place in a very different context, and in some ways they offer a far subtler notion of the process of subconscious modification than those of recent anxieties surrounding 'false memory syndrome'. For Cobbe, the 'fallacies of memory' are not deliberately implanted but are the inevitable result of memory always being a representation, never the thing itself. Her aim here is to debunk what she sees as prevailing myths about memory as well as to mourn the loss of a knowable Past on which present identity depends. 'That dear Past, by whose grave we are standing all our later life ... to know that what we deem we recall so vividly is but a poor shifting reflex – hardly of the thing itself only of our earlier remembrance of the thing – this is sad and mournful' (p111). But there is also a sense here in which Cobbe is able to contemplate the 'abyss' of amnesia because, for her at least, identity rests on a larger concept, one which exists beyond memory, and which is at once expressed through, and transcends, a sense of the mind's own materiality. As with her other articles exploring aspects of the unconscious mind and the current state of mental science, Cobbe was writing for a general audience, at a time when psychology was rapidly becoming established as an important medical specialism and a growing intellectual discipline, but before its boundaries had hardened and while it was developing a 'scientific' language. Her pieces first appeared in popular middle-brow publications such as *Fraser's* and *Macmillan's Magazine*, journals which responded to the widespread fascination with the powers of the mind in mid-Victorian culture and which aimed to explain new developments in mental science to an expanding middle-class readership. A professional journalist, as well as being a feminist who was fascinated by new developments in science, and who embraced the idea of natural selection even though she was unable to reconcile Darwin's later theories of sexual selection and moral development with either her feminism or her own brand of idealist Theism, Cobbe's position relative to the medical and scientific establishment was in some ways marginal.[2] But her discussions of contemporary psychological theory were read and responded to both by the magazine's general readers and by the writers whose work she discussed, and this gives her a significant part in the complex debates of mid-nineteenth-century psychology.

In this essay I consider some of the ways in which memory – a key term that simultaneously shaped the notion of the self as autonomous agent and undermined the idea of unified self-identity – became a crucial means of linking psychic and social identity in nineteenth-century culture. I will do this by exploring how two figures at the heart of the medical establishment – Henry Holland and William Carpenter – as well as Cobbe herself, analysed memory as part of a wider debate on the nature of subjectivity and the limits of individual autonomy. It is not difficult to see how the fears surrounding the unreliability of memory that Cobbe so eloquently expressed formed part of a wider sense of cultural anxiety surrounding modernity in the mid-nineteenth century – how the fragility of personal and historical recollection threatened the continuity of past and present on which tradition and social stability rested. Here, though, I want to tease out the different concepts of consciousness that lay behind these anxieties, and to look at how they were explored in very different ways *within* the heart of the 'dominant culture', emphasising that we need to scrutinise our own interpretative framework in reading the ways in which the Victorians analysed the self.

It is now widely recognised that the three key intellectual revolutionaries of the nineteenth century – Karl Marx, Charles Darwin and Sigmund Freud – were not towering giants standing in splendid isolation, but figures that reworked and transformed debates current within their contemporary culture. Yet while it is generally acknowledged that concepts which now seem characteristically 'modern' – above all the development of psychoanalysis – drew on psychological debates that had been developing throughout the nineteenth century, we still tend to read these debates teleologically (perhaps inevitably) in the light of our own preoccupations and paradigms. The nineteenth-century concept of the 'unconscious' did not directly prefigure Freud's – it did not involve, for example, a concept of repression which is itself latent – but neither was it based on notions of a stable self: nineteenth-century psychologists were fascinated by the 'obscure recesses of the mind' even as they wished to penetrate and control its elusive workings. Cobbe's analysis of the ways in which specific cultures reinvent and reconstruct individual and collective memories in the act of narration acts as a kind of cognitive border for the ways we think about the relationship between dominant and marginal forms of knowledge in mid-nineteenth-century mental science – and about how specific debates about unconscious memory focus some broader questions about personal and political subjectivity and the nature of cultural authority as 'authorship'.

For the distinction between orthodox and the heterodox, 'weird' and mainstream, science is continually breaking down in the complex debates that made up nineteenth-century mental science. Binary models of cultural authority – in which 'other', alternative forms of knowledge, and, by implication, social identities and practices, exist beneath or against the dominant one – quickly become unsatisfactory when one starts to unpack the precise meanings of particular debates within a given cultural formation. I don't think that any single theoretical paradigm – either Foucault's analysis of discursive formations, Raymond Williams's still useful description of a culture being made up of dominant, residual and emergent forces, or Gillian Beer's account of the mutual assimilation of scientific and narrative fictions – adequately describes this complexity. Studies such as Adrian Desmond's *The*

Politics of Evolution; Roger Smith's studies of the history of physiological psychology; Roger Cooter's book on phrenology in early
nineteenth-century radical culture; and Alison Winter's work on
mesmerism in mid-nineteenth-century England, all extend the reaction
against 'internalist' accounts of scientific gentlemanly traditions, showing how emergent theories developed out of radical or non-conformist
secular contexts, beneath and often in opposition to the elite, Anglican,
Oxbridge-dominated establishment.[3] In very different ways they
demonstrate the inextricability of specific forms of scientific knowledge from the social, political and institutional contexts in which they
are produced. However in showing how particular paradigms could
develop into new kinds of dominant models (as in the case of evolutionary theory), or into residual forms (as with phrenology), or into
various modes of heterodox therapies (as with mesmerism), these studies suggest, either explicitly or implicitly, that there are no clear lines of
either incorporation or exclusion that connect the 'dominant ideology'
of a particular moment with the social and political positions of writers and practitioners, or with the concept of what forms legitimate and
illegitimate knowledge *within* those theories.

This in turn raises the question of how we might see a discursive
formation as including various forms of contradiction and tension,
without simply falling back into a vague bricolage which it's hard to get
any critical purchase on. One way of approaching this problem is to
take apart the 'marginal': Alison Winter's impressive work on
mesmerism, in particular, makes it clear that there is no straightforward
correlation between an 'alternative' therapeutic movement and a
precise set of political or cultural meanings. Mesmerism gained its
appeal and generated anxiety as a means of both exploring and control-
ling the self during the 1830s and 1840s, partly because it offered a
flexible discourse that blurred the boundaries between the material and
the metaphysical and could be used to support widely differing theories: of the self, the forms of latent memory, of the nature and causes of
mental derangement. While increasingly denounced by the medical
profession, it attracted a wide range of groups and interests, including
Radicals, Utilitarians, Tory evangelicals, middle-class Unitarians and
Whig aristocrats. Thus particular methods and even texts could be
interpreted in radically different ways: artificial somnambulism could
be seen to be emphasising the importance as much as the limits of self-
control; it could be seen as a levelling force, based on a materialist
analysis of the mind, as in the writings of Harriet Martineau.
Alternatively it could be pressed into service to support a higher spiri-

tual authority, manifested by the superior power of the mesmeriser over his subjects, as in the work of Chauncy Hare Townshend. This turns attention back to how we might think about contradictions within the 'dominant', which is what I want to focus on here.

Mesmerism and, emerging from it in the 1840s, James Braid's concept of hypnotism, was one of the more spectacular means of conceiving the mind as 'containing' a set of latent traces which emerge in extraordinary or limit states such as dreams, artificially induced or spontaneous states of trance, 'double consciousness' or insanity. However, it was only one aspect of mental physiologists' fascination with the elusive movements of memory, and it is in their sense of the *weirdness* of its everyday workings, and its continual connection with different conditions of alterity, that one can detect tensions within the dominant formation – practical, institutional and theoretical – even as it was being defined. The analysis of memory's breakdown or decay – the results of accidents, old age and cerebral disease – was a central part of the newly professionalised specialism of mental pathology, and had a practical bearing on the growing network of state and private asylums by the 1850s, but studies of double consciousness and other forms of mental dissociation were pursued not only to draw boundaries between healthy and morbid mental states, but also to explore the general working of the brain and the mind and the way in which identity itself is shaped. The actual mechanisms underlying memory and forgetting may have only become the subject of systematic study in Europe in the late nineteenth century, with Hermann Ebbinghaus's statistical experiments in Germany and, in France, Eugene Azam's analysis of the multiple personalities of subjects under hypnosis, and Pierre Janet's studies of the psychic effects of trauma.[4] But this work was deeply indebted to earlier developments in mental science: T.A. Ribot's influential study of diseases of memory (which Nietszche cites in *The Genealogy of Morals*), for example, owed much to the work of the prominent figures of British Psychology in the 1850s and 1860s – William Carpenter, Alexander Bain, Herbert Spencer and G.H. Lewes.[5] Indeed, it was partly because memory *was* so central to the concept and study of the self in the mid-nineteenth century that it was not separated from other aspects of the study of the relationships between the mind and the brain.

Yet how exactly did memory work, and what were the implications of the wide range of metaphors and models used to explain it: *not* the tablet so much as the palimpsest; the room with many doors and windows leading in and out; the photograph; or concentric circles of conscious and unconscious thought? Do we unconsciously assimilate all our past experience and how is this experience inscribed on the brain and nervous system? How mutable is latent thought, and what processes govern its subliminal transformation? What are the causes and functions of forgetting as well as remembering; how and why are memories triggered, and what is the relationship between physiological, intellectual and emotional response? Above all, what power relationships are implicit in the act of recollection and forms of latent mental life? 'Is memory a distinct and sovereign power, exercising independent autocratic authority?' asked the eminent alienist Forbes Winslow in 1860. 'Or is it one of the results of a *combined* or *complex* operation of several of the mental faculties?'[6] His contemporaries were acutely aware of the social, moral and ontological issues that these questions raised. 'It is the Consciousness of Agreement between our present and past mental experience which constitutes our experience of personal identity', stressed William Carpenter, reiterating an old truism. 'Without it we would live in the present alone; for the reproduction of past states of Consciousness would affect us only like the succession of fantasies presented to us in the play of the imagination'.[7] Self-identity, then, breaks down in the uncanniness of memory, as the radical otherness within the self emerges in this succession of fantasies.

In exploring the ways in which identities are created through the interaction of conscious and latent memory, mid-nineteenth-century physiological psychologists were critically transforming phrenological models – the materialist analysis of how active or latent propensities are localised in parts of the brain – and eighteenth-century associationist theory, which, like Cartesian philosophy and Kantian metaphysics, had posited that identity can only exist in time through the subjective recognition of past ideas. While the key figures of mid-century physiological psychology – William Carpenter, Alexander Bain, Herbert Spencer and G.H. Lewes – all criticised associationism for its idealism and abstraction, each drew on associationist discourse in developing evolutionary models of consciousness in which the self performatively learns habits of actions, thought and feeling through repetitive mental gestures that become embedded as mental reflexes and incipient instincts embodied in evolving organisms. However not only is it risky to simplify the diverse ways in which these writers interpreted notions of embodied or unconscious memory in their interrogations of habit, reflex or instinct – it is also important to emphasise that associationism itself was not a unified discourse that could simply be modified in the light of new physiological models and adapted for evolutionary ends.

For in certain respects the associationist tradition is one of the clearest examples of a dominant theory based on an unstable concept of mental dominance. Developed by Locke and Hume, whose concepts of rational and regulated selfhood were based on the notion that both consciousness and identity are products of the complex processes of recognition and association that make up experience, associationist philosophy was given a specifically materialist dimension in the mid-eighteenth century by David Hartley's concept of physiological vibrations which, he argued, carved channels in the nerves and brain in a process of repetitive association between ideas, muscular reflexes and motions which made sympathy based on physiological correspondence the basis of moral sense.[8] Hartley's materialist psychology became one of the cornerstones of Unitarian rationalism, and James Mill's development of associationist principles into a theory of absolute self-identity and self-surveillance grew out of and reinforced Utilitarian philosophical radicalism.[9] This is one of the clearest examples of the connections between political and mental economies, in which the collective good of proper self-management is based ultimately on control of the mind. It is both developed and modified in John Stuart Mill's concept of moral agency, in which character is ultimately self-created, even though the conditions which surround it may be beyond individual control.[10] With its emphasis on self control and its hostility to all forms of idealism (manifested most clearly in J.S. Mill's scathing attack on William Hamilton),[11] it suggests a profound split within associationism itself, in which Mill's utilitarianism is pitched against the more dynamic theory of consciousness that was developed by the Edinburgh philosophers Dugald Stewart, Thomas Brown and William Hamilton himself. This theory was fostered in the close connections between medicine and philosophy that flourished in early nineteenth-century Edinburgh and Glasgow universities, which tended to stress the continual process of interaction between the conscious and the unconscious mind.

In this adaptation of associationist precepts, Dugald Stewart had drawn attention, at the end of the eighteenth century, to the classical distinction between the conscious recollection of specific events, in which the mind selects from and determines its own processes of thought, and memory itself – the far more elusive mass which forms its raw material – and had emphasised that all acts of recollection are performative, involving active conception and reinterpretation.[12] Reworking Lockean principles twenty years later, Thomas Brown had replaced the concept of association with that of *suggestion,* in which the mind makes spontaneously creative and emotional links between present and past impressions and correspondences.[13] Developing these theories, William Hamilton argued that the mind works through three degrees of latent mental modification: firstly, that which we consciously recall, secondly, subliminal memory emerging in extraordinary states, and finally, the everyday process through which all thought proceeds through the unconscious assimilation of latent associations.[14] To illustrate his theory of latent thought, Hamilton drew on specific case studies of double consciousness, the most famous being the story, which Coleridge had made popular in his critique of Hartley, of the uneducated German girl who mysteriously started speaking Greek and Hebrew in a state of fever. Hamilton used this story to make the point that *all* experience is assimilated even though it passes out of conscious memory.[15] And in the mid-nineteenth century Hamilton's theories were defended most rigorously against Mill's utilitarianism by E.S. Dallas in *The Gay Science* – his extraordinary and eclectic analysis of aesthetic pleasure based on a theory of the unconscious or the 'Hidden Soul'.[16] Yet this distinction between two strands of associationism, the one rationalist and utilitarian, the other emphasising latent memory and mental marginality, continually breaks down. James Mill had been Dugald Stewart's admiring student, just as Dallas had been Hamilton's, and the intellectual hot-house of early nineteenth-century Edinburgh, feeding the English medical establishment, was in many ways as much part of the dominant culture as the Oxbridge Anglican elite. The two strands (if they can be called such) continually interwove, and to explore this I now look briefly at how two figures of different generations, both at the heart of the emergent mental science establishment by the 1850s, explored the working of latent memory and conscious recollection, before returning, finally, to Frances Power Cobbe.

HOLLAND ON MEMORY, IDENTITY AND TIME

Henry Holland and William Carpenter both came from provincial Unitarian backgrounds and had become key members of the London medical establishment by the time they developed their work on mental physiology. But the contrasts are equally telling. Born in 1788, first cousin to Elizabeth Gaskell and Darwin's second cousin on the Wedgwood side, Holland never held a teaching post at any of the large London hospitals nor did he work as an alienist in a public or private asylum. Instead, he pursued an extraordinarily lucrative career in private practice, supporting a lifestyle which, mimicking that of his wealthy patients, enabled him to spend each autumn in extensive travel. Holland's wide acquaintance transected London's social, political and intellectual worlds, moving from the radical intelligentsia to the conservative social elite, and ranging across three generations. As he tells us in his *Recollections of Past Life* – a memoir which scatters famous names in all directions – he was the friend of Anna Barbauld and Walter Scott in his youth and of George Eliot in later life, while his clients included Queen Caroline, Queen Victoria, and six prime ministers.[17] What his *Recollections* also imply – not least through their dreadful snobbishness – is how his position as society doctor helped shape the development of his writing. For it was his privileged niche in private practice, with the means and leisure to pursue his ideas, that contributes to the speculative tone of his analysis of the mind that pervades his influential book, published in 1852, *Chapters of Mental Physiology*, in which he developed and expanded the psychological material of his earlier popular collection of essays, *Medical Notes and Reflections*, which had appeared twelve years before, in 1840.

The specific cultural contexts in which Scottish associationist psychology developed has, therefore, an important bearing on Holland's discussion of the place of memory in consciousness. Holland's Dissenting background was more of the successful business than the politically radical kind. As a well-heeled medical student, he quickly became involved in Edinburgh's elite cultural and literary circles, and while he remained politically unengaged, he became friends with Francis Jeffrey, founder and editor of the staunchly Whig *Edinburgh Review*, and his elegantly-written essays on a range of scientific topics to the *Edinburgh*, and later to the conservative *Quarterly Review,* consolidated his professional position. During the first half of the nineteenth century, then, Holland spanned intellectual and social positions that would become increasingly detached: carrying his social and intellectual status as a successful private physician into the emerging field of mental science, and self-reflexively bringing together associationist and physiological approaches in the analysis of memory.

Chapters on Mental Physiology doesn't claim to offer a coherent theory of consciousness or an overview of the relations between mind and brain, but the way Holland organised the free-standing essays is telling. Anticipating William James's much later *Principles of Psychology,* the chapter 'On the memory, as affected by age and disease' comes after two essays on the perception of time: 'Mental consciousness in relation to time and succession', and 'Time, as an element in mental functions'. But it also comes before one of Holland's most influential pieces, 'On the brain as a double organ', an essay which had a significant impact on debates about double consciousness when it first appeared in *Medical Notes and Reflections*, and was one of the main inspirations behind A. L. Wigan's extreme manifesto, *The Duality of the Mind*, written in 1844, which argued that we each have two entire distinct and separate cerebra, each with its own memory and powers of concentration. Holland rejected Wigan's crude physiological determinism, suggesting that double consciousness often takes the form in which 'complete trains of thought are perverted and deranged, while others are preserved in sufficiently natural course to become a sort of watch upon the former'. He argues that this should be understood primarily as a form of disordered association 'where the mind passes by alternation from one state to another, each having the perception of external impression and appropriate trains of thought, but not linked together by the ordinary gradation, or by mutual memory'.[18]

Moreover, to explain this, Holland refers to his earlier discussion of 'mental consciousness in relation to time and succession', in which he describes the multiplicity of consciousness, not in abnormal states but in everyday life, and 'our inability to measure by time these momentary passages of mental existence; crowding upon each other, and withal so interwoven into one chain, that consciousness, while it makes us aware of unceasing change, tells us of no breach of continuity' (p187). Here 'double consciousness is a kind of slowed down version of the constant shifts and gradations the mind subconsciously assimilates as it passes through time, where mental existence in time undercuts the consciousness of agreement between past and present in a proliferation of identity which for us now, after William James and Henri Bergson, seems characteristically 'modernist'.[19] 'For the swift consciousness we have only those names of "transitive states", or "feelings of relation"', James would write in 1890. 'As the brain-changes are continuous, so do all these consciousnesses melt into each other like dissolving views. Properly they are but one protracted consciousness, one unbroken stream'.[20] Forty years earlier Holland, too, explored this process:

> Some object of sense is before the mind to the momentary exclusion of others; thought follows such perception, excluding for a time all objects of external senses; remembrances crowd upon thought, and furnish it with ever-changing subjects; passion and emotions are blended in the same current, but equally under constant change and succession. Volition in some cases governs and guides the sequence;

and selects, as it were, the objects of present perception and thought. At other times the mind seems submitted to the changes of state, which comes upon it unbidden and despite the will ...[21]

'We have, in the instrument of examination, the actual thing to be examined', Holland continues, recognising that understanding memory involves reflection on the object of study itself – on the interconnection between the brain as a set of physiological processes and the mind responding to them. Moreover while the mind has extraordinary power of focusing attention on one mental representation or physical state, it is the multiplicity of past impressions which cumulatively produce the emotional texture of consciousness. Volition here 'is a limited faculty', Holland argues, 'corresponding with that wonderful combination of voluntary and involuntary acts which pervades, or rather constitutes every part of our existence' (p61). It's too simple to read Holland's work as somehow determined by his social and cultural position, but I'd like to suggest that he was able to explore the limits of consciousness, volition and conscious memory without either engaging in specific debates about the classification and treatment of insanity or aligning himself with a heterodox movement such as mesmerism, partly because of his privileged position as a practising physician – on the one hand at the heart of the medical establishment, on the other, marginal to formal institutions. Though less idealist, some of his arguments are, for example, strikingly similar to that of the critic E.S. Dallas who, like Holland, developed Hamilton's notion of 'latent mental modification' in developing his theory of the 'Hidden Soul'. Both Holland and Dallas saw the unpredictability and apparent spontaneity of memory as 'a power that belongs even more to the unconscious than the conscious mind'. Both recognised, for example, that when we attempt to recollect a lost memory we set in train a series of associations, while acknowledging that this attempt is frequently frustrated and it is often better to turn one's mind in a completely different direction in order to set in place the 'automatic machinery' of hidden memory that surrounds the will. 'The miracle here, is when memory halts a little,' Dallas noted, 'and there arises the strange contradiction of a mind knowing what it searches for, yet making the search because it does not know'.[22]

At the same time, as a practising physician, Holland's reflexive uncertainty allowed him to bring together specific cases and speculative hypotheses without either ranging them in a specific causal order or subjecting them to an ultimate authority and this eclecticism may have contributed to the usefulness of his work to contemporary mental science. His work points not only to the limits of consciousness, but to the limits of contemporary knowledge of it, without bordering on the mystical. Although self-identity is 'made up of the knowledge and thousand memories of the past', he argues, it is never clear whether consciousness is a 'series of acts and states...in unbroken sequence', or 'a wide and mixed current, in which, various sensations, thoughts, emotions and volitions ... coalesce and coexist'.[23] This means that he concurs with the prevailing view that both memory and attention 'may be enlarged by effort and cultivation' while laying stress on the limits of volitional control. The essay 'Of memory, as affected by age and disease' includes detailed cases of specific forms of memory failure – such as forms of aphasia and 'mental dislocation' caused by cerebral trauma, and the decay of short-term memory with advancing age – cases where it is clearest that 'of all the intellectual faculties [memory] depends most on *organised structure* for whatever concerns its completeness, its changes and decay' (p152). He maintains that while 'the *dislocation* of memory' may partly be explained by clearly physically identified causes, these depend on 'observations of the faculty in its natural state', and both, like the limits of memory itself, 'are unseen and inaccessible to our research'. Indeed Holland freely confesses that memory baffles systematic enquiry: 'The metaphysician, who is here treading on the same ground with the physiologist and physician, equally fails of reaching any conclusion which can be admitted within the pale of exact science' (p145). He sees memory not as a specific faculty but as a series of functions, which cannot be reduced to any one conceptual metaphor, explained systematically: 'It is manifest that there is a line or limit here, at which both reason and imagination are arrested ... '. He goes on, 'Even when expressly using the powers of recollection, the mind seems almost consciously to be exerting itself on something *without*, which is imperfectly submitted to the will' (p152). How does this compare with William Carpenter?

VOLITION AND REFLEX: CARPENTER'S UNSTABLE HIERARCHIES

As a well established figure by the 1830s, Holland played a part in fostering William Carpenter's career, and as Alison Winter has noted, Carpenter depended on the approval of Holland and other orthodox figures such as John Henslow to establish his at the time unorthodox syntheses of *Principles of General and Comparative Physiology*: his rise to the position of premier figure in British physiology by the 1850s was by no means inevitable.[24] While Holland moved away from his Unitarian origins, Carpenter remained dominated by its rationalist theology – its view of a material universe shaped by natural laws ultimately determined by a rational God. The son of a Unitarian minister and one of a family of reformers – his sister, Mary, was active in setting up ragged schools in Bristol and active also in prison and criminal reform – he was trained in Hartley's principles of association before studying in Edinburgh and becoming profoundly influenced by radical French theories of the unity of organic structures.[25]

Carpenter's work builds totalising morphologies which extend across the vegetable and the animal, the animal and the human, and the physical and psychic, worlds. Holland and Carpenter are thus self-reflexive in very different ways, and this is partly indicated in their institutional positions. While Holland worked in private practice, Carpenter endeavoured to dominate and transform medical education, striving to break the conservative Anglican Oxbridge monopoly on English science and shift the centre of gravity to London. His textbooks and encyclopaedias, popular with a general as well as a specialist audience, became standard medical reading throughout the second half of the nineteenth century, and the psychological sections of the 1855 *Principles of Human Physiology* were expanded into *Principles of Mental Physiology* in the early 1870s. Carpenter thus moved from an oppositional position within orthodox science to a dominant place defining and even policing the boundaries of legitimate psychology by the mid-1850s.

The most obvious aspect of Carpenter's mental physiology is his preoccupation with the power of the will in the face of unpredictable mental reflexes. In the 1855 edition of *Human Physiology* he rejects thoroughgoing materialism, denying that 'Man is but a *thinking machine*, his conduct being entirely determined by his original constitution, modified by subsequent conditions beyond his control', and responding, puppet-like, to external sensations.[26] Instead he sets up a modified dualism, in a rising hierarchy of automatic mental functions.

Here ideas as well as sensations and emotions respond automatically to stimuli, and while there is normally a gradual progress whereby sensations become ideas linked to emotions, rising to intellectual processes controlled by the will, these intellectual responses too, can become *ideo-motor* reflexes when the will is suspended. People in states of natural and artificial somnambulism, he argues, are the examples *par*

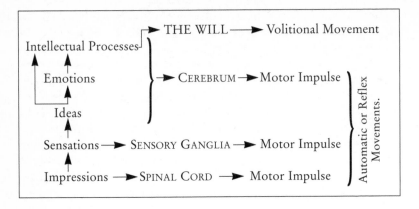

Carpenter's model of mental reflexes[27]

excellence of 'mere thinking automata – their whole course of thought and of action being determined by suggestion conveyed from without', although as he later elaborated, this state is generated by the displaced will of the subjects themselves, through their own state of heightened expectancy, as much as the imaginary power of the mesmeriser.[28]

This means that despite his insistence on the potential of the will either directly or indirectly to control this complex structure of voluntary and automatic responses, Carpenter's mental hierarchy remains an inherently unstable one. In an image that he shares with his friend Frances Power Cobbe, he compares the relationship between the conscious and unconscious mind to that of a frisky horse controlled by a skilful rider: 'the horse furnishes the power', while, 'the rate and direction of the movement are determined by the Will of the rider'.[29] Carpenter thus strives to give the will overarching authority, where states of mesmeric trance are signs not of latent or subliminal selves but of the internalised colonisation of an 'emptied out' identity that, implicitly at least, lacks a history and therefore a memory. But if we place his analysis of ideo-motor reflex in the light of associationist concepts of mental modification, his overall analysis of unconscious cerebration becomes more complex than his discussion of automata suggests. For despite his stress on volition, Carpenter concedes that the will 'can *originate* nothing; its power being limited to the *selection* and *intensification* of what is actually before the consciousness... no one has ever *acquired* the creative power of genius'.[30] He shares the contemporary fascination with Coleridge, whose anecdote of the German girl who spoke Greek and German during a fever became one of the meta-narratives of nineteenth-century discussions of latent memory and was the ultimate example of the ambivalent power of unconscious mental life. The 'unconscious' for Carpenter thus is both an empty and a vigorous place, where the self is either at its most puppet-like or its most productive, and this has an important bearing on his discussion of how conscious recollection and latent memory interact.

For Carpenter, in line with both Kantian and associationist premises, self-identity relies on the subjective recognition of the past, and this depends firstly on the vigorous training of the power of recol-lection in the present – the conscious mind's 'sovereign authority' to range through and select from its mass of latent material through indi-rect colonisation rather than conscious control. Like Holland, he acknowledged the futility of forcing the mind along a train of recollec-tion in trying to remember an event, but he directly follows James Mill in claiming that one can indirectly control the memory by 'fixing atten-tion upon one or more of the ideas already present to the mind...the very act of thus *attending* to a particular idea, serving not only to inten-sify the idea itself, but also to strengthen the associations by which it is connected to others'.[31] But in *Mental Physiology* he lays far greater stress than Holland does on the formation of early associations in childhood, and the powerful force of these emotions to modify the brain, continually and unconsciously:

> Here again, it would seem as if the material organ of the Feelings tends to *form itself* in accordance with the impressions habitually made upon it; the Emotional state seems often to be determined by circumstances of which the individual has no Ideational consciousness ... a mode of influ-ence which acts with particular potency on the minds of children and is a most important element of their moral education .... [For] The concep-tions of childhood will long remain latent in the mind, to reappear at every hour of weakness, when the tension of the reason is relaxed and the power of old associations is supreme. (p540-3)

And this suggests a different archaeology of consciousness to the one suggested in his responses to mesmerism – one in which the repet-itive associations of habit become ingrained into a moralised unconscious, embodied in the accumulated memory of habit, whose end point is both the evolving organism, and the conscious self.

Carpenter's theory of the reflex action of the mind can clearly be linked to his ideological and institutional position as a radical Unitarian at the heart of the medical establishment. It was this position that helped to legitimise the study of the unconscious mind – to bring it into the sphere of the 'dominant' while reinforcing the boundaries between orthodox and marginal modes of knowledge; he places both within a developmental paradigm in which latent memory in childhood has a crucial place. In *Mental Physiology* he modifies the widespread view that every fleeting thought is registered on the brain, arguing that it is uncertain 'whether *everything* that passes through our Minds thus leaves its impression on their material instrument'. It is only certain categories of associations that are transformed into automatic reflexes – those habitual modes of thought and feeling which affect the growth of the brain in childhood, together with 'single experiences of peculiar force and vividness, such as are likely to have left very decided "traces" although the circumstances of their formation were so unusual as to keep them out of ordinary associational remembrance'. But Carpenter then makes a significant shift from forms of recovered memory to the act of recollection. Giving Mill's distinction between the 'experiencing self' and the 'witnessing self' an explicitly physiological base, he describes how the sudden recall of immediate sensual associations (such as tears arising from the recollection of a painful event) is changed by the fact that it has been registered as an idea of an emotion in the brain. Conversely the 'storing up of ideas in the memory' is also 'the psychological expression of physical changes' – and here the photograph is the most fitting metaphor. 'Though we are accustomed to speak of Memory as if it consisted of an *exact* reproduction of past states of Consciousness,' he concludes, 'yet experience is continually showing us that this reproduction is very often *inexact* ... that reminiscence really represents, not the actual occurrence, but the modified trace of it' (p453-6). To illustrate this point he cites Frances Power Cobbe's story of her 'conscientious friend' who so radically misremembered her performance of table-turning, which brings us back to Cobbe's ambivalent concept of memory.

CONCLUSION
'Whenever we bring memory to the test it is habitually found to be defective.' I opened by suggesting that Cobbe was able to contemplate the unreliability of memory by seeing identity as resting on a concept of consciousness that existed beyond its empirical truth. I want to conclude by noting how Cobbe's ambivalent sense of identity in time opens up another set of tensions within the dominant, touching on many of the questions about ancestral memory and the

subliminal self that preoccupied late nineteenth-century psychology. As she noted in her autobiography, it was mainly through Carpenter that Cobbe met the major scientific figures of day; she was introduced to him by his sister Mary Carpenter who she lived with in the late 1850s, teaching in Mary's ragged school and working in women's reformatories. But despite their shared commitment to philanthropy and belief in a rational yet transcendent natural law, Cobbe was no Unitarian, and found Mary Carpenter's austere lifestyle hard to stomach. She came from a wealthy, conservative Anglo-Irish family, inheriting a meagre allowance of £200 a year on her father's death (compare that with Holland's £5,000 p.a. made in private practice!) which she supplemented by her journalism. Rejecting Orthodox Christianity and the idea of the afterlife in her teens, she remained preoccupied by questions of morality and mortality; her first book *An Essay on the Theory of Intuitive Morals,* written at home while looking after her aged father, was an explication and defence of Kantian transcendental idealism. Here she commends the *Critique of Practical Reason* as positing an absolute and universal Moral Law of rational free agents, based on a unified self-consciousness that is independent of the perception of the empirical world. While Cobbe later acknowledged that these concepts of transcendental unity and absolute Moral law needed to be revised in the light of evolutionary theory, they remained her 'fundamental laws of mind' and in some ways they both explain and compensate for her apparent relativism in 'The fallacies of memory'.[32]

Yet while Cobbe seems to deny any concept of a 'deep self' by arguing that our remembrance of memory is as unreliable as our remembrance of fact, elsewhere other concepts of memory and identity come into play, which at times reinforce, at others clash with this 'fundamental law of mind'. In 'Darwinism in morals', Cobbe applauded Darwin's development of Spencer's concepts of inherited or organic memory in the *Descent of Man* in so far as it underlined a teleological interpretation of humanity's animal ancestry – and this would feed into her concept of animal rights that underpinned her anti-vivisection campaigns. She attacked Darwin and Spencer not for their evolutionism so much as for their moral relativism – their argument that 'our moral sense is nothing but the experience of utility organised and consolidated through all past generations', and she uses Wallace's claim that natural selection cannot explain the development of altruism to reinforce her concept of a transcendent moral law.[33] Here humanity's unconscious memory – its animal ancestry, embodied in shared instincts, expressions and reflexes – is amalgamated into a teleological unity. But 'Unconscious cerebration: a psychological study' continually circles round the problem of how to reconcile the conscious self and the embodied memories of the unconscious mind; again coming back to Forbes Winslow's question that had exercised both Holland and Carpenter: 'Is memory a distinct sovereign power, exercising independent autocratic authority? Or is it one of the results of a *combined* or *complex* operation of several of the mental faculties?'

Cobbe starts and concludes with a weird exaggeration of the magnetised subject – that of the Teraph or 'old Hebrew necromancers', 'the decapitated head of a child, placed on a pillar and compelled by magic to reply to the questions of the sorcerer' – and here the mind is a set of reflexes performing the functions of Thought and Memory in which the 'thinking brain' is separated from the 'conscious self'.[34] Surveying the different forms of unconscious activity so widely discussed by mid-century mental physiologists – dreams, trance, drunkenness, the 'fairy work' performed by the mind during sleep, latent memory, the automatic actions of skills such as weaving or piano playing – she argues that Carpenter's theory of unconscious cerebration is the fullest attempt to give latent thought a physiological explanation, describing it in readily understandable terms. Finally, Cobbe tries to press Carpenter's hierarchy of mental reflexes into the service of her own form of transcendental idealism. She attempts to tread a fine line between materialism and anti-materialism by drawing, as Carpenter does, on the image of the horse and rider to suggest a modified dualism of conscious and unconscious mind: 'We are not Centaurs, steed and rider in one, but horsemen, astride on roadsters, which obey us when we guide them and when we drop the reins...canter off without our permission' (p333). But in the process, she manifests the paradoxes inherent in Carpenter's theory of automatic reflex as much as her own, for here it is the Will, the conscious self which ultimately becomes the Teraph, the disembodied head, in Cobbe's formulation, precisely because the cords of memory are severed. Cobbe is finally driven to a spiritualist explanation to account for the continuity of the self, for consciousness can only exist in time in Kant's metaphysics as much as in associationism, and this means that the conscious self must be based on a process of amnesia that it has itself forgotten, but which is, nonetheless shaped by hidden memory.

The sense of a coherent personal and political subjectivity depended on a concept of memory and identity that was recognised as being provisional and unstable in the mid-nineteenth century. Here I've explored some of the implications of this in the growing field of mental science, and it is risky to extrapolate from these into the explicitly political sphere: I've wanted to avoid over-simple formulas in which different discourses can be read off each other. But today's disciplinary boundaries – between philosophy, psychology, biology and social theory – did not apply in the mid-nineteenth century, and most writers were acutely aware of the broader implications of their work in their discussions of the self and the ways in which it might be imagined. What emerges here is not one political subject in the mid-nineteenth century, but a sense of the complexity of subjectivity shaping social identity, and here the fascination with the marginal, the elusiveness of subjectivity, does not necessarily serve progressive political ends. Nineteenth century mental science embodied both sides of an ambivalent 'modernity': on the one hand the stress on progress, rational self control, empirical analysis – on the other a fascination with the elusiveness of consciousness, the division and complexities within the self. For the three figures considered here, memory had very different kinds of implicitly political meanings: for Holland it meant an eclectic shifting between positions and identities that would have an indirect impact on literary modernism; for Carpenter, a continuing liberal Utilitarian reformism, based on a concept of a regulated but ultimately elusive unconscious, that would contribute more to the development of neuroscience than psychoanalysis; for Cobbe, a belief in Kantian transcendentalism – of a self that exists through and beyond materiality – underpinned both a profound political conservatism, and an insistence on the rights of women and the claims of beasts, in a concept of natural law that has re-emerged in modern debates on animal rights. None of these defined the dominant culture, but all of them contributed to it, in different ways reinforcing the liberal concept of the self – that we shape our own character – while also revealing its underside: that this self is shaped through the continual interaction of conscious and unconscious memory. Today, when the dominant legacy of nineteenth century psychology is, on the one hand that branch of evolutionary psychology developed by neurobiologists, on the other, therapeutic debates about the 'truth' of memory, we need to remember this complex history.[35]

NOTES

1. Frances Power Cobbe, 'The fallacies of memory', *Hours of Work and Play*, N. Trubner & Co., London 1867, pp88-89.
2. On Cobbe's relation to nineteenth-century scientific debates more gener-

ally, see Evelleen Richards, 'Redrawing the boundaries: Darwinian science and Victorian women intellectuals', in Bernard Lighten (ed), *Victorian Science in Context*, University of Chicago Press, Chicago 1997.

3. Adrian Desmond, *The Politics of Evolution: Morphology, Medicine and Reform in Radical London*, University of Chicago Press, Chicago 1989; Roger Smith, 'The background of physiological psychology in natural philosophy', *History of Science* 11 (1973); and 'Does the history of psychology have a subject?', *History of the Human Sciences*, 1:2 (1988); Roger Cooter, *The Cultural Meaning of Popular Science: Phrenology and the Organisation of Consent in Nineteenth-Century Britain*, Cambridge University Press, Cambridge 1984; Alison Winter, *Mesmerised: Powers of Mind in Victorian Britain*, University of Chicago Press, Chicago 1998.

4. See Ian Hacking, *Rewriting the Soul: Multiple Personality and the Sciences of Memory*, Princeton University Press, Princeton 1995.

5. T.A. Ribot, *Les Maladies de la Memoire*, Balliere, Paris 1881.

6. Forbes B. Winslow, *On the Obscure Diseases of the Brain and Disorders of the Mind*, 4th edition, John Churchill and Son, London 1868, p232.

7. William B. Carpenter, *The Principles of Mental Physiology*, Henry S. King & Co., London 1874, pp454-455.

8. For a useful overview of associationism, see Maurice Mandelbaum, *History, Man and Reason: A Study in Nineteenth-Century Thought*, Johns Hopkins University Press, Baltimore 1971; also Karl M Figlio, 'Theories of perception and the physiology of mind in the late eighteenth century', *History of Science*, 12 (1975), pp177-212.

9. James Mill, *Analysis of the Phenomena of the Human Mind* (1829); new edition with notes by J. S. Mill, Longmans, Green and Dyer, London 1869.

10. This is most clearly spelt out in J.S. Mill's *A System of Logic Ratiocinative and Inductive*, *The Collected Works of John Stuart Mill*, vols. 7 and 8, J.M. Robson (ed), Routledge and Kegan Paul, 1974. See Janice Carlyle, *John Stuart Mill and the Writing of Character*, University of Georgia Press, Athens and London 1991.

11. In his *Examination of William Hamilton's Philosophy* (1865), Mill used Hamilton as an exemplar of what he saw as the 'intuitive' approach to the study of the mind.

12. Dugald Stewart, *Elements of the Philosophy of the Human Mind*, 2 vols, 1792; 6th edition, T. Cadel & W. Davies, London 1818, I pp403-407.

13. Thomas Brown, *Lectures on the Philosophy of the Human Mind*, Edinburgh 1820.

14. William Hamilton, *Lectures on Metaphysics and Logic*, H. C. Mansel (ed), 4 vols, 1859; 2nd edition, William Blackwood and Sons, Edinburgh 1861, I, pp347-349. For an overview of this material, see Jenny Bourne Taylor

and Sally Shuttleworth (eds), *Embodied Selves: An Anthology of Psychological Texts, 1830-1890*, Oxford University Press, Oxford 1998.

15. S.T. Coleridge, *Biographia Literaria* 2 vols, Rest, Fenner, London 1817, I pp108-116.

16. E.S. Dallas, *The Gay Science*, 2 vols, Chapman and Hall, London 1866.

17. Henry Holland, *Recollections of Past Life*, Longmans, Green & co., 1872.

18. Henry Holland, *Chapters on Mental Physiology*, Longman, Brown, Green and Longman, London 1852, pp186-187.

19. William James is usually credited with first using the term 'stream of consciousness', while Henri Bergson's, *Time and Free Will: An Essay on the Immediate Data of Consciousness* (1889) had a strong influence on early twentieth-century modernism.

20. William James, *The Principles of Psychology* 2 vols., Henry Holt and Co., New York 1890, I, pp247-248.

21. Holland, *op. cit.* pp46-47.

22. E.S. Dallas, *op. cit.*, I, p210.

23. Holland, *op. cit.*, pp48-50

24. Alison Winter, 'The construction of orthodoxies and heterodoxies in the early Victorian life sciences", in B. Lightman, *op. cit.*, pp36-43.

25. On Carpenter's career, see Desmond, *The Politics of Evolution*, *op. cit.*, pp210-222, and on the political implications of his work, Robert M. Young, *Mind Brain and Adaptation: Cerebral Localisation from Gall to Ferrier*, Oxford University Press, Oxford 1970, and *Darwin's Metaphor: Nature's Place in Victorian Culture*, Cambridge University Press, 1985.

26. W.B.Carpenter, *Principles of Human Physiology* 5th edition, John Churchill, London 1855, p548.

27. From *Principles of Human Physiology*, *op. cit.*, p446.

28. *Ibid.*, p548.

29. Carpenter, *Principles of Mental Physiology*, *op. cit.*. p24.

30. *Human Physiology*, *op. cit.*, p590.

31. *Ibid*, p602.

32. On Cobbe's, life and developing ideas, see her autobiography, *Life, by Herself*, 2 vols, William Bentley, London 1894; and Barbara Caine, *Victorian Feminists*, Oxford University Press, Oxford 1992, pp103-149.

33. F.P. Cobbe, 'Darwinism in morals', in *Darwinism in Morals and Other Essays*, Williams and Norgate, London 1872, p5 and *passim*.

34. F.P. Cobbe, 'Unconscious cerebration', in *ibid.*, p305.

35. For a fascinating discussion of contemporary debates on memory and the neurosciences, see Steven Rose, *The Making of Memory: from Molecules to Mind*, Bantam Book, London and New York 1993.

'Here with the Karroo-bushes and the red sand'

OLIVE SCHREINER AND COLONIAL SELF-RELIANCE

CAROLYN BURDETT

Looking back at the work of his mature years in the final chapter of his *Autobiography*, John Stuart Mill notes that *A System of Logic* was intended to exemplify the doctrine that 'all knowledge [derives] from experience'. Adapting the eighteenth-century associationist tradition in philosophy, Mill sought to demonstrate that the 'notion that truths external to the mind may be known by intuition or consciousness, independently of observation and experience, is ... the great intellectual support of false doctrines and bad institutions'.[1] Mill believed that utilitarianism could use associationist philosophy in order to drive away an irrational intuitionism which had hitherto bedevilled philosophical thought and had thus helped to support, and keep potent, social institutions and political formations anathema to a rational, liberal and modernising world. The political subject Mill wished to call into being is capable of relinquishing the lures of superstition for the sterner but ultimately truthful exercise of senses governed by reason.

Mill is, of course, responding to the extraordinary set of changes generally known as European modernity, changes which were in the process of consolidation during the latter half of the nineteenth century. During that period, Darwinian evolution provided an increasingly powerful set of terms through which relations between the self and the organic and social worlds were studied. When Christianity began to unravel as the primary means of distinguishing good from bad, a new grounding for a moral economy was sought in biological and organic life: the evolutionary account formulated by Darwin and others promised to provide truths of all sorts – about the human organism, the human psyche, and the social world that humans make. Darwin himself was attracted to the psychological aspects of associationism – the notion that the mind links ideas in chains of thought, developed by Locke and David Hartley[2] – seeing it as compatible with a naturalistic explanation of human development. Associationist psychological concepts allowed Darwin to conceive of human thought and behaviour as the product of natural forces, of the interaction between organism and environment, thus dispensing with the need to understand mental states as deriving from intuitive ideas.[3]

Despite the purposiveness in life and history that Darwinian evolution seemed to promise, the final decades of the century saw argument about the nature of the social world return with full force to the issue of human irrationality. The bloody conflict in far-away South Africa, with which one century was seen out, and the next seen in, provoked considerable disillusion amongst reform-minded liberals about the effects of evolutionary thinking on social life. The New Liberal Leonard Hobhouse, for example, in his 1904 *Democracy and Reaction*, laments the degradation of cultural and ethical life, commenting: 'But after all, by far the most potent support [for this adverse change] ... has been ... the belief that physical science had given its verdict in favour – for it came to this – of violence and against social justice'.[4] Hobhouse was attacking the 'might is right' rhetoric of social Darwinists which he (correctly) saw as a misunderstanding of Darwin. He was appalled by the biological fatalism or determinism which resulted, and in which human reason is ousted by the forces of more or less unconscious instincts. Equally worrying though, Hobhouse argues, is the reversion to 'the easy rule of authority and faith' of a society daunted by the unceasing tasks of reason, improvement and progress.[5]

The theological world-view that optimistic and positivistic-minded intellectuals of the 1860s and 1870s had believed to be entering its death-throes indeed proved more tenacious than many might have imagined. In the socially turbulent years at the end of the nineteenth century, the moral consensus that a tradition of liberal rationalism had hoped to achieve, alongside political democratisation, was palpably lacking. Like Hobhouse, therefore, other commentators turned to ideas of human irrationality, or the effects of instinct, in order to explain the failings of a rational utilitarian account of social life. In his very influential 1894 work, *Social Evolution*, Benjamin Kidd argued that, far from signalling a superstitious past to be rolled away by the forces of rational modernisation, religion constituted an 'ultra-rational' (or non-rational) element essential for evolutionary success. For Kidd, the interests of the social organism and the interests of the individual are inevitably antagonistic, and reason cannot resolve this antagonism because reason is, fundamentally, self-oriented. Neither is it only liberal individualism which is implicated in Kidd's critique of reason: socialism, as a 'rational' attempt to foster social interests, if implemented, would be biologically self-defeating because it would reduce conflict and lead to stagnation and degeneration. The only efficacious integrative principles in society are non-rational. Human progress, Kidd argues, has resulted not primarily from rational or intellectual forces, but from the ethical systems deriving from religion, which confer evolutionary advantage in the struggle for survival.[6]

Kidd's adaptation of Darwin appalled those committed to rational evolution. The self-proclaimed socialist and eugenist Karl Pearson attacked Kidd promptly, but *Social Evolution* surely helped to compound Pearson's belief that a trained élite of professionals had ultimately to control the uneducated (and potentially irrational) masses in order to foster the good (and well-managed) society.[7] Between Pearson's increasingly dogmatic state socialist managerialism and the reaction of a liberal such as J.A. Hobson – who saw, in the jingoism provoked by the war in South Africa, 'an instinctive display of some common factors of national character which is outside reason'[8] – the reformist agenda looked increasingly bleak. Legitimating the political identity of the working masses through the franchise brought about a panicky emphasis on the unmodified instincts fuelling a potentially unruly and dangerous urban mob. Irrationality (or instinct) began to figure as part of the justification for thoroughgoing forms of social control, with the corollary that 'reason' itself was defined more and more in instrumental and mechanistic ways.

There were, however, enthusiasts for modernisation and social transformation who were able to imagine a more productive vision of the modern subject and its relation to the world. One such was the South African-born writer, Olive Schreiner. Born in the Cape Colony in 1855, Schreiner was the daughter of missionary parents. Early on, she rejected her parents' evangelical Christianity and found, through her largely informal and unguided reading, both revelation and solace in texts which comprise a roll-call of nineteenth-century intellectual debate, including Buckle, Vogt, Goethe, Mill, Darwin, and Spencer. The conviction that in change is evolutionary meaning, and that science might prove a guide to its truth, were ideas which Schreiner greeted with a passion borne of her sense of isolation and unbelonging in the stultifying atmosphere of colonial South Africa. For her, England was 'home' – home not least to the ingredients which would make up a modern and better world, released from the thrall of God-*fearing*. In 1881, aged 26, she travelled to England and soon began to meet writers and intellectuals such as Havelock Ellis, Karl Pearson and Edward Carpenter. By the end of the century, however, and having returned to the country of her birth, she had become one of the most outspoken critics of the British empire – and the forms of modernity with which it was associated – as Sir Alfred Milner, South Africa's High Commissioner, and the Colonial Secretary, Joseph Chamberlain, took Britain to war against the two Boer republics, the Transvaal and the Orange Free State.

The work I wish to look at here, however, predates Schreiner's long and arduous final falling out with the forms taken by metropolitan progress, although it does outline the version of reason and progress which she was formulating. My focus will be on one chapter from Schreiner's most famous novel – the only one to be published in her lifetime – *The Story of an African Farm*, which she wrote in her early twenties while employed as a governess on a series of Cape Colony farms. Published in England in 1883, it made her an instant literary celebrity, its two themes seeming to speak directly to the mood and temper of its metropolitan audience. These themes are carried by the novel's two central protagonists, Lyndall and Waldo. One theme is the position of women. This is Lyndall's story, and it made her the proto-type of the 'New Woman' who was to become such an important fictional figure in the 1890s. Lyndall's formidable feminist eloquence was surely a key reason for *African Farm*'s popularity.

I will chiefly be concerned, however, with the second protagonist, Waldo. His task in the novel is to chart the painful processes of lost faith and the search for meaning in a world seemingly governed by a capricious and cruel nature. It is in Waldo's story that Schreiner demonstrates her extraordinary intelligence of response to the turbu-lent ideas of history and change she was encountering. Fiercely committed to reform and social transformation, Schreiner reached out to embrace and put to work the currents of modernisation which saw, in science and scientific method, the route to a newly enlightened truth. At the same time, however, she took with her the differences of her colonial context and identity and *used* them as a way of showing the metropolitan culture what, in its own thinking and self-conception, might be missed or occluded.

The chapter I am concerned with occurs towards the beginning of the second part of the novel.[9] In Part I, the boy Waldo has had to confront the terrifying prospect of a world shorn of meaning and design. His faith in a benevolent God gone, he sees nothing beyond caprice and cruelty, epitomised in the rascally trickster Bonaparte Blenkins whose arrival on the farm heralds a testing time for Waldo. Although Bonaparte eventually overreaches himself and flees the farm, it is not before Waldo has lost his devout old father, Otto, his faith, and his belief that anything can make the world a meaningful place to be. The European stranger who appears towards the beginning of Part II and lends the chapter its title – 'Waldo's Stranger' – offers salvation to Waldo in the form of an allegory. Requesting leave to rest himself and his horse for a while, the stranger relates the narrative as a response to a wooden post which Waldo is carving for his father's grave. This is the novel's famous allegory of the Hunter after Truth, which was later reprinted in Schreiner's 1890 collection of allegorical writings, *Dreams*.

The allegory is a parable of the triumph of a positivist, or scientific, worldview to set against the false dreams and lures of a human God and immortality. To strive after truth means renouncing the consolations of religion and of the body; it means long arduous work scaling the 'mighty mountains of Dry-facts and Realities' (p166), and accepting the tiny, partial contribution an individual can make to the accumulation of knowledge: a process which defines scientific endeavour. The stranger's words have a convulsive effect on Waldo who feels that, for the first time, he has been given an intellectual and imaginative guide to help make sense of the 'confused, disordered story' of his life and world (pp159-170). When the stranger departs, he leaves Waldo a book. Early on in what would turn out to be a life-long correspondence with Havelock Ellis, Schreiner explains that Waldo's stranger was based on an experience of her own:

> The book the stranger gives to Waldo was intended to be Spencer's *First Principles*. When I was up in Basutoland with an old aunt and cousin, one stormy, rainy night, there was a knock at the door, they were afraid to go and open it, so I went. There was a stranger there, like Waldo's Stranger exactly. There was no house within fifty miles so he slept there; the next morning he talked with me for half an hour; and then I never saw him again. He lent me Spencer's *First Principles*. I always think that when Christianity burst on the dark Roman world it was what that book was to me. I was in such complete blank atheism. I did not believe in my own nature, or any right or wrong or certainty.[10]

In another letter to Ellis, Schreiner explains more explicitly what

Spencer meant to her: 'He helped me to believe in a unity underlying all nature'. Spencer provided her, in other words, with 'the whole theory of evolution' by which she could understand the world as meaningful.[11]

By the 1870s, *First Principles* had gained Spencer a reputation as a hugely influential thinker.[12] Published in 1862, it inaugurated Spencer's *Synthetic Philosophy*, in which he determined successively to treat biology, psychology, sociology and morality from an evolutionary viewpoint and to show that all life and existence is governed by immutable laws. *First Principles* attempts philosophically to account for the knowledge science produces. Science aims to bring law-like regularity to otherwise uncoordinated facts: philosophy's task is to discover the ultimate generalisations to which all laws conform. Spencer argues that the entire knowable universe – inorganic, organic and the social and human forms of life Spencer called 'superorganic' – develops according to a law or formula of evolution. This law is defined as 'an integration of matter and concomitant dissipation of motion; during which matter passes from an indefinite, incoherent homogeneity to a definite, coherent heterogeneity'.[13]

The law of evolution functions via various primary physical laws, namely the 'Indestructibility of Matter', the 'Persistence of Force' and the 'Direction of Motion'. The law of evolution describes the process by which this force is redistributed into progressively more complex forms. This process is not infinite, as evolution tends towards what Spencer calls 'equilibration', 'the ultimate establishment of a balance'. This cosmic equilibrium presupposes harmony between its parts – including a harmony between 'man's mental nature and the conditions of his existence' – which will result in 'the greatest perfection and the most complete happiness'.[14] Spencer was able to furnish his argument with abundant examples: germinal forms evolve into complex living creatures; human creatures make ever more complex social groups. Modern civilisations are complexly ordered in their various industrial, bureaucratic and political parts and are clear evidence of the 'progress' which is at the heart of Spencer's theory. It is this progressive aspect of Spencer's evolutionary theory which had such an impact on the ideas associated with 'social Darwinism' (which owed less to Darwin, especially the Darwin of *Origin of Species*, than to Spencer).

Spencer's own political life was begun as a Radical, committed to the sanctity of the individual. An advocate of ending aristocratic privilege via the nationalisation of land, he also supported Mill and other Radicals in the Governor Eyre controversy. By the final decades of the century, however, Spencer's form of individualism and laissez-faire were increasingly associated with socially conservative liberalism. In his early *Social Statics* Spencer emphasised the functioning of morality as a set of rules or guides to the 'highest conceivable perfection', obtainable through the eventual adaptation of man to his environment.[15] In the 1892-revised edition of *Social Statics*, however, the equilibration which signalled social perfection Spencer saw as only abstractly achievable, in infinite time. As adaption advances, the forces driving evolutionary change diminish and so the processes of advance slow, and dissolution sets in.[16] Thus Spencer's insistence that anything hampering the forces of adaptation – which latter involves the dying away of the least well-adapted – must be resisted, including all forms of social welfare aimed at alleviating the conditions of the poorest and most vulnerable of a state's citizens.

While Schreiner continued to acknowledge a debt to Spencer, she was deeply opposed to the socially reactionary implications of his work. In her later, unfinished, novel, *From Man to Man*, there is an extended critique of the Spencerian doctrines of struggle, competitiveness and survival and an advocacy instead of global and holistic development.[17] It is the idea of evolutionary connectedness that Schreiner found so compelling in Spencer's *First Principles* – the idea of a joined-up world. Part II of *African Farm* begins with a chapter called 'Times and Seasons', where Waldo's story is recapitulated in an abstract, first person plural narrative. Here, following the storms of a decaying faith, the narrator finds enlightenment and mental solace in an exploration of the natural world and the discovery of both beauty *and* regularity. Thus the pattern of blood vessels in dead lambs or birds is the same shape as the thorn tree, or the metallic tracery on rocks, or the flow of water from a dam. 'Times and Seasons' takes its title from the famous passage in *Ecclesiastes*. *Ecclesiastes* explores contingency: all things are in continual flux; times and seasons are presumably fixed by God, but their rationale remains obscure to the humans they affect.

The abstract narrative voice in 'Times and Seasons' reworks the deliverance from this absolute contingency as the revelation of a romantic conception of natural harmony. More specifically, the last section of 'Times and Seasons' can be seen as a rewriting of one of Schreiner's favourite poems, Emerson's 'Each and All'. The poem argues for an aesthetic based on respect for harmony and wholeness, and the interconnectedness and interdependence of the natural world. Thus the narrator picks delicate shells from the shore and takes the 'sea-born treasures home' only to find 'the poor, unsightly, noisome things/Had left their beauty on the shore' – because their beauty is part of a *whole* scene. Only through the pursuit of the truth of this interconnected world and one's place in it, rather than the fantasy that its beauty can be jealously sequestered for oneself alone, will 'the perfect whole' become apparent.[18]

In *African Farm* however – as with the rest of her work – Schreiner is not merely reworking evolution as a romantic narrative. In this early work is an intimation of her life-long attempt to challenge the opposition between rationalism and romanticism. Much of the formal innovation of her writing – again in both *African Farm* and her subsequent fiction – is the result of attempts to find a narrative and form appropriate to the vision of a reformed rationality (and it is in the delicately used rhythms of archaic allegory that she comes closest to doing so). *African Farm* proved so popular to its 1880s audience because it seemed to address the central 'questions of human nature and human action', including the 'great question of the human heart, What is the hereafter?' It also – according to Edward Aveling, in his review of the novel – knows that the only answers to make sense in the modern world are scientific ones.[19] But just how straightforward is this apparent discovery of 'science' as a solution to the 'great questions' *African Farm* addresses? There is, in fact, a warning note at the centre of Schreiner's narrative which is a forceful plea against the dogmatic certainties of which Victorian science so often stands accused.

Let me return, then, to Waldo, listening to the sweet voice of his stranger. On the face of it, it seems indeed that Edward Aveling is right. The tormented youth is given a vision of scientific modernity as his 'way out'. The stranger is, of course, thoroughly coded as cultured 'European'. His well-dressed appearance is described as 'French-looking', and his voice is metropolitan-melodious; his recasting of St Paul, 'I am a man who believes nothing, hopes nothing, fears nothing, feels nothing' (p159)[20] – identifies him as a sceptical modern. For Waldo, his life spent on a Boer ostrich farm where there is only One Book: 'Ah! That man who believed nothing, hoped nothing, felt nothing; *how he loved him!*' (p159). But what, in the end, does Waldo's salvation-by-scientific truth amount to? What does the revelation of Spencerian evolution and progress open up for him? Waldo yearns to go out into 'the rare wonderful world [which] lay all beyond' the farm, from where the stranger, with all his intellectual riches, has come (p171). When he eventually does so, however, he returns never to leave again. The 'rare wonderful world' teaches him about social power and oppression, and about the body- and spirit-dulling consequences of relentless manual labour, but little else. Waldo's story suggests that, although the farm is deadly, 'outside' may in fact be worse. The narrative of bourgeois enlightenment and modern progress is stymied, and neither realism nor romance are fully adequate fictional forms in which to represent the farm inhabitants' peculiarly colonial plight.

For Waldo is, above all, a complex representation of colonial identities. He is a culturally and 'racially' hybrid figure: German-born, he is a striving modern, captivated by John Stuart Mill's views on political economy and Herbert Spencer's on evolution. But he is also associated with Boer pastoralism in his shuffling, *velschoen*-clad gait, and with black Africa (another character, Gregory Rose, describes him as always 'muttering to himself like an old Kaffir witch-doctor!' (p231)). It is Waldo who is arrested by signs of the Cape's lost people and culture. Towards the beginning of the novel, he finds Lyndall and her cousin Em sitting under a shelving rock. Relaying the information that a stranger named 'Bonaparte' had arrived at the farm, he listens to Lyndall's impassioned imaginative reconstruction of Napoleon Bonaparte's imperial ambition only to interrupt her with a reminder of the much closer-to-home account of colonisation told in the 'Bushman' paintings which decorate the rock against which the girls are seated. For Waldo, the 'glorious' tale of European expansion Lyndall is telling ignores the suffering wrought by colonisation, just as the girls fail to see the evidence of the inglorious destruction of the life and culture of the Cape's indigenous population which is virtually under their noses.

It is, however, in the chapter 'Waldo's Stranger' that the importance of Waldo's colonial status is most intriguingly and subtly asserted. On the face of it – as I have indicated – the chapter charts the bringing of 'European' knowledge (especially scientific knowledge) into the culturally and intellectually impoverished (and 'pre-modern') colony. Waldo is shocked, however, when, after pouring out to the stranger the 'confused, disordered story' of his painful quest for self-enlightenment, the stranger enquires if he is happy at the farm. At first Waldo thinks he is being ridiculed for the puny insignificance of his mundane life and world. He soon recognises, however, that the stranger is quite serious and that what he is recommending to Waldo is a version of *self-reliance*. At first sight it seems a strange suggestion, for Waldo has had to be pitifully self-reliant through all his brief, lonely and troubled life. At the very moment his isolation is assuaged in the overwhelming relief of realising that others, too, think as he does, his deliverer recommends that he stay, alone, 'here with the karroo-bushes and the red sand' (p171).

The stranger justifies his advocacy of Waldo's staying on the farm by explaining that a great, historic change is taking place, in which the traditional, sacred world is disappearing to be replaced by something new. The transition, he says, is a time of uncertainty and danger. The moral laws on which religion 'has artfully fastened itself, and from which it has sucked its vitality' (p171), may prove to be good and true, but people are bewildered and unable to tell truth from distortion: having cast off religious faith, they are morally adrift. In telling Waldo to stay put, the stranger qualifies the message of the 'Hunter' allegory: that truth is had by following the stern disciplines of scientific endeavour; rather, on his South African farm, Waldo may be able to know something that 'Europe' does not: 'Stay where you are ... The time may yet come when you will be that which other men have hoped to be and never will be now' (p172).

When Willie Bertram, the original of Waldo's stranger, lent his copy of *First Principles* to the young Schreiner, he also advised her to read Emerson. She bought a copy of the first series of the *Essays* in 1874. In the notes he wrote about Schreiner in the first stages of their life-long friendship, Havelock Ellis records that at the time she was very unhappy and thinking about suicide; reading Emerson, particularly 'Self-Reliance', helped her to recover.[21] 'Self-Reliance' is a romantic, Rousseauesque call for the acceptance of one's own truth and integrity as the basis for moral living. Such acceptance demands a ceaseless battle against the ruthless pressures of social conformity:

> The magnetism which all original action exerts is explained when we inquire the reason of self-trust. Who is the Trustee? What is the aboriginal Self, on which a universal reliance may be grounded? What is the nature and power of that science-baffling star, without parallax, without calculable elements, which shoots a ray of beauty even into trivial and impure actions, if the least mark of independence appear? The inquiry leads us to that source, at once the essence of genius, of virtue, and of life, which we call Spontaneity or Instinct. We denote this primary wisdom as Intuition, whilst all later teachings are tuitions.[22]

The stranger's emphasis on Waldo's *location* – 'here with the karroo-bushes and the red sand' – indicates that the boy's 'self' is a specifically colonial entity. Waldo is portrayed as intimately related to the land. Frequently represented as lying or squatting close to the ground, he functions as a kind of metonym for the African landscape. In recommending to him a self-reliance predicated on his relation with the land, the stranger seems to suggest that the positivist scientific knowledge he offers to Waldo (in the allegory and in *First Principles*) needs in turn to be mediated or leavened by a different kind of 'knowledge' which belongs to the farm.

This knowledge is based on Waldo's sensuous and intimate relation with the sparse and uncompromising beauty of the land. It is a romanticism, in other words, that is specifically colonial. It suggests a kind of truth (about morality and, by implication, about ways of knowing) that is lost or inaccessible to the metropolitan culture, not despite but because of the latter's positivist and scientific character. There are '*in*calculable elements', the text seems to suggest, which are necessarily inaccessible to scientific method. Scientific rationalism is thus ushered onto the African farm, but is then questioned or mediated: Waldo must maintain a 'science-baffling', non-calculable knowledge born of his colonial identity. Yes, *African Farm is* a powerful confirmation of scientific modernity and the ways in which it frees and releases humans from the constraints of tradition, custom and superstition. But it also suggests that 'rational' knowledges must always have space for different kinds of wisdom – and, by implication, that the metropolitan 'centre' must be able to hear the truth which can only be had at the colonial 'margin'.

In addition, as I have already indicated, romantic naturalism is not offered here as a *resolution* of Waldo's story (a number of critics, including J.M. Coetzee and Stephen Gray have, indeed, emphasised the way in which the landscape in *African Farm* is hostile to the white inhabitants, offering them no roots or belonging).[23] The landscape may be an overwhelming natural phenomenon but it is also always a fully historical one. For example, the farm's ostriches tell, *sotto voce*, a story of colonial economics. Ostriches had been farmed in the Cape from the first half of the nineteenth century, but production expanded considerably under the influence of British economic and developmental practices. British settlers brought with them entrepreneurial habits associated with a highly dynamic and competitive industrial society, as well as access to capital and a knowledge of European markets. Thus the first incubator for breeding ostriches was a British innovation. It helped in the expansion of an industry the export revenue for which tripled between 1869 and 1874 as farmers responded to the growing demand for ostrich feathers by the European fashion industry.[24]

Towards the beginning of the novel, in the scene I have already mentioned, when small Lyndall and Em are sitting under a rock with their backs to the 'old Bushman-paintings' which cover its surface, the year is identified as 1862, the 'thirsty summer' of a devastating drought in South Africa. Set just prior to the boom in ostrich farming, the novel is also set on the cusp of South Africa's economic transformation into a world-exporter of minerals. Lyndall has picked an ice-plant leaf and fastened it to her pinafore, noting how its crystal drops look like diamonds. Her dream of wearing diamonds in her hair alerts us to Schreiner's own historical advantage in knowing that, by the 1870s, the Colony's economy had been transformed by the discovery of diamonds. *The Story of an African Farm* is thus also the story of colonisation and economic transformation, given to us in brief in this chapter 'Plans and Bushman-Paintings'. Its first stage, signified by the paintings, tells of Afrikaner settlerdom and the dispossession of the San in the conflict for land and cattle which accompanied white colonisation of the Cape Colony ('Now the Boers have shot them all', Waldo says of the artists whose paintings cover the rocks (p50)); while the 'plans' of the chapter's title hint at what is to come in the economically-driven transformation of South Africa into an industrialised mining economy. It is this history which Schreiner was to live with, sometimes in almost unbearable intimacy, and from which she concluded that an unmediated capitalism produced catastrophic effects for human beings.[25]

In the early years of the 1890s, a young South African farmer called Samuel Cronwright wrote to the famous Olive Schreiner (who had recently returned to South Africa from England, and whom he was soon to meet and marry) in order to express how strongly her book, *The Story of an African Farm*, had affected him: 'I am like Waldo listening to the sweet voice of the Stranger'.[26] In *African Farm*, the stranger is a metropolitan bringing knowledge into the colony. In so far as Schreiner stands in the place of the stranger, she turns the tables and takes her colonial knowledge to the metropolis. In her famous preface to the second edition of *African Farm* – seen by many critics as a statement of the book's prototypical modernism – Schreiner talks of the reader's perplexity at a plot in which a man might appear only to leave behind 'no more substantial trace than a mere book'. Her own 'mere book' Schreiner signed 'Ralph Iron', although the pseudonym did not long disguise her youthful female identity. She and Waldo and Em thus share out between them Emerson's given names, but Schreiner also borrows directly from 'Self-Reliance' for her family pseudonym. 'Trust thyself: every heart vibrates to that iron string', is Emerson's injunction to the would-be self-reliant.[27] The paradox which distinguishes this flexible, tenacious ore, wrought iron rather than cast, and therefore capable of movement and life, marks it out from the hard and impervious ore of capitalist production. The latter, according to Max Weber, in the end produces an 'iron cage' by which modernity itself is imprisoned.[28] Schreiner's colonial self-reliance, wrought in the heat of an African sun, signs off the first of a lifetime's writerly efforts to cast modernity and progress differently.

NOTES

1. J. S. Mill, *Autobiography* [1873], Penguin, Harmondsworth 1989, pp171-172.
2. See Jenny Bourne Taylor and Sally Shuttleworth (eds), *Embodied Selves: An Anthology of Psychological Texts 1830-1890*, Clarendon, Oxford 1998.
3. Greta Jones, *Social Darwinism and English Thought: The Interaction Between Biological and Social Theory*, Harvester, Sussex 1980, p14.
4. Leonard T. Hobhouse, *Democracy and Reaction*, T. Fisher Unwin, London 1904, pp83-84.
5. *Ibid.*, pp79-80.
6. Benjamin Kidd, *Social Evolution* [1894], Macmillan, London 1885. See also D.P. Crook, *Benjamin Kidd: Portrait of a Social Darwinist*, Cambridge University Press, Cambridge 1984.
7. Pearson defended socialism against Kidd in an article in the *Fortnightly Review*. It is reprinted in Karl Pearson, *The Chances of Death and Other Studies in Evolution*, vol. 1, Edward Arnold, London 1897, pp103-139. See also Donald A. MacKenzie, *Statistics in Britain 1865-1930*, Edinburgh University Press, Edinburgh 1981, pp90-91; and for a longer discussion of Pearson see my *Olive Schreiner and the Progress of Feminism: Evolution, Gender, Empire*, Palgrave, London 2000.
8. J.A. Hobson, *The Psychology of Jingoism*, Richards, London 1901, p18.
9. Olive Schreiner, *The Story of an African Farm* [1883], Penguin, Harmondsworth 1971, pp155-173. Subsequent page references will be given in the text.
10. Richard Rive (ed), *Olive Schreiner Letters, vol. 1 1871-1899*, Oxford University Press, Oxford 1988, p36.
11. *Ibid.*, pp37, 90.
12. See J.W. Burrow, *Evolution and Society*, Cambridge University Press, Cambridge 1966.
13. Herbert Spencer, *First Principles* [1867], Routledge/Thoemmes Press, London 1996, p396. See also Michael Taylor's, 'Introduction', ppxii-iii.
14. *Ibid.*, p517.
15. Herbert Spencer, *Social Statics* [1851], Routledge/Thoemmes Press, London 1996.

16. Spencer, *First Principles*, *op. cit.*, pxv.

17. Olive Schreiner, *From Man to Man* [1926], Virago, London 1982, pp195-223.

18. Ralph Waldo Emerson, 'Each and All', in Stephen E. Whicher (ed), *Selections from Ralph Waldo Emerson*, Riverside Press, Boston 1957, p413-414.

19. Quotations are from, respectively, Henry Norman, 'Theories and Practice of Modern Fiction', *Fortnightly Review*, 34, December 1883, excerpts quoted in Cherry Clayton (ed), *Olive Schreiner*, McGraw Hill, Johannesburg 1983, p69; and Edward B. Aveling, 'A Notable Book', *Progress: a Monthly Magazine of Advanced Thought*, 1, 1883, excerpts quoted in Clayton, *op. cit.*, p68.

20. cf. I *Corinthians* 13. 7: 'Charity ... Beareth all things, believeth all things, hopeth all things, endureth all things'.

21. See Rive, *op. cit.*, fn. 1, p40.

22. Ralph Waldo Emerson, 'Self-Reliance', in Whicher, *op. cit.*, p156.

23. J.M. Coetzee, *White Writing: On the Culture of Letters in South Africa*, Yale University Press, New Haven & London, 1988, pp. 64-6; Stephen Gray, 'Schreiner and the Literary Tradition', *Southern African Literature: An Introduction*, David Philip, Cape Town 1979.

24. See Mordechai Tamarkin, *Cecil Rhodes and the Cape Afrikaners: The Imperial Colossus and the Colonial Parish-Pump*, Frank Cass, London & Portland 1996, pp20-23.

25. For a much fuller discussion of these issues, see Burdett, *op. cit.*

26. S.C. Cronwright-Schreiner, *The Life of Olive Schreiner*, Unwin, London 1924, p232.

27. Emerson, 'Self-reliance', *op. cit.*, p148.

28. Max Weber, *The Protestant Ethic and the Spirit of Capitalism* [1904-5], Routledge, London 1992, p181: ' ... the care for external goods should only lie on the shoulders of the "saint like a light cloak, which can be thrown aside at any moment". But fate decreed that the cloak should become an iron cage.'

Politics in the Nursery

SEBASTIAN KRAEMER

In this short essay I take a developmental view of how a human baby becomes a political animal, starting with the first social relationship, which is that between infant and caregiver (almost always the mother). This little society grows from two to three to larger numbers, but there is a limit, after which we live, as Benedict Anderson states so memorably, in an 'Imagined Community', in a state or a nation.[1] Membership of such a large group tends to encourage primitive concepts about what it is one belongs to, often defined by vague idealisations that depend on the exclusion of those who are not members. The political subject, including the potential reader of this book, is not such a sophisticated individual as he or she may believe. We have very basic desires which drive the process of belonging.

In the beginning there are two. The baby comes out, looks for company, and is at least as keen to make contact for social purposes as for feeding, so the face and the breast are both targets. Although a baby's eyesight is good, s/he can only focus on relatively near objects, an arrangement which is ideally suited to intimate conversation. This is what usually happens: mother holds baby to her face and talks in the way that most of us can hardly help doing when confronted with a tiny human, or indeed any immature mammal. Babies do not understand the language but they do get the message. If we did not speak to infants as if they could understand us they would not learn to speak, or think, later on. The purpose of this instinctive process is to provide optimum conditions for the development of mind and body. Merely feeding a baby and keeping her or him warm will not do. Attentive company is also necessary, otherwise the baby's brain will not develop properly, and the regulation of body systems – blood pressure, for example, as well as temperature, growth hormone production and heart rate – will be upset. What has this got to do with politics?

The political subject is a person, or more properly a personal state of mind, which refers to the relationship we have to the country or region we inhabit, of which we are citizens.[2] It is not usual to adopt a developmental perspective rather than a historical one, when considering political process: how, that is, social groups came to exist, how they tried to exert power one over the other and so on. Few writers consider the origins of political consciousness. It is somehow 'given' that we are interested, sometimes compulsively, in the machinations of power, in particular the drama of the relationships between the men (and it usually *is* men) at the top. Even the politically ignorant tend to have a view on the soap opera aspect of politics.

This reflects our political training in the nursery. From the start we have an acute sensitivity to the social skills of our partner, usually mother, soon to be joined by others: father, grandparents and later childminder or nanny. Does she get it? Here I am, in this little body that I can barely control, and her job is to work out what I need her to do now: change the nappy, get the wind out, feed me, hold me, put me down but, most important of all, to talk to me about what is happening to me, so I can begin to make sense of it all. For other mammals this is far less of a problem, as they are born with greater motor skills than we are. Because their brains are relatively small, birth comes later in the development of the individual. Humans are uniquely immature at birth, and most brain growth takes place outside the womb – where there is room for the head to expand – in the first two years of life. It is during this time that we acquire basic social skills, but also the physiological and neurological structures that will take us right through life. These skills and structures will largely determine our capacity to regulate states of arousal, emotion and attention.

Political consciousness evolves directly from these early interactions, which are far more influential than anything the education system can provide later on. You can and should introduce children to history and democracy, but their basic positions on social justice and political strategy are already in place before they go to school. Although there is a fiercely intellectual and rational tradition in politics, it is also a passion, a constant passion for its practitioners, and from time to time for the citizen too. We may like to think that we make entirely rational political choices, but this is far from the whole story. The emotions we bring to citizenship are just as powerful as those that we bring to intimate relationships: to love and sexual desire. Consider your motives. Why follow this or that party, theory, or programme? What is the goal you seek to achieve? You might say, perhaps with some embarrassment, that your goal is a peaceful and orderly world with everyone going about their business. This may well be based on your recollection of childhood, especially if you were born in the 1940s or 1950s in Western Europe, when from a child's point of view, life may have seemed just like that. Or you might, even though from a different generation, have a more vengeful goal in mind, of an enemy to be defeated, even destroyed. This may be derived not from nostalgic longings, but from painful experiences of injustice and rage against another, more powerful, person or group of people.

The arrival of a younger sibling can also provoke disturbing reflections on how babies are made, even with the pleasurable anticipation of a future playmate. Adult language is not adequate to describe this mental and emotional turbulence, some of which may never have been articulated, but which provides a template for later beliefs about the way the world should be. These revolutionary experiences have to be managed somehow, and our (relative) success or failure in doing so affects our perceptions and judgements in later triangular relationships: in families, for example, and in friendships, work and political groups. This is not a reductionist point of view. I am not saying that political passions are 'merely' or 'nothing but' derivations from early life, but that these experiences powerfully colour our later views. And they can of course be modified. One of the addictive aspects of political discourse is that it never needs to stop. Like religion and psychoanalysis there is always something more to be said that just might make a difference.

After that first mother-baby relationship the crucial steps in learning to relate to others begin with the arrival of a third person.[3] Whatever the family structure, the realisation that one was conceived by a woman and a man together does not merely add another number, it also removes the infant from the centre of the universe, just as Copernicus shifted the Earth from its position. Whether the father is present or absent, the discovery of his role as co-procreator is a terrible shock, but is also a spur to deeper understanding: three dimensional thinking.

> If the link between the parents, perceived by the child in both love and hate can be tolerated in the child's mind it provides him with a proto-

type for an object relationship of a third kind in which he is witness, not a participant. A third position then comes into existence from which object relationships can be observed. Given this, we can also envisage being observed. This provides us with a capacity for seeing ourselves in interaction with others and for entertaining another point of view whilst retaining our own, for reflecting on ourselves whilst being ourselves.[4]

Although many individuals affect 'no interest' in politics, all of us, except the most autistic or psychotic, are, like our not so distant cousins the wolves and other animals who run in packs, involved in group processes of an intensely primitive kind. We constantly observe how others are getting on with each other and how we get on with them. We need to know where we stand. As the anthropologist Gregory Bateson put it: 'Severe pain and maladjustment can be induced by putting a mammal in the wrong regarding its rules for making sense of an important relationship with another mammal'.[5]

The difference between humans and other group living mammals is the intensity of the social relationship that *precedes* group membership. The position you take up in your first peer group, at nursery, was influenced by family relationships. If your caregivers could stand the stress of looking after a demanding and dependent infant and enjoyed conversations with you, and loved you most of the time (hate is allowed, probably even necessary, as long as it does not overwhelm love), then you came out of infancy prepared to trust others, to be curious, generous, able to share and enjoy things with your peers and to stand up for yourself when you felt unfairly treated (and, later, to stand up for others). This is secure attachment and around two thirds of populations studied are able to act in this way.

If, on the other hand, the primary caregiver (usually mother) is out of tune with the baby and there is nobody – such as a father, grandmother or childminder – to share the task with, then the poor child gets a different message and is likely to be wary or aloof in her or his social interactions, repeating with peers what s/he has picked up from that first relationship. This sounds hard on mothers, but they do carry an enormous responsibility, even when the task is shared out with the father or someone else closely involved. And the patterns run through the generations. The kind of parenting you do is affected by the kind of parenting you had.[6] A variety of styles of relating can emerge, depending on mismatches at the beginning.[7] When caregivers are inconsistently attentive and more in need of care than able to give it, the result is a child who clings because s/he has to keep an eye on mum rather than the other way round. Less common is the avoidant infant who behaves as if s/he did not need looking after: an adaptation to physically present but mentally absent care. A more disturbing pattern is shown by children who are mostly afraid of their parents, though they are of course still dependent on them. These children are quite frozen with anxiety, even terror, because of violence or rage from, or between, parents.

Even in the toddler years it is possible to predict the way a child will tend to behave as an adolescent and adult. Such predictions are not always right, but are more so than most social scientists would like. After all, the point of politics is to change the world, so it is alarming to find that some qualities are relatively unchangeable. The value of being able to chart these patterns of relating is that they appear to be quite stable over time and have been reliably observed in different populations. They seem largely independent of genetics, education, social class or intelligence. Many people seek to challenge their personal history by deliberately being different from their parents, but, to their surprise, often find that they have brought their parents with them into the next generation, hearing the echo of parental voices as they shout at their own children or partners. Change is possible, but not through will power alone. Growth requires new relationships, and some of us are fortunate in the partners we find, or the friendships we form, including of course political ones. Psychotherapeutic help also comes into this new-relationship category. Cultural change, which could include greater respect for interpersonal skills (and therefore for women who tend to have them in greater measure), might encourage the expression of human qualities previously disregarded or undervalued. In a society devoted to war, different kinds of attachment, more anxious and obedient, less reflective and thoughtful, might be promoted.[8]

I doubt that one could predict a person's place on the political spectrum from early relationships, but it might be possible to say what style they would adopt: how rigid, for example, or how angry, how competitive, how cruel, how obedient, how utopian, how Machiavellian, how ambitious, how diplomatic. Likewise the broad political goals a person seeks are influenced by nursery experience: justice? peace? freedom? equality?

Real historical events, such as war, migration and other social traumas, must also have their impact, but even these are modified by the parents' reactions to them. I suggest that the 'silent majority' of the public includes a large proportion of contented (i.e. securely attached) individuals, while the passionate activists will be those whose early experience was stressful and required great struggles to be overcome.

The part one plays in any group is affected by the quality of early care. One's hatred or enjoyment of conflict, for example, or the desire to lead or to follow, will show up in a group, whatever the task. For most people the important thing is to be accepted and, because much political activity takes place in groups where debate is expected, this can present problems. Some beliefs, if expressed, would mean expulsion from the group. Belonging usually takes precedence.

Also, the political subject can forget her or his ultimate purpose, so engaging is the immediate process. Bion described the astonishing stupidity that can overcome even sophisticated and educated people when they have to work together.[9] In spite of having the correct information, individuals find themselves unable to stick to the meeting's primary task and instead become preoccupied with irrelevant matters such as the interesting relationship developing between two other members of the group, or with the conviction that someone will lead this group and 'solve all our problems for us'. Such collective daydreaming is always going on, and can easily disable the group's work. Our hopes for democracy have to be tempered with respect for the primal processes – envy and rivalry in particular – that undermine our capacity for useful work in groups. The fact that over 600 people can meet regularly without violence in such a place as the British House of Commons is evidence of many centuries of learning and regulation: the taming of the wolf-pack within us all. Again, this is not to detract from political ambitions, but to emphasise the immensity of the task of real co-operation between people. Even in a post-modern world, tribal processes cannot be removed from human behaviour. They have to be understood as part of it.

Like a thrilling story, political drama is captivating in itself. Who is going to lead this group? How will we keep out so-and-so? What is happening to our opponents? When the object of the exercise is eclipsed by these otherwise ordinary preoccupations, the result is very dangerous indeed. Under such conditions people will kill others without concern. Even when objectives are not forgotten, the passions of membership can simplify and pervert them. In the nastiest scenarios, there is not enough room and people have to be moved out. This is a fairly constant process in history, most memorably in the expanding Germany of the late 1930s and in Yugoslavia recently. It seems unbelievable that these expulsions and murders are meant to achieve a happy society where everyone can live in peace together afterwards, but that is the idea. Such is the power of the imagined community. You cannot know everyone in it, but you feel that all are your brothers and sisters. Like dogs we drive out the ones that do not smell right.

Attachment to parental figures and the pressures of the group are both very basic forces in human life. They have biological roots, which means that we have to respect their power. This is not the same as believing that everything that we do is genetically determined, that we are mere Darwinian items or selfish genes. Quite the reverse. Human thought is extraordinarily creative and, at its best, both gracious and free. But if we base political understanding on theories that regard human nature in one dimension only – either essentially selfish, or essentially generous – we do ourselves an injustice.

NOTES

1. B. Anderson, *Imagined Communities: Reflections on the Origin and Spread of Nationalism*, Verso, London 1983.
2. If we are not citizens of anywhere, then we are in serious social difficulties. Refugees and other stateless persons suffer so greatly because they have no rights. This is experienced as not belonging anywhere, not being cared about. This lack of attachment is precisely analogous with the neglect and abandonment of individual children by parents or others.
3. The term 'object relationships' is used by psychoanalysts because it is about the object of our desires.
4. R. Britton, 'The Missing Link; Parental Sexuality in the Oedipus Complex', in J. Steiner (ed), *The Oedipus Complex Today: Clinical Implications*, Karnac, London 1989, p87.
5. G. Bateson, *Steps to an Ecology of Mind: Collected Essays in Anthropology, Psychiatry, Evolution and Epistemology*, Granada, St Albans 1973, p248.
6. M. Steele, H. Steele & P. Fonagy, 'Associations among attachment classifications of mothers, fathers, and their infants: Evidence for a relationship-specific perspective', *Child Development* 67, 1996, pp541-555.
7. J. Belsky, K. Rosenberger. & K. Crnic, 'The origins of attachment security: 'classical' and contextual determinants', in S. Goldberg, R. Muir & J. Kerr (eds), *Attachment Theory; Social, Developmental, and Clinical Perspectives*, The Analytic Press, Hillsdale NJ, 1995.
8. S. Kraemer, 'Promoting resilience: changing concepts of parenting and child care', *International Journal of Child & Family Welfare*, (in press).
9. W. Bion, *Experiences in Groups*, Tavistock, London 1961.

Mass Psychology and the (Re)Analysis of the Self

STEPHEN REICHER

ON THE SUBJECT OF HISTORY

If the forward march of reason seems to have come to a shuddering halt, it is due as much as anything else to an encounter with the mass politics of the twentieth century. Confronted with the spectacle of Nuremburg rallies, and with that awful path from the massed rank of the faithful to the piled masses of their victims, can we do other than conclude that our rationality is at best fragile and easily overwhelmed by collective forces? Radical pessimism and rampant irrationalism seem the only responses commensurate with the scale of the tragedy. And with the all too frequent reminders from Rwanda, from Kosovo, from East Timor and from many other places, we cannot console ourselves that such things are behind us.

If the scale seems relatively new, the tragedy certainly is not. From the beginnings of written history one encounters the same despair whenever mass action is contemplated. Since Herodotus commented that 'there is nothing less understanding and more proud than the blind mass',[1] a brief swipe at the 'crowd', 'mass', 'mob' or 'multitude' has been almost obligatory in the work of social thinkers. Perhaps Kierkegaard was the pithiest of them all: 'You must know the opinion of the mass in order to know what to do: the opposite'.[2] However, it was not until the late nineteenth century (particularly in the febrile and insecure French Third Republic) that the aphorisms were given a theoretical infrastructure. Of all those who contributed to the development of crowd psychology, only one – Gustave Le Bon – continues to be acknowledged.[3] The reasons for his enduring popularity are interesting in themselves and will be addressed later. For the present, his model can be briefly summarised. Le Bon argued that when people are submerged in a crowd such that they are indistinguishable from others, their conscious selves are lost and they gain a great sense of power. With the loss of self goes a loss of control and a loss of rational judgement. Crowd members simply go along with whatever idea or emotion is suggested to them. In particular, they are helpless before suggestions emanating from the 'racial unconscious', a common substrate to which we revert when our conscious self is lost. Because the racial unconscious is primitive and barbaric, crowd behaviour shows similar characteristics. In one notorious passage Le Bon declares that:

> It will be remarked that among the special characteristics of crowds there are several – such as impulsiveness, irritability, incapacity to reason, the absence of judgement and of the critical spirit, the exaggeration of the sentiments, and others besides – which are almost always observed in beings belonging to inferior forms of evolution – in women, savages and children, for instance.[4]

Psychology is often criticised for being sexist, racist and ageist. It takes a great psychologist, like Le Bon to achieve all three in a single sentence.

However unpalatable Le Bon's forms of expression might be, his account is hard to dismiss in so far as it seems to capture and explain the constant excesses of crowd action. Natalie Zemon Davis provides an all too vivid description of such excess in her study of religious riots in sixteenth-century France, culminating in the St Bartholemew's Day Massacres of 1572.[5] These events continue to exert such a fascination upon the French imagination that they have been the subject of the recent and highly successful film *La Reine Margot*. The rioting between Catholics and Protestants resulted in many deaths, but the killings were only the start. Catholics then proceeded to attack the bodies of their victims. Heads were hacked off and mounted on sticks. Bodies were sliced open and the entrails torn out. Genitalia were carved from corpses and displayed as trophies. Equally, Protestants were not satisfied with mere murder. They defecated in the holy water of Catholic churches, they smeared excrement upon the holy vestments. They used the holy oil to clean their boots. As Davis exclaims, the horror and the extremity of such acts understandably drive us into Le Bon's arms – and indeed many earlier analysts used Le Bon to account for the riots.[6] Surely, people must have lost their minds to act in these ways.

And yet, even amidst the horror, there is a pattern to the events. If both Catholics and Protestants indulged in excess, their targets can be seen to be different: Catholics targeted the body, Protestants targeted the Church. Moreover, these patterns begin to make sense when viewed in terms of the participants' collective understandings. The riots were on the issue of heresy, and heresy for Catholics was located in the body of individual Protestants. Hence these bodies had to be obliterated. Conversely, for Protestants, heresy lay more in the collective rites of Catholicism – the so-called 'demonic mass' – than in the bodies of individual Catholics. Hence it was the artefacts of the mass which became targets of desecration. The riots display not only pattern, but ideologically coherent pattern. To argue that action is irrational and uncontrolled is to miss (or rather, as I will argue further on, to obscure) such coherence. So, even in its very heartland, at the point where it seems most secure, the irrationalist position can be seen to be fatally flawed. Its theoretical underpinnings – and in particular the notion that individual identity is the sole measure of rational and controlled behaviour – are found to be equally wanting even in their apparent pomp. It may well be true that individuals in crowds act in ways that appear to go against their individual self-interest and may even put them at personal threat. However, this is not to say that subjects simply act against their interests. What has to give is not the notion that people in crowds act in interested, meaningful and controlled ways, but rather the notion that the individual self is the sole arbiter of interest and control. As the great historian of the French revolution, Georges Lefebvre, notes, Le Bon's account was only possible because of his ignorance and distance from the phenomena he purported to explain. Lefebvre argues that closer examination leads to a very different conclusion: perhaps it is only in the crowd that individuals transcend their petty day to day concerns and are guided by the larger collectivities to which they belong.[7]

To paraphrase, perhaps it is only in the crowd that individuals become the subjects of history. One therefore emerges from what first seemed like the heart of darkness with the realisation that we have not encountered irrationality but rather we have discovered the need to reconceptualise rationality. We have not been faced with the loss of self but with the emergence of social selfhood. The challenge before us is therefore to extend our understanding of what self means and hence what it means to pursue self-interest. In the broadest terms, can such an extended use of the concept provide a means of understanding how ideological constructs can come to be reflected in the patterned behaviour of crowd members? Can we refashion the self so that it provides the point of pivot between social constructs and individual actions? In order to understand the nature of this task, and also what is at stake, we need first to address some origins.

THE CONTEXT OF ANTI-COLLECTIVISM

After millennia of antipathy, why did anti-collective sentiment coalesce into theory only in the late nineteenth century, and why in France? The broader context for the birth of crowd psychology (and thence, of social psychology more generally) was the rise of industrialisation and the rapid growth of an urban proletariat increasingly distanced both ideologically and physically from those who employed them.[8] This led to a chronic concern with how the social order could survive such altered social relations. Such concerns led to a range of intellectual reactions which can be gathered together under the rubric of mass social society theory.[9] What these shared in common was the idea that the loss of traditional hierarchies had caused the masses to become rootless and made them prey to any passing influence – however pernicious. Sheer numbers combined with lack of restraint placed the very existence of settled social life under threat. That is, in a classic move, challenges to an existing social order in the name of an alternative social order were transformed into an opposition between order and chaos full stop.[10] Resistance and rebellion were rendered as mindlessness, as pathology, as pure negativity. If the mass represented an imminent threat to society, the crowd as the mass in action represented the apocalyptic moment at which the threat would turn into reality. The crowd represented all the nightmares of the nineteenth-century bourgeoisie and, as Susanna Barrows has documented, it came to incorporate all the other contemporary symbols of social fear and social breakdown: fears of independent women and the demise of patriarchy were incorporated into a crowd as essentially feminine; fears of alcoholism and the loss of social discipline were rendered as the crowd as a metaphorical or literal drunkard.[11] Crowd psychology arose as a discipline which was only concerned with understanding crowds in order to facilitate their repression.

It arose in France because the French elite, more than most, had reason to fear the crowd. For them, the apocalyptic moment was not simply a nightmare but something they had seen with their waking eyes. As Eleanor Marx Aveling puts it in her introduction to Lissagaray's History, the Paris Commune of 1871 'was the first attempt of the proletariat to govern itself'.[12] The fact that the bourgeois defeat was temporary and that the Commune was repressed with bloody efficiency (Lissagaray estimates that some 30,000 people were shot by the troops of 'law and order') was scant consolation and did little to diminish the fear of revolutionary crowds. The Third Republic which emerged out of the Commune remained fatally weak; it was buffeted by clerical unrest, by populist enthusiasms, but most of all by the relentless rise of working class agitation. For the French bourgeoisie, crowd psychology was not an arcane interest consigned to obscure academic tomes, but rather a matter of survival which was publicly debated through the pages of popular society magazines.[13]

All these themes come together in the person of Gustave Le Bon. Le Bon was born into a provincial family with a long heritage of bureaucratic state service. He himself trained as a medical doctor and experienced the Commune first hand as head of ambulance services. Le Bon's horror at what he saw motivated him to study how to instruct the masses and guide crowds in order to act as an antidote to the 'blind social revolutionary'. This ambition increasingly framed his efforts. In his later years Le Bon ran a luncheon club to which he invited the prominent right-wing politicians of his time and where he sought to convince them of his ideas about the guidance of crowds. What marked Le Bon out from his contemporaries, then, was not so much his theoretical innovation (in large part he plagiarised and popularised the work of others) but rather his activism.[14] This marked another contrast between Le Bon and his fellow crowd theorists and explains his enduring success. Whereas they simply diagnosed the problem, Le Bon also suggested a cure. That is, he did not simply comment on the furious energies of crowds and their danger *to* the social order, he sought to explain how these energies could be harnessed *for* the social order. Indeed his book *The Crowd* is as much a primer for any budding right-wing orator as a work of theory. As Moscovici puts it, the importance of Le Bon is that he doesn't just comment on mass phenomena, he was central to the creation of the mass politics of the twentieth century.[15]

By now, though, it may be apparent that there is a dilemma to be resolved – or, rather, two. In the previous section, I argued that Le Bonian psychology was based on ignorance and is incapable of explaining the patterns of crowd action. In this section I have argued that Le Bon's ideas were highly influential and were used to extreme effect. Why should such a flawed theory prove so popular and how can such erroneous ideas be so practical? At one level, these questions are somewhat parochial. However, in answering them, larger questions have to be confronted concerning both the nature of self processes and also the importance of the self in ideological processes. By analysing how things are done wrong, we can, perhaps, gain some insight into how to get them right and how important it is to do so.

Le Bon's popularity can be explained as resulting from a double bias in his work. On the one hand, he had a clear political bias – an antipathy to the predominantly working class crowds of his era. On the other hand, he had a perspective bias. He viewed crowds as an outsider. This is clear in his basic concept of submergence. Le Bon assumes that people lose their selves because they cannot be distinguished from others. Now it may be true that when one gazes on a crowd it is hard to tell one face from another. However, when one is in a crowd one characteristically knows many of the participants. Indeed one of the joys of crowd participation is the experience of recognition.[16] Le Bon's psychology therefore represents the projection of an external consciousness upon the consciousness of insiders. The political bias explains why Le Bon's ideas were so congenial to the elite. In effect, his model constitutes a psychological mechanism which gives substance to the claims of mass society theory. Acts of contestation or struggle by one class against another are transformed into asocial and mindless acts by the simple expedient of removing one of the classes from the picture and hence rendering a contextualised understanding impossible.

If, for instance, mineworkers demonstrated because of their terrible conditions and if such collective acts led them into conflict with the mine owners' security forces, with the police or with the army, all that remains after the theoretical filter has been applied is the crowd alone, acting as if in a void. A decontextualised account of the phenomena that need to be explained demands an explanation which is similarly decontextualised. Hence Le Bon's individualistic account of identity and his notion of identity loss both flow from and underpin the refusal to consider crowds in their settings. Such psychologisation – by which I most definitely do not mean psychological explanation in itself, but rather an account which frees psychological processes from their socio-historical moorings and therefore resorts to accounts of socially contingent action in terms of fixed properties of mind – is a form of naturalisation, one of the primary modes of ideology.[17] In the case of crowd psychology, the notion that crowds are inherently mindless and inherently destructive serves a number of ideological functions. Firstly, the perspectives of crowd members are obscured and their grievances are denied. If, as Martin Luther King famously declared, crowds are the voice of the powerless, crowd psychology silences that voice. Equally, by declaring crowds to be inherently destructive, all responsibility for violence is removed from the social order in general and its representatives in the immediate context. John Stevenson has shown that, of over 600 people killed in crowd disturbances from 1700 – 1832, all but a handful were killed by army or militia.[18] Crowd psychology doesn't even allow you to question these forces since they are absent from the picture. Finally, if crowds are so dangerous and so irrational, it follows that they cannot be dealt with by reason but only with a big stick.

So, in addition to silencing and excusing, a decontextualised psychology underpinned by a decontextualised notion of the self legitimates repression of those who challenge the status quo. These are major returns and they illustrate the political dangers that flow from a refusal to accept the social bases of action and their mediation through collective selfhood. It could easily be argued that, for the elite, such returns strongly outweigh the minor inconvenience of distorting the character of crowd action. However, it is unnecessary to impute such cynicism, or to assume that the elite appreciate the meaningful character of crowd action prior to twisting the story to their own ends. Indeed, the irrationalist account not only serves their interests. It also reflects their perspective. For if crowd action reflects the collective identities and collective understandings of participants and if, from the outside, one has no access to those understandings, it becomes impossible to appreciate the patterns and meanings inherent in what is done.[19] Behaviour does indeed seem meaningless and random. If the bases of rationality are obscured, it becomes easy to put the behaviours down to a loss of rationality. What is more, by taking perspective into consideration it is possible to explain why a wider public, who do not share the interests of the elite and who might even have political sympathies with crowd members, nonetheless endorse the Le Bonian view. If you see a crowd and you see the crowd being violent and you discern no pattern to that violence, how can you accord sense to the behaviours and how can you be sure that you might not be the next target? Accusations of mindlessness and sentiments of fear are common to observers of crowds, whatever their social position. Whether the importance of collective identity for collective action is neglected through hostility or incapacity, the results are the same.[20]

Political and perspective bias might well explain the popularity of classic crowd theory. However this only sharpens the horns of the second dilemma. How can bias co-exist with effectiveness? How can one sway the masses through the application of a theory that patently misrepresents the nature of mass psychology? Since he views crowd members as intellectually incapacitated, Le Bon instructs the would-be demagogue to dispense with reasoning. Rather, it is necessary to use simplification, affirmation and repetition to move crowds. As he puts it: 'Affirmation, pure and simple, kept free of all reasoning and all proof, is one of the surest means of making an idea enter the mind of crowds ... Affirmation, however, has no real influence unless it be constantly repeated, and so far as possible in the same terms'.[21] These prescriptions are echoed by the practitioners. To quote Hitler: 'The receptivity of the great masses is very limited, their intelligence is small ... In consequence, all effective propaganda must be limited to a very few points and must harp on these in slogans until the last member of the public understands what you want him to understand by your slogan'.[22] But if the premise is false and members of crowds and masses are not so gullible, why should simplistic slogans work?

The answer is to be found by looking a little more closely at the rhetorical practices of Le Bon's supposed disciples as well as those of Le Bon himself. While he may have written of crowds as if they reverted to a single and unchanging racial unconscious, in practice his project was to win them from the cause of class to that of nation. In other words he sought to replace one social categorical basis for collective action with another. Similarly, both Mussolini and Hitler sought to use national identity as a basis for mass action. Moreover they sought to root their vision of the nation in historical and mythological themes and thereby make a contingent version of the category appear as a timeless essence. In Mussolini's case, the *romanitá* (cult of Romanness) was at the heart of his contemporary politics.[23] Hitler drew on the romantic conservative strain of nineteenth-century *volk*ish-nationalist thought in which the cult of the nation, a racial and specifically anti-Semitic definition of national community, and the idea of heroic leadership, were all central. In a mixture of actual and mythological pasts, Hitler was self styled as part Frederick the Great and part Siegfried.[24]

Putting these elements together, Hitler's rhetoric, and that of the Nazi Party more generally, achieved an elision between the leader, the Party and the nation such that Hitler was able to define for members of the *Volksgemeinschaft* (national community) what it meant to be German.[25] This was exemplified in the words of Rudolf Hess which formed the climax of the 1934 Nuremburg rally (and of Leni Riefenstahl's film of the rally, *Triumph des Willens* – Triumph of the Will): 'The Party is Hitler. But Hitler is Germany, just as Germany is Hitler. Hitler! Sieg Heil!'. Such rhetoric is clearly highly stylised and highly condensed. For some, such form is in contrast to content. It indicates that Hitler practised as he preached, at least when it came to his oratory, and did not tax the attendant masses by attempting to communicate complex ideas – or even any ideas at all. Stern, for instance, argues that: 'At the party rallies at Nuremburg the content drops out altogether and the 'exchange' between the Leader and the masses becomes pure ritual: (Hitler:) *'Deutschland!'* (Answer:) *'Sieg Heil'*.[26] However, such ritualised exchanges are only possible because of a wealth of understanding that is so well known, and known to be shared, that it requires little to be invoked. Many key elements of the Nazi world view are here. The exchange is framed by the naming of the national community, and it is Hitler who takes the position of invoking the name. The audience responds with the Nazi greeting and the greeting to Hitler as *Fuhrer*. There may only be three words here, but they serve to instantiate an understanding of the category which frames the action of the collective (German identity), an understanding of how that category is defined (in racial and hierarchical terms) and an understanding of who represents the category (the leader – Hitler).

The importance of style, then, is not that it substitutes for substance, but rather that it allows the substance – the various constructed dimensions of identity – to be taken for granted. These dimensions don't need to be spoken, to be put on view and hence to invite the possibility of alternatives. The power of this rhetoric therefore lies in the ability simultaneously to construct categories and to hide all traces of construction. This can also be seen as Le Bon's gift to the mass politician: an understanding of how to employ culture posing as nature. Affirm, simplify and repeat, but, above all, do not allow the categorical basis upon which such formal devices operate to be available for questioning. The individualistic concept of identity along with the concept of a racial unconscious work in tandem to deflect any unwelcome attention. For, if there is no social basis to the ideas that guide us, if the members of the collective have lost any basis for choosing amongst the ideas that are suggested to them and if the sole psychological mechanism that remains (the racial unconscious) is both non-intellectual and fixed, then it follows that one cannot alter the grounds of crowd action, ideas are irrelevant to the guidance of crowd action and even when individuals are alone and ideas are relevant to their action, these ideas are selected on idiosyncratic grounds. To search for the social categorical grounds of crowd action or to seek to contest the grounds that are offered would be a triply futile exercise.

All in all, it could be argued that Le Bon understands the importance of mythology to crowd action full well and he offers that understanding as a weapon. However what makes it a weapon is that, rather than clarifying how myths are invoked to mobilise masses, he and those who follow him mythologise the foundations of mass mobilisation. So it is not that the practice succeeds despite the theory. Rather, what makes for bad theory is what makes for an effective totalitarian practice. To spell it out, it is through the denial of the social nature of selfhood that a specific social identity can be smuggled in and used to instantiate a particular model of social relations. Therefore, if you ignore the issue of identity or if you take its nature for granted, it will come back to haunt you. To presuppose that identity will take a given form is to presuppose one partial view of subjects and their social relations. It is both to advance one's politics and to deny others a democratic choice of politics. I do not think that it is an exaggeration to state that a fully democratic politics is impossible without opening the processes of identity to inspection. The stakes are that high. They are that high because of the relationship between collective identities and collective practice. It is this relationship which needs fuller exploration if we are to understand the nature of identity, how identity allows an articulation of social and individual levels of explanation and why it is so important to get it right.

IDENTITY IN PRACTICE

I have now addressed two domains which, above all others, are meant to be characterised by lack of identity and hence by lack of ideas: crowd action and mass rhetoric. In both cases, we have discovered not only that identity is present but also that it plays a key role in the patterning of phenomena. If identity is so central in the very areas which are supposed to be the mark of its absence, one must at least pause and consider whether there are any cases in which it is safe to ignore its role in the shaping of action. I will pursue this point with one more example.

For many academics and many commentators, nationalism is the most central force of our era. Yet for every voice raised in favour of national self-determination, there are voices raising the dangers of chauvinism, exclusionism and of ethnic cleansing. In the British context, those who call for Scottish independence – the Scottish National Party (SNP) – are matched by those defending the Union and decrying the siren voices of the nationalists. One might expect, therefore, that national identity would prove to be more central in the rhetoric and the politics of the SNP than in that of the other parties – especially the Conservatives who opposed even the devolution of powers to a Scottish Assembly within a United Kingdom framework (a policy supported by the Labour and Liberal Democrat parties which became reality in May 1999). However that is not the case. To take but one of many examples, the Conservative candidate in North East Fife for the 1997 general election, a certain Adam Bruce, was portrayed on his leaflet clad in kilt and sporran and sporting the sword of his distant ancestor, Robert. Bruce, along with multitudes of his fellow Tories, declared that he was fighting for Scotland. They repeatedly insisted that they deferred to no one in their pride as Scots. Indeed they declared their support for the Union on the grounds that it reflected Scottish values and was good for Scotland. Wherever one looked, amongst Unionists, devolutionists and separatists, all started their arguments from Scottish identity and the Scottish national interest.[27]

This example is not meant as an argument for the necessity of national identity. Indeed there were those who contested its relevance and its morality. But they largely stood outside of the electoral fold. Indeed, for those who sought to appeal to the electorate in general, the use of an identity which included all within its boundaries and through which all could be appealed to was all but ubiquitous. That is the point of my example. Collective identities serve to constitute a common audience into a single community who can thereby be enjoined to act in a common way. Moreover, to the extent that the speaker is able to construct him or herself as part of that community, he or she is at one with the audience and able to speak for them. Collective identities therefore serve to make collective mobilisation and collective influence possible. To the extent that different speakers seek to mobilise the same audience they are likely to speak in terms of the same choice of identity. What I am arguing, then, is that identity may always be implicated in the organisation of social practice. However, as a corollary, the nature of identity will always be a function of the practices in which it is implicated. This leads to an apparent paradox, which at the same time is crucial to unravelling the role of identity in social action. On the one hand, identity is essential to human collective action (I would argue that it is essential to all rational human action, in the Weberian sense of behaviour based on the selection of appropriate means to reach given ends; however I don't have the space to argue the case here). On the other hand identity is essentially constructed and will either vary or else stay constant as a function of the nature of those practices to which it is oriented.[28]

If our politicians all used Scottish identity to appeal to an identical audience, their construction of the contents of Scottishness varied profoundly in relation to their different projects of mobilisation. For SNP politicians, the Scottish psyche was inherently egalitarian and inherently different to the English such that the Scottish desire for a radical society could not be achieved while yoked to England. For

Labour, the Scottish psyche was also egalitarian and open to the public services, but also had much in common with the English, such that the radical future must be achieved within the United Kingdom. For Conservatives, Scots were natural entrepreneurs whose dynamism was only possible through the larger Union. The enactment of this Scottish psyche through Conservative policy would brook no tampering with the constitution. All sought to naturalise their constructions in Scottish history, in Scottish culture, even in the Scottish landscape. Sometimes they even used the same figures and the same commonplaces to ground their constructions. In each case, identity was central to the appeal. In each case, the substantive construction of identity was radically different. In each case the formal relationship of identity to proposed mobilisations was identical.

We are now in a position to draw a number of conclusions. Firstly, there is a danger in restricting the term 'identity politics' to particular forms of social mobilisation which are oriented towards the validation of particular forms of difference – gender, 'race', sexuality and so on. All politics is identity politics in the sense that the promotion and organisation of particular forms of social relations is achieved through the construction of identity, whether or not the explicit celebration of the category is an end. Indeed, just as national identity can be used to promote Union rather than independence, so, for instance, gender identity could be used to argue against a politics based on gender differentiation. Indeed, it could be argued that the very use of the term 'identity politics' to denote particular forms of practice is yet another example of limiting the choice over what identity means and what flows from it.

Secondly, it is possible to describe the art of politics more as the craft of identity construction and to describe politicians as 'entrepreneurs of identity' – though the term can be extended to anyone concerned with the persuasion or mobilisation of others: social movement activists, religious and other missionaries, advertisers and so on. The effective entrepreneur will be one whose performance in all its dimensions – from dress, posture, tone and style through to the content of what is said – work together in order to underpin a coherent model of identity.[29] To return to Hitler at Nuremburg, an understanding of the messianic power of his rhetoric would need to start with the moment where his arriving plane cast the shadow of a cross on the crowd to the final tumultuous exchange between the raised figure of the *Fuhrer* and the massed ranks of the crowd bound together in Speer's monumental architecture.

Thirdly, an acceptance of the ubiquity of selfhood must necessarily co-exist with a reconceptualisation of the nature of the self as something which is defined collectively as well as individually and whose substantial definition – in terms of the boundaries of inclusion, the characterisation of prototypical group members and the understanding and values associated with group membership – is always open to contestation. Often we presume that because identity has such material consequences there must be something equally solid and permanent as cause. The reverse is true. It is precisely because identity is so consequential that it is so disputed. Moreover, in a world that is constantly changing, one's room for manoeuvre would be severely constrained if the font of action were fixed.

Fourthly, if it is necessary to revise our notion of self, it is equally important to revise our usage of self related terms: self-esteem, self-efficacy and many others, most notably self-interest. As we have seen, the starting point for accusations of collective irrationality is the claim that individuals do not act in terms of self as indicated by their willingness to sacrifice self-interest. People willingly put themselves at individual risk with little indication of individual gain. In Timisoara, members of the Romanian crowds bared their chests before the guns of the Securitate and declared that it was better to die than to live with Romania unfree. More mundanely, one can find repeated examples of individuals in crowds who go to aid unknown others who are in danger of being arrested, thereby putting themselves in danger of being arrested. All this makes little sense at an individual level. However it is a very different story if one accepts that people may define themselves at a collective level, that interest is the maximisation of that which is a good as defined by reference to collective values and that which accrues to the collective rather than the individual. Thus a good to fellow ingroup members can be a good for one's collective self. Just as an injury to one can be an injury to all, so a benefit to one can be a benefit to all. Altruism therefore flows not from an abnegation but from an extension of the self. If one accepts this, it becomes relatively straightforward to explain phenomena of cohesion and solidarity and to account for people pulling their weight rather than forever seeking a free ride. Phenomenal feats of logic are required only if one seeks to explain collective action while starting from the absolute assumption that people always seek to maximise their individual self-interest as against the interest of other individuals.

Fifthly and finally, while it is an understandable and comforting reaction to brand barbarism as mindless, one must beware of confusing expressions of moral repugnance with explanations of why the repugnant occurs. Those who kill and maim and deface usually do so with all too clear a view of why they are acting and why they must act as they do. The problem is less that they lack a sense of themselves in the world, but rather that they follow that sense to the end without questioning. If there is pathology in their actions, it is not psychopathology. They are not intellectually impaired. Rather, it is sociopathology. The problem lies in the nature of the identities they enact and the understandings associated with those identities. As I have argued at length, the problem also lies in the way that particular positionings of the subject can be made to seem natural such that the actions that flow from such positions become equally hard to question. As Umberto Eco suggested in writing *The Name of the Rose*, a world which excludes all doubt is in danger of burning all to the ground. The response to barbarism must therefore be to contest the theory and politics which reduces the many forms of identity to a single choice. To bemoan identity loss in a mass society is not only a useless response to the problem, it is part of the problem.

NOTES

1. Quoted in S. Giner, *Mass Society,* Martin Robertson, London 1976, p4.
2. Quoted in P. Riewald, *L'Esprit des Masses,* Delachaux & Niestle, Neuchatel 1949, p325. Author's translation from the French.
3. Le Bon's book, *The Crowd: A Study of the Popular Mind*, Ernest Benn, London 1895, translation 1947, is possibly the most widely read social psychology text of all time. His ideas survive, albeit in a sanitised and more technically sophisticated form, through the work of deindividuation theorists. For a recent review and critique see S. Reicher, R. Spears and T. Postmes, 'A social identity model of deindividuation phenomena' in W. Stroebe & M. Hewstone (eds), *European Review of Social Psychology*, Vol. 6, Wiley, Chichester.
4. Le Bon, *op. cit.*, p40.
5. N.Z. Davis, 'The rites of violence: religious riot in sixteenth century France', *Past and Present*, 1978, 59, pp51-91.
6. Davis is not alone in showing this to be so. There are many studies which reveal the order under the apparent chaos of crowd events. Perhaps the most impressive studies are those dealing with food riots which, if anything is a candidate for atavistic behaviour, would seem to foot the bill. Surely, people get hungry and instinctively grab what sustenance is available. Yet closer studies show that the conditions under which food riots start, the forms they take and the ways they develop, are all guided by

collective notions of legitimate practice and concepts of rights. The classic example is E.P. Thompson, 'The moral economy of the English crowd in the eighteenth century', *Past and Present*, 1971, p50, pp76-136. See also W. Reddy, 'The textile trade and the language of the crowd at Rouen 1752-1871', *Past and Present*, 1977, 74, pp62-89.

7. G. Lefebvre, *Etudes sur la Revolution Francaise*, Presses Universitaires de France, Paris 1954.

8. Gareth Steadman Jones, *Languages of Class,* Cambridge University Press, Cambridge 1989, provides a compelling account of this separation.

9. See S. Giner, *Mass Society*, Martin Robertson, London 1976, for an analysis of mass society theory.

10. The move is akin to what John Thompson calls 'expurgation of the other', *Ideology and Modern Culture*, Polity, Oxford, 1990, p65.

11. S. Barrows, *Distorting Mirrors,* Yale University Press, Yale 1991.

12. Lissagaray, *History of the Paris Commune*, New Park, London 1976.

13. See Robert Nye's account of the crisis of democracy in the Third Republic and the links to crowd psychology, *The Origins of Crowd Psychology*, Sage, London 1975.

14. Le Bon was highly successful in this enterprise – and his influence extended beyond his luncheon circle and even beyond his lifetime. Both Mussolini and Goebbels acknowledged Le Bon's influence – see S. Moscovici, *L'Age des Foules*, Fayard, Paris 1981 and R. Nye, *op. cit.* Adorno and Horkheimer note how Hitler's account of crowd psychology and how to direct crowds is taken clearly from Le Bon and that 'Mein Kampf' could be seen in some respects as a poor person's, 'The Crowd', in *Aspects of Sociology*, Heinemann, London 1973.

15. Moscovici, 1981, *op. cit.*

16. Aveni, 'The not so lonely crowd: friendship groups in collective behaviour', *Sociometry*, 1979, 40, pp96-99, provides evidence of acquaintance patterns in crowds. My own work provides examples of the pleasure people derive from feeling part of a known community even in the midst of a riot, see for example S. Reicher, 'The St Pauls riot: An explanation of the limits of crowd action in terms of a social identity model', *European Journal of Social Psychology*, 14, pp1-21.

17. For an analysis of naturalisation as an ideological technique see Thompson, 1990, *op. cit.*

18. J. Stevenson, *Popular Disturbances in England 1700-1832*, Longman, London.

19. David Smith, in his analysis of the Tonypandy 'riots' of 1910,'Tonypandy 1910: Definitions of Community', *Past and Present*, 87, pp158-184, likens crowd behaviour to a language. The metaphor can be extended. Like a

language one doesn't know, crowd action can seem like a meaningless babble of sound to those outside.

20. For an analysis of outside views of the St Paul's 'riot', see S. Reicher & J. Potter, 'Psychological theory as intergroup perspective: a comparative analysis of 'scientific' and 'lay' accounts of crowd events', *Human Relations*, 1985, 38, pp167-189.

21 Le Bon, 1895, translation 1947, *op. cit.* pp124 -125.

22. Quoted by D. Welch, *The Third Reich: Politics and Propaganda*, Routledge, London 1993, p11.

23. See R. Visser, 'Fascist doctrine and the cult of the Romanita', *Journal of Contemporary History*, 1992, 27, pp5-22.

24. See L. Greenfeld, *Nationalism*, Harvard University Press, Cambridge, Massachussetts 1992; I. Kershaw, *The 'Hitler Myth'*, Clarendon Press, Oxford 1987.

25. See N. Baynes, *The Speeches of Adolf Hitler,* 2 Vols., Oxford University Press, London 1942; Kershaw, 1987, *op.cit.*

26. Quoted in J. Stern, *Hitler: The Fuhrer and the People*, Flamingo, London 1984, p39.

27. This evidence is taken from a comprehensive study of Scottish politicians. See N. Hopkins and S. Reicher, 'Constructing the nation and collective mobilisation: a case study of politicians arguments about the meaning of Scottishness', in C. Barfoot (ed), *Beyond Pugs Tour: national and ethnic stereotyping in theory and literary practice*, Rodopi, Amsterdam 1997; N. Hopkins and S. Reicher, *Social Identity and the Nation*, Sage, London, in press. See also G. Morton, *Unionist Nationalism*, Tuckwell, East Linton 1999.

28. See, however, Reicher, 'Three dimensions of the social self', in M. Oosterwegel and R. Wicklund (eds), *The Self in North American and European Culture*, Kluwer, Dordrecht 1994. See also Reicher and Hopkins, *The Identity of Social Psychology*, Sage, London (forthcoming).

29. See G. Mosse, *The Nationalisation of the Masses*, Cornell University Press, Ithaca 1991.

On the Subject of New Labour

ALAN FINLAYSON

Does New Labour's 'project' seek to re-politicise the relationships and practices that constitute contemporary citizenship? Tony Blair has written of 'finding new ways to enable citizens to share in decision making that affects them' and of the need to 'encourage public debate on the big decisions affecting people's lives'. He has spoken of a 'drive to "reinvent" national government' and declared it 'incumbent on us to improve its image and effectiveness', stating that 'open, vibrant, diverse democratic debate is a laboratory for ideas about how we should meet social needs ... we want to revitalise the ethic of public service'.[1] Third Way theorist Anthony Giddens demands the 'democratising of democracy', arguing that 'The crisis of democracy comes from its not being democratic enough' before calling for a renewal of civil society, an expansion of the role of the public sphere and a cosmopolitan outlook for the state.[2]

Added to this rhetoric are a number of New Labour policies that seem to be potential motors of a radical transformation in both the conduct of British politics and attitudes toward it. Numerous commentators have pointed to the scale of constitutional reform initiated by the Blair government and argued that there is an unstoppable movement toward new forms of pluralism, decentralisation and renewed civic engagement that will break conservative hegemony and allow new forms of radical politics to emerge.[3] Directly elected mayors for London and, presumably, other large cities, may renew interest in the relevance of municipal action. Citizenship classes in schools surely suggest an interest in revitalising the democratic tendencies of our society while devolution of Westminster power forms a key plank in what the Blairites sometimes call 're-connecting' with the people. Certainly there is potential here for an enhanced politicisation of British life.

But the policies, indeed the general perspective of the government, are contained within a set of assumptions about the nature of our present social and economic arrangements and the direction of their development that do not complement a desire to politicise or democratise society. On the contrary they lead to the encouragement of a kind of self-government, an individualising of citizens such that they become the object of their own political practice. Curiously, this proceeds on the basis of de-politicising selfhood through turning it into codified practices and techniques while reducing the explicit role of the state to that of facilitating individuals in this quest for their own individualisation.

The intention of this chapter is to open up and expose these assumptions and tendencies that inform third way thinking and action without always being sufficiently explicit to receive conscious evaluation, even by those who draw on them. This is particularly the case with conceptions of 'the subject'. The effective power of concepts of subjectivity resides precisely in their generally 'un-thought' nature. We take for granted some conception of who or what we are, derive judgements and generalisations from it, and place the whole beyond question because doing so seems to be essential for continuing to be and act. This is even more the case when self-hood is believed to be the object of continual invention and creation. The open-ended, or self-creating subject is just another mode in the history of discourses of subjectivity. It no less a way of founding our political perceptions on supposedly solid ground just because it claims that the ground is no longer solid. It is even more so for being the only mode available.

The concept of the subject is central to contemporary political analysis. 'The modern' in both political theory and practice can be characterised, if only partially, by the centrality it affords to a particular sort of individualised rational subject. A philosophical concept of the person as a unique self, in possession of a singular and coherent individuality, relating to an external world via the faculty of reason, entails a particular vision of the social, and political, agent. That agent, because of its unique faculties, can be held to require sovereignty over itself and its private affairs as well as freedom to determine, with other such subjects, the rules of conduct that will govern public affairs. It is this subject that can form a social contract with others and thus set the framework, and limits, of public, political life.

Such a conception has made possible revolutionary political ideas and practices. It is hard to think of concepts such as human rights (to liberty, free speech and political participation for example) without assuming a singular, rational will to claim and exercise them. Furthermore, the implication of this belief is that there is an essential equality to human subjects: that our mutual capacity to reason necessitates some form of democratic political structures to which none can be subjected without their consent. For Kant the motto of Enlightenment was 'Have courage to use your *own* understanding'; a state of affairs that necessitated freedom 'to make public use of one's reason in all matters'.[4]

We might say, then, that the liberal vision of the subject made possible modern forms of state and democratic politics. But we could reverse this formulation and suggest that modern forms of state, democracy and social organisation pre-supposed the Enlightenment individual; that they were driven to bring about its invention and formalisation. In so doing, the kind of 'ideal' subject envisaged was circumscribed and limited in various ways. Far from being a transcendent and eternal truth it was a historically dependent conception, a product of its time. That subject was generally conceived as masculine, specifically European and property owning, while the labouring subject required freedom in as much as he could then set about the business of selling his labour. Yet, these limitations aside, the concept provided the terms and tools for its own critique, for the demand that it be applied to all regardless of their race, gender or economic situation.

This 'liberal' notion of political and social subjectivity was very quickly challenged from different political standpoints. A conservative such as Burke, specifically taking on the claims of the French Revolution to have founded a new order of liberty, finds the capacity for the individual to reason freely to be curtailed by passions and prejudices. The latter form the essential bedrock of custom and convention with which it would be folly to tamper. For Burke the individual is foolish. It is only the species that, through the slowly developing interaction of history, experience and learning, can be wise. The application of abstract principles to the social order is an illegitimate intrusion bound to end in despotism and destruction.

From the left the Enlightenment subject came to be seen as a fiction supporting the ideological claims of bourgeois society. The rights that attached to the subject could thus be regarded as what Lenin called 'constitutional illusions', for a 'thousand obstacles' ensured they could never be exercised. Later Marxist critical theorists came to argue that subjectivity belonged to the ruling classes and was denied to the alienated labourer.

Though their motivations and arguments are different these two angles of critique of the liberal political subject have some ideas in common. The claims of liberal enlightenment make the individual subject the basic unit of politics and social organisation. It is from the nature, capacities and rights of that individual that appropriate political, social and legal structures are derived; their purpose is to facilitate, encourage, foster and (if necessary) limit. In taking issue with this subject both conservatism and socialism proposed something else as the object of politics. Challenging the notion that the individual is either the beginning or end of politics they looked instead to forms of collective. For the conservative this is a collective divided into 'little platoons' secured in place thanks to the rigours of the great chain of being and its necessary hierarchy. For socialism, and in particular Marxism, it is the movements of the mass that are the object of politics and that will determine historical development. It is specifically the proletarian mass that must take on the responsibility of advancing humanity.

Both positions present a fundamental challenge to the notion of the liberal subject while simultaneously failing to remain uncontaminated by it. It is quite possible for conservatism and socialism to conceive of the collective in question as itself a kind of subject writ large. Thus conservatism comes to embrace the unity of the nation striving to manifest its innate reason and exercise its God-given capacities, while socialism can conceive of the mass proletariat as a historically given, unified actor that must be allowed to exercise its power as the universal subject. In other words while the liberal subject comes in for criticism it is still possible for the thought of the subject to persist in such a way that further critique is necessary. It is this that, amongst other schools of thought, post-modern or post-structuralist thinking has sought to do.

Here the sources of the subject are de-centred away from innate or naturalistic foundations and from the laws of history or economy. Instead the subject is understood to emerge from 'contingent' historical forces and the relations of power that animate them. The pre-cursors of such a conception hardly need re-stating – Marxist arguments have already been mentioned – but we could also rehearse the Freudian 'discovery' of the unconscious or the centrality given to language by much philosophy and social science in the twentieth century. Both trends displace the roots of self-hood from our own purely internal will into a network of structures and flows that make up the social universe; to the representations and habits of thought into which we are socialised and from which we draw our narratives of self. But the crucial development here is that subjectivity itself becomes politicised. For the liberal vision the individual subject was a secure entity which could then go forth and be a citizen, engage in debates, formulate or challenge laws. For the conservative the collective subject of the organic community was a shell formed through the ages that made civilisation and social, political, interaction, possible. And for the vulgar Marxist, political requirements could be derived from the status of the collective proletarian subject within the greater movement of history. All three place subjectivity outside, or prior to, political engagement. But the post-structuralist comes to see 'the subject' as something that emerges from particular, and historical, configurations of power. Foucault, for example, made available to us the question of how political subjects are created. Rather than seeing power as some-thing that exists independently of the rational subject (such that it can be legitimately or illegitimately exercised, that one can be shielded from it through rights and so forth), Foucault contends that it is power that constitutes such subjects. 'Rights' and 'responsibilities' are not neutral concepts or properties that can be derived from or attached to the independent subject. Different regimes of power produce different kinds of truth about the subject, creating new kinds of subject, subjected to new formulations and practices of power. In this way the subject becomes intelligible as a historical formation and not as the name for a trans-historical essence.

But it also becomes clearly political – indeed Balibar argues that the notion of the subject does not receive a full philosophical formulation until Kant when it emerges in conjunction with post Revolutionary notions of citizenship.[5] But more than this, politics can be understood as a process that is reliant on notions of subjectivity around which it can cohere. As Laclau has argued, it is the subject which forms the fixing point of ideological discourses, which do not merely seek a response from a subject that is already formed and waiting for political rhetoric to invite its participation but to create the subject of their own discourse, defining it as the natural mode of being.[6] For Stuart Hall ideology is the process of articulating 'into a configuration, different subjects, different identities, different projects, different aspirations. It does not reflect, it constructs, a "unity" out of difference'.[7] Politics is the process from which identities derive definition and a sense of their interests through articulation in the public realm of contestation.

Such theoretical positions make it possible to engage in a particular sort of analysis of a phenomenon such as New Labour, one that tries to establish what sort of subject it seeks to produce – to 'interpellate' within its rhetoric and to 'construct' through new forms of state-led exhortation and inducement. Here we can ask questions about the sort of subject New Labour conceives to be the key actor in social change and development; about the ideal subject/citizen of an ideal New Labour world – the kind of person it portrays as liberated or enhanced by its policies. We can ask about the kinds of exclusions at work – does New Labour draw on partial gendered assumptions about 'normal' identity? Does it accommodate diversity of race or sexuality within its conception of a reinvigorated national polity? What is the place of rhetorical scare figures (the single mother, the pregnant teenager, and the deviant male adolescent) in the securing of New Labour's ideological vision? In what ways do new regimes of welfare seek to discipline and direct people into taking on certain sorts of behaviour, lifestyle and moral orientation towards themselves?

Such questions certainly proliferate. This short essay can only partially address some of them. We shall focus on the first question about the kind of subject that motivates social change. From this we shall offer a general picture of the 'ideal' New Labour subject. In so doing it is necessary to pretend that there is a greater degree of uniformity and coherence to New Labour than is really the case. But analysis, like politics itself, must always begin with a little creative construction and with the invention of its own subject.

NEW LABOUR: POLITICS, THEORY AND THE SUBJECT

New Labour has been described as the most radical government of the century and as lacking all substance, composed only of image. Michael Freeden has argued that New Labour's ideology includes aspects of Socialism, Liberalism and Conservatism articulated together in a way that redefines them.[8] Others have simply pointed to the Clinton strategy of triangulation and reduced New Labour to nothing other than a cynical attempt at attaining power. One could also throw in the influence of North American communitarianism, of ethical Christian socialism, in which Blair is known to have an interest, or indeed of Labour's own traditions and previous attempts at 'modernisation' – as advocated by Gaitskell and Wilson for example. Nor should one forget the framework of 'post-Thatcherism' within which present politics is shaped.[9]

That such a range of elements have been adduced as the key to New Labour suggests that we are tending to see only small parts and to mistake them for the whole. Perhaps, rather than ask *what* New

Labour is we should begin by asking *how* New Labour is possible, what configuration of social conditions, what form of political conjuncture, made New Labour thinkable? The substantive political theories and strategies identified as elements of New Labour are parts of its 'conscious' ideology – the doctrines and dogma that are drawn upon in the formulation and justification of policy and outlook. But we need also to look at something like its 'spontaneous' ideology, that clutch of taken-for-granted assumptions and prioritisations that inform its decisions and assessments. New Labour formulates political and policy claims on the basis of beliefs about current social, economic and cultural conditions from which there are derived generalisations about the way society needs to be re-ordered.

The neo-liberal shift of the 1970s and 1980s was predicated on the assumption that the Keynesian welfare state had fallen into crisis because it was too lumbering to maintain competitiveness in an increasingly flexible economy. The impediments to improvement were identified as trade union protectiveness and complacency on the part of a liberal, public service élite. The former were systematically undermined while the latter were forced to submit to the discipline of the market. Financial institutions were opened up to greater global circulation and the entrepreneur became the guiding spirit of the liberated market. But Thatcherism could not maintain confidence in the new regime it sought to construct partly because of blindness to the necessary social dimension of such reforms. It is not enough to introduce new entrepreneurs to the discipline of the market and free them from government interference. The state must necessarily play a role in creating the appropriate conditions. The entrepreneur requires the continuing technological innovation which he or she can exploit and a workforce already capable of working with it (not to mention a consuming public that can use the goods and services on offer). The only body that can act to bring about or encourage these conditions is the state. It can initiate training schemes, for example, and can give tax breaks to encourage investment as well as launch television advertising campaigns.

Furthermore, hostility to the social dimensions of economic policy prevented Thatcherism from recognising the cultural underpinnings to any market society. As one time Thatcherite John Gray has argued: 'the central dilemma of the age ... is how revolutionary changes in technology and the economy can be reconciled with the enduring human needs for security and for forms of common life'.[10] Those human needs are of course essential to the success of the changing economy and it is incumbent on the state to find ways of engendering 'trust', 'community', and legitimacy, for the new regime.

The key to New Labour is this belief in the necessity of responding to economic and technological change allied to a conviction that only it can fully do so, that only New Labour understands the breadth, as well as the depth, of what such a transformation entails. For Blair the world 'has undergone a veritable revolution of change. Our young people will work in different industries, often those of communications and design, not old mass production'. Social democracy must be redesigned to match up to these conditions where work is more flexible, not tied to old routines of nine-to-five and a job for life, where more women are in work and, above all, where forces of economic globalisation demand new adjustment. This sense of newness pervades Blairite rhetoric which is filled with phrases evoking 'a world with its finger on the fast forward button; where every part of the picture of our life is changing'.[11] Addressing the TUC annual conference in September 1999 Blair stated that 'The challenge of the new economy is the fundamental issue of our time'.

Similarly, a Demos collection on The Third Way refers to 'the profound forces of globalisation, which have sharply altered the operating environment for government. Governments can no longer easily erect barriers to the exchange of money, regulate precisely what media their citizens consume, insulate their economies from global business cycles or pursue autonomous defence strategies'. The core challenge is that of 'achieving the transition to an economy based on intensive application and development of knowledge'.[12] Or, as Blair puts it in his explanation of The Third Way: 'Just as economic and social change were critical to sweeping the Right to power, so they were critical to its undoing. The challenge for the Third Way is to engage fully with the implications of that change ...[to aim for] ... a dynamic knowledge based economy founded on individual empowerment and opportunity, where governments enable, not command, and the power of the market is harnessed to serve the public interest'.[13]

Giddens's analysis shares this conviction that certain specifiable social conditions demand a new form of politics. Old ideas of socialism are obsolete and our concepts of knowledge and control need to be rethought to fit a society too complex, too fluid and diverse, to be managed by a central state. Social relations cannot now be assumed or relied upon. We are open to more risk in social encounters and require new forms of trust. Old forms of authority must be replaced by dialogic forms of democracy and new forms of solidarity based on a 'new balance between individual and collective responsibilities'.[14] This also means recognising the opportunities and possibilities of risk, the chances it creates for new forms of lifestyle. Hence Giddens calls for a 'social investment state' that develops an entrepreneurial culture, offering protection in a way that encourages risk and opens possibilities facilitating our embrace of the knowledge economy.[15] Third Way politics should 'help citizens pilot their way through the major revolutions of our time: globalisation, transformations in personal life, and our relationship to nature ... '.[16]

We have then a vision of a world that is undergoing epochal change, that is accelerating due to the forces of advanced technological production and globalisation. It is a society that, as a result of its own productive tendencies, is increasing the opportunities for individual autonomy and the expression of variety and difference. The task of government is to enhance and increase these tendencies; to introduce the conditions for the structural competitiveness of the state; and to encourage the autonomisation of lifestyle which is both cause and effect of the former. From within this vision Thatcherism can be understood as having been a necessary project though one that failed to appreciate the extent of its task. New Labour will fulfil that vision by extending the logic of economic modernisation across the social and cultural field. Government will be modernised so that everyone can e-mail their MP. The health service will be modernised so that we can receive consultations via the internet. Policy formulation will be based on a fluid and mobile analysis of social conditions and the outcomes of government action – thinking will be 'joined-up' and 'holistic'. The welfare and educational systems will not only be modernised but will become tools for modernising the population, encouraging within us the requisite attitude of adaptability and self-responsibility that will help us to be entrepreneurs – in business, in the public services, or in our communities.

But it cannot do so in the 'old' ways, through government intervention, legislation or anything so crude as taxing people. For Perri 6 'Culture is now the centre of the agenda for government reform, because we now know from the findings of a wide range of recent research that culture is perhaps the most important determinant of a combination of long-run economic success and social cohesion. The mistake of both statist left and laissez-faire right was to ignore this fact'. Educational achievement cannot be enhanced without 'a shift in the mentalities of parents and children towards valuing education and investing time and energy into it'; law and order requires changing the cultures of the people who live in areas with high crime rates; environmental improvement rests on changing attitudes to energy efficiency, and unemployment requires addressing not only economic barriers to the long-term unemployed 'but also their own cultural and attitudinal handicaps'.[17] This is nothing less than a project aiming to create new kinds of subject, to fit new kinds of economic and social conditions and to bear the weight of new risks and new kinds of work – to invent what Giddens calls 'responsible risk takers'.[18] It is, in Nikolas Rose's phrase, an etho-politics which 'seeks to act upon conduct by acting upon the forces thought to shape the values, beliefs, moralities that themselves are thought to determine the everyday mundane choices that human beings make as to how they lead their lives. In etho-politics, life itself, as it is lived in its everyday manifestations, is the object of adjudication'.[19]

Where once the state had to intervene to make society and its citizens fit for the new industrial economy (by forcing people off land and into cities, by developing disciplinary education systems to begin training them) now the state must intervene to bring about the people of the knowledge economy. They will be the true reflexive individuals, a new kind of permanently revisionist self, an empowered and mobile subject (geographically, economically and psychically) who is his/her own entrepreneur of selfhood. As a corollary the state will cease to be a tool of direct intervention but will become merely an enabler, while those individuals and the associations of which they may be part move in to fill the space left by the state. This is 'a double movement of autonomization and responsibilization'. People and organisations are set free yet they must also take on the burden of establishing moral direction and exercising responsibility.[20]

NEW LABOUR'S SUBJECT (AND SUBJECT)

There are two subjects in play here. We will distinguish them through capitalisation – a Subject and a subject. The former is related to the way in which the process of 'modernisation' and the growth of the knowledge economy is itself conceived. The second is related to the way in which individuals in that economy are to be 'made up'. We shall begin with the Subject.

In a 1994 pamphlet outlining his vision of socialism Blair criticised socialism for allowing itself to become 'time limited': 'The problem with an ideology based on a particular economic prescription or time-limited view of class is that it may be valid for one time, but quickly becomes historically redundant. Society or the economy changes and the disciples of the ideology are left trying to fit the world to the ideology and not the ideology to the world'.[21] The changes he has in mind are the familiar ones of economic globalisation, expansion in service industries, the spread of consumer culture, changing patterns of employment and the knowledge economy. Five years ago Blair already saw that the task for New Labour was to 'equip and advance the individual's ability to prosper within this new economy'.[22]

This perspective finds itself revived at various points in Blair's writings and speeches. In 1994 he declared that 'satellite and communications technology are the nerve centre of a new information economy – doing for the next century what roads and railways have done for this one' and so argued for massive expansion in education. [23] In 1995 he presented 'proposals to equip our people and businesses for new technological and economic challenges, and to change the basis of this country's thinking of the last 100 years ... education is the best economic policy there is. And it is in the marriage of education and technology that the future lies. The arms race is over. The knowledge race has begun'.[24] 'Education is for life' he said. 'This is hard economics. The more you learn the more you earn. That is your way to do well out of life ... This combination of technology and know-how will transform the lives of us all', he continued, before announcing a plan by which BT would, in return for market access, connect 'every school, every college, every hospital, every library in Britain'. In 1996 'the Age of Achievement' was to be built on new technology' and by 1997 modernisation and innovation were found to be 'in the blood and bones of the British'.[25] All these speeches and writings are peppered with references to the new economy, the new world, the new generation, the challenges of the next millennium. This reaches a peak in the pamphlet on the third way when it is made clear that 'The challenge for the Third Way is to engage fully with the implications of that change'. Number one in a list of key policy objectives is 'A dynamic knowledge-based economy founded on individual empowerment and opportunity, where governments enable, not command, and the power of the market is harnessed to serve the public interest'.[26]

New Labour's claims about the need to update the constitution, reform welfare, renew education are contained within these assumptions about the pace of change and the revolutionary impact of new technology. But in imagining this process something strange happens. New Labour is making claims based on its convictions about the changing nature of the present and its superior knowledge of them. But the processes themselves take on an air of inevitability. Since they are irreversible the political and social challenge is to live up to them – we must, in Blair's words, 'modernise or die', thus transforming 'a conjectural state of affairs into an historical necessity'.[27] As Michael Rustin points out: 'It is a notable and defining fact about 'New Labour' that for the first time the power of capital and the markets which empower it are regarded as merely a fact of life, a reality to be accommodated to, and not a problem, a force to be questioned and resisted. The abstractions of 'globalisation', 'individualisation', even 'informationalism', can be used to reify the real agents and interests which dominate the contemporary world'.[28]

As Demos make clear, the tasks of 'how to balance prosperity with social inclusion, capitalism with community, how to modernise welfare systems, public services and labour markets, how to deepen democracy … ' occur against the background of the 'profound changes being wrought by globalisation of industries and market forces'.[29] In other words, globalisation and the knowledge economy are but the framework in which we operate and not themselves something we can operate upon. To be sure, Demos states a need for 'ideals' and not merely technocratic skills but they turn this economic environment into a terrain on which we are free to make our own choices but from which we cannot escape. The choices cannot be reconfigured so as to question that terrain itself. Third way thinking does not see this modernisation process as an unalloyed good nor as an entirely uniform and mono-directional process. But it does see it as a process outside of us, to be dealt with and lived up to.

This is related to claims to superior knowledge. Demos claims that politics must be based on 'clear values and a clear understanding of what motivates people'. Where past ideologies have based themselves on assumptions about human nature, 'Today we have a better understanding of the foundations of human nature. We know more about how evolution shaped our drives, our instincts as well as our capacity to co-operate.' Policy towards the objectified economy must be formed on the basis of objectifying human beings – faced with a world that is beyond our control we must strive to develop the best knowledge about it so we can fit into it. A bastard child of Spinoza and Kant, this philosophy of freedom gives only because it has already taken away. As Leadbeater argues, there is no way round the global knowledge economy. 'We have to go through it…we have to steel ourselves to press on, not really sure what lies ahead, but knowing that retreat is no alternative'.[30] We need to re-design institutions 'to enable them to withstand the gale around them'. Anything else would be the pointless activity of a Luddite King Canute.

New Labour's Subject is not a rational enlightened individual, but neither is it the 'net-nerd' clicking between the share index and pornography before purchasing designer goods from a digital TV sales channel. The Subject is not a person at all. It is this thing, this economy, this knowledge economy. The process of 'modernisation' or globalisation is the Subject that is the motive force of social and political change. It has most of the key characteristics of a person in late capitalist society – it is dynamic, it has needs, it has demands, it must be appeased lest it turn on you, it must be understood, analysed and encouraged to go in particular ways but it has rights too and shouldn't be interfered with too much. Like an acknowledged drug habit this particular inevitable revolution in the forces of production must be fed – only then can we avoid the terrifying destruction of withdrawal.

This is a very anti-political logic. The globalising knowledge economy becomes part of the given context of political action, not something that might be the object of challenge, change or reform. This is why, in the *Marxism Today* special issue on Blair, Stuart Hall, Eric Hobsbawm and David Held all take on the government for treating globalisation as an autonomous, non-political process, echoing earlier criticisms, for example in the journal *Soundings*.[31]

Labour modernisers are part of a vanguard movement that believes it has grasped the flow of history and social forces. That flow leads in the direction of expanding autonomy and renewed democracy but in order to be brought about requires the strong and determined leadership of those who understand. In order to free up individuals for the new economy and society, yet maintain the cohesion of the social order, the state must take a strong hand in producing those individuals. It must not do so by imposing a direction upon them but by cajoling them into accepting that the economy is an inexorable force to which we must match up. We must be free to act in the new economy but we must act freely in the right way. So the story of the New Labour subject does not stop with the reified globalising info-tech economy. Given the status afforded to this process it becomes essential to generate the kind of individual who can bear the responsibilities of existence in this new brave new world.

For social democracy the subject was a producer, a worker. But, as Leadbeater repeatedly points out, consumption in the knowledge economy is part of the process of production. In buying access to Microsoft products, to the ideas the new technologists provide for us, we buy the right to make things with them and in turn market them.[32]

Capitalist markets always needed to train their consumers, to generate individuals who recognised their need for a new product and were capable of using it. Advertising, especially in the post-war period, has gone to great lengths to educate consumers not only about what is available but about why new goods are worthwhile and how they can be used. In a hyper-commodified society, where the weightless predominates over the solid, this becomes an even greater requirement. Many of the new technologies do not offer anything that will, strictly speaking, improve the material quality of life. Luxuries are no doubt welcome, but they are, in an important sense, superfluous. This is why we require some training in order to properly recognise our new needs. The 'creative industries', such as advertising, and the horizontal integration of markets in, for example, entertainment, are increasingly important as a way of ensuring that I do want that video, that particular shirt or that particular video game (and that I want it now, in this financial year). The thrust of innovation is shifting from refining productive or carrier technologies to designing the mechanisms that sell the content to me, that teach me how attractive and desirable a product really is and reassure me that I am capable of using it – the mechanisms that train me in my job as consumer where in turn I can produce more. All of which links in to discourses of a 'postmodern', ever-developing subjectivity and the fusion of 'the aim of manufacturers to sell products and increase market share with the identity experiments of consumers'.[33]

Hence New Labour's economic and welfare policies are both oriented towards the reproduction and regulation of a particularly paradoxical economic subject: one that is immersed ever more in the sphere of productive consumption in order to forge an identity that is separate from it. For the state this presents problems since it wants and needs people to engage in the activity that keeps the weightless economy floating but at the same time it must manage a society which is opening itself up to a proliferation of activities that cut across the very social and moral structures that constitute it. The enabling state thus becomes also an 'exhortatory state' seeking to change 'identities' and 'govern by culture' instead of direct regulation. Just as the knowledge economy needs new kinds of individual so it requires a new kind of state to manage and mould the new citizens.

For Giddens we need to find ways of ensuring social solidarity and stability in this time of fragmentation, but the 'new' individualism demands, and is creating, a new moral order. Family life, sexual intimacy, the meaning of work are being re-shaped by this transformation.

Where the neo-liberal 'economic man' was left untouched by interfering government, so as to be able to maximise his own calculating judgement, now he must turn that judgement upon himself, developing a general moral framework but above all investing in himself so as to be able to respond to the ever-shifting environment. Education, for example, becomes an investment in the enhancement of individualised human capital, the purchase of knowledge, an investment in a consumer durable.

This is necessarily a disciplining process since it requires people to be equipped to deal with this dynamic economy – they can flourish differently within it but it is the horizon up against which they cannot go. This is one reason why the third way embraces the shift from the concept of equality to that of inclusion. It is not that the third way is anti-equality but that equality to be and live how we want to (as Mill might have seen it) contradicts the demands of economy. Thus we are not all equal in our rights to be 'old' labour or to be inactive in the formal economy. But we should all have free and equal access to the labour market even if we have to be forced into it. The concept of inclusion assists in turning a generalisable notion of equality (in lifestyle, and in ability to exercise our freedoms, to make the 'constitutional illusions' real) into a specific kind of equality. For though social inclusion is used to refer to membership of a wider culture and to the exercise of citizenship, it is clear that these all derive from inclusion within the workforce. In his 1999 conference speech Blair stressed that, 'We aren't just workers. We are citizens proud to say there is such a thing as society and proud to be part of it'. He spoke of 'the liberation of human potential not just as workers but as citizens'. But that liberation referred to the hitherto wasted talents of 'the many' and was allied to the argument that 'Talent is 21st century wealth. Every person liberated to fulfil their potential adds to our wealth'. His declaration of citizenship segued into a discussion on social values and respect, on tackling crime.[34] Once again the liberty of the subject and his/her fulfilment is related to the fact that such liberty is now an economic necessity since growth depends on 'creative investment', while citizenship, most revealingly, is tied into a communitarian rather than republican imagination.

The key policy areas where this sort of vision takes shape are those which most directly enter into the lives of citizens, primarily education and social security (though rhetoric around personal health would be of interest here also). These two policy areas are closely linked in the minds of the present government. Education forms the key part of plans to tackle social exclusion and is crucial to the welfare-to-work strategy. As the welfare green paper made clear: 'A skilled workforce is essential to a modern economy, and high educational standards offer people their best chance of a secure and prosperous life'.[35]

New Labour's welfare strategy revolves around these core notions of work and exclusion with education as the hinge that links them. In the words of the Commission on Social Justice, welfare is to be productive of both social justice and economic efficiency. It is to be about promoting personal autonomy, choice and the 'confidence and capability of people to manage their own lives.' For Giddens we should shift the notion of redistribution of wealth to that of the redistribution of possibilities: 'The cultivation of human potential should as far as possible replace "after the event" redistribution' or, in Blair's terms, 'the redistribution of opportunity'. Ruth Levitas describes this sort of welfare discourse as 'social integrationist' in which the poor are seen to lack not power but work.[36] The emphasis of policy is on making people responsible for themselves through assisting them in getting into the labour force. Ruth Lister further describes it as the discourse of RIO (Rights, Inclusion, Opportunity).[37] To receive benefit claimants must undergo an interview to discuss how they will find work. The 'something for nothing welfare state' will be ended and replaced by the balance of rights and responsibilities.[38] As Levitas also points out, the emphasis on 'employability over employment' is revealing. Because the new economy cannot itself be touched, so as to increase jobs available, policy must focus on the unemployed themselves in order to make them capable of working for it. Here, the New Deal for Lone Parents is indicative.

But one of the key developments of New Labour welfare policy is an emphasis on the individualisation of service delivery and with it the encouragement of responsibility for gearing up for the new economy. We have 'tailor-made packages' of help. Personal advisers can identify individual needs so that people may be 'empowered to seize the opportunities to lead independent lives' as they foster in themselves the skills that attract employers. Service will be 'customer-focused' and we will have Individual Learning Accounts to invest in that education which is an investment in ourselves. New technology will further this simultaneous 'autonomisation and responsibilization'; for example kiosk technology will make it possible (necessary) for people to access information for themselves.

Education, as we have already seen, is taken by some in the government to be the key route out of poverty or social exclusion. It is not seen primarily as an introduction into the moral or traditional culture of the nation nor as a way of empowering individuals to think openly and freely. Primarily it is seen as the mechanism by which individuals can equip themselves, and by which the national economy can feed itself, with the appropriate skills for the new economy. Education was the key site for the production of economically usable individuals in the industrial revolution, disciplining them, ordering them, encouraging them to keep time and instilling in them the skills and knowledge necessary for worker efficiency. For Demos this is an out-dated and unhelpful mode of education. We need citizens who 'learn to learn' and do so across their lives.[39] Knowledge has to be understood as open-ended and contextual. Education systems shouldn't aim to distil fixed blocks of information into their students but should aim to produce autonomy, responsibility and creativity. Schools and universities should open up to 'the overlapping, mutual networks of community and economic life.' Funding should be individualised, parents enabled to claim it back if they educate children at home.

But this freeing up, decentralisation and diversification of education comes with its necessary corollary. In place of 'a single public education infrastructure, governments should concentrate on establishing the standards, outcomes and underlying bases needed to support learning opportunities'.[40] Parents' home-schooling should be supported 'as long as they can demonstrate their ability to achieve the outcomes and quality standards which governments must continue to set and monitor'.[41] Decentralisation is thus accompanied by a tightening up of what the newly freed are permitted to do and, once again, the underlying motive is the need for us to shape up to the new economy. The education system described by Bentley mirrors in its structure the shape of the knowledge economy – the manner of schooling is thus as important as its content. The opening up of schools to industry and business can become a way of tying the skills taught back into the demands of economic 'necessity', making schools responsible not to society as a whole but to the demands of the economy. Already we see the possibility that extension of choice in education simply becomes an expansion of market choice with parents empowered as consumers offered choice via league tables of examination performance. The *Young Fabians* have advocated differential pricing of university tuition fees, a recent pamphlet declaring that the purpose of Higher Education is to 'produce employable people'. Certainly it should produce 'critical thinkers' but this is because 'undergraduates who have been trained to question accepted truths to construct wider principles from evidence, and to ask penetrating questions will be in high demand from any employer'. Luckily however 'the same critical skills that make these students so attractive to employers will also make them fit citizens for a democratic, free-thinking polity'.[42] Thus the danger that individual self-development becomes swamped by demands from the labour market is resolved because the two are conceived as coincident. The authors are cautious enough to insist that Higher Education 'should not be a Gradgrindian feeder to convert schoolchildren into fodder for the labour market'[43] but this marketing of higher education through differential pricing is itself part of a training for the new economy and the new world. Its very form is an exercise in consumer choice that thus encourages students to become good purchasers and sound investors in their own human capital – free floating subjects of a weightless economy.

Educational and welfare policy can thus be seen as mechanism by which the new subjects of the new economy are to be formed. They are to be individuated yet also habituated to the particular kind of autonomy that the knowledge industries can promote. They are subjects whose responsibilities for themselves and their communities must be borne through schooling oneself in permanent transformation and adaptation, as we employ an individually focused form of natural selection upon ourselves and our own attributes.

This developing discourse of subjectivity is found throughout New Labour rhetoric and policy – it is there in the exhortations to new kinds of self-oriented moral construction that are intended to reawaken our desires for communality. The New Labour individual is also part of 'one nation' and part of a community to which he or she owes obligations and within which the key characteristics of trust and cohesion can be developed. Rose places emphasis on this dimension, arguing that New Labour represents 'governance by community'.[44] The point here has been to suggest that New Labour's vision of the ideal subject is that of the reflexive individual who regards his or her self as a form of capital to be processed, refined and invested. Thus it reveals to us, once again, that part of the innovation of New Labour is to allow economistic discourses to flood across categories and come to inform everything. That is what it means now to be modern.

CONCLUSION

At one level the emergence and meaning of a movement such as New Labour (and it is not a unique development, but is mirrored across western capitalist democracies) is really quite simple. Under Capitalism, as we all know, 'all fixed fast-frozen relations with their train of ancient and venerable prejudices and opinions, are swept away, all new formed ones become antiquated before they can ossify'.[45] Such an effect has been intensified by electronic media and communications systems, which allow capitalism to function faster, as well as the direct transmission of varied visions and expectations. Under these conditions the moral orders of tradition, as Giddens knows, begin to collapse, exposing us to an ever greater sense of uncertainty yet also increasing freedom from the weight of the past. But the lack of shared, binding, principles undermines capitalism itself. It is what we used to think of as an internal contradiction. As a result the acts of committee management that used to define the bourgeois state become less feasible. Pluralisation of values and lifestyle demands new kinds of governmental strategy oriented towards facilitating the fast flow of capital and goods while developing new kinds of self-governing individuals who can exist in the new environment.

The main purpose of this chapter has been to examine and expose some of the ways in which this can be observed in the developing third way. As such, there is nothing intrinsically critical about what has been said. After all, one might well accept that the economy is an objective process, that it is and should be the alienated expression of a range of disparate human desires and that this is the best way to mediate such desires. But such a perspective should be recognised for what it is – an anti-political one that removes the political dimension from subjectivity in order to make conflict between individuals and their socio-economic environment an individual, moral, responsibility rather than a collective one. The challenge becomes that of managing change, of achieving the inevitable transition with the minimum of fuss.

It is certainly not my intention to suggest that we should ignore 'globalisation' or that we should refuse to embrace any new technology. Nor am I arguing that taking account of developing trends, thinking about how people function and so forth has no place within political life. I am not about to refuse some of those things New Labour seeks to offer – more opportunity, for example, accountability and efficiency, a dynamic economy, and a proper response to the possibilities of new technology. These are hardly terrifying prospects. Indeed new forms of technology very probably do possess the capacity to improve aspects of the lives of many millions. But they will not do so of themselves since technologies possess no capacity for self-direction. The political question is how are we to envisage these new forms of social and economic potential? What is to be the focus that guides their implementation – their capacity to liberate us from old forms of futile desire and helpless drudgery or the necessity that we attune ourselves to the economy and accept our drudgery as the price of inclusion? After all work in a telephone call centre is no less sweatshop drudgery for the fact that it is high tech.[46]

The point is not that momentous transformations should be ignored or refused but that they should be treated as transformations that we are bringing about and as if we can, and should, think about how they should be dealt with. Is it not possible that human agency is capable of forming an economic regime that seeks to satisfy human needs rather than extend desire as far as is profitable? It is to the credit of New Labour that it recognises unflinchingly that changes in the mechanisms of production and exchange are underway and that they have the potential to undermine many, perhaps all, of the ways in which we organise ourselves and our economy; that they challenge our perceptions of gender roles, the nature of families, the meaning of work; that they make possible new forms of autonomy. Only a party of the left could ever realise that capitalism can 'play a most revolutionary part'.

But these processes can go in many directions. They may continue in ways that benefit those who score most in the capitalist economy. But they are also fracturing and pluralising in ways that are both positive and negative. This is why our understanding of politics and the political nature of such change is so important. For this fragmentation and pluralisation opens up numerous spaces of dislocation where conflicts and disputes about the organisation of society and the distribution of its goods break out. It is possible that this new economy and these new kinds of social arrangements will allow us universally to recognise the intrinsically political nature of subjectivity and thus, paradoxically, its inapplicability as a universal category; that the social is nothing other than a constantly evolving network that cannot be understood by appeal to some point outside itself – tradition, God, history, economics.

To realise this the economy has to be subordinated to the political. This was indeed what 'old' socialism and social democracy forgot. It is ironic that these projects have foundered at just the point where such a vision could be made possible because the economy can no longer be conceived as a separate, isolated element within a social totality, nor as the foundation point for its structures; a historic moment where the embeddedness of economics within social life should become apparent and its reification impossible; where our rallying cry could be 'politicise or die'.

But the danger is that New Labour is beginning to conceive this pluralisation and fragmentation as necessitating an extension of forms of governance rather than the recognition of a welcome degree of ungovernability. For the former perspective, governance must become concerned with policing individual endeavours to contribute to a unified social body. For the latter, political life has to be regarded as intrinsic to all social relations, and government is about the mechanisms of allowing conflict to play itself out rather than the forging of artificial and enforced consensus.

Perhaps those behind the New Labour throne do realise this. Perhaps they think that when they have taken the iron hand and shaped us all up then they can recede, and their state can wither away. If so, this is a dangerous strategy and there is historical precedent to prove it. For the moment it is enough to remind ourselves that, 'The problem with an ideology based on a particular economic prescription or time-limited view of class is that it may be valid for one time, but quickly becomes historically redundant. Society or the economy changes and the disciples of the ideology are left trying to fit the world to the ideology and not the ideology to the world'.

By way of acknowledgement I should like to thank Wendy Wheeler for twisting my arm and making me write this as I found it interesting and worth doing in the end. I particularly acknowledge her patience in waiting for the text to be completed. While this is an original piece some of the arguments and points made in this chapter have been employed in other articles I have written on New Labour and the Third Way and the journals where these have appeared deserve acknowledgement: Alan Finlayson (1999) 'Third Way Theory', Political Quarterly, Vol. 70(3), pp. 271-279; 'New Labour and the Third Way: Re-Visioning the Economic', Renewal, Vol. 7, No. 2, 1999, pp. 42-51; 'Tony Blair and the Jargon of Modernisation', Soundings, 10, Autumn 1998 pp. 11-27.

NOTES

1. Tony Blair, *The Third Way: New Politics for a New Century*, The Fabian Society, London 1998, pp15-17.
2. Anthony Giddens, *The Third Way: The Renewal of Social Democracy*, Polity, Cambridge 1998, pp69-78.
3. See for example Andrew Gamble, 'After the Watershed, the Conservative Eclipse', in Anne Coddington and Mark Perryman (eds), *The Moderniser's Dilemma*, Lawrence and Wishart, London 1998, pp15-31; Stewart Wood, 'Constitutional Reform – living with the consequences', *Renewal*, 7, 1999 (3), pp1-10.
4. Immanuel Kant, 'An Answer to the Question: "What is Enlightenment" ', in Hans Reiss (ed), Kant, *Political Writings*, Cambridge University Press, Cambridge 1996, pp54-60.
5. Etienne Balibar, 'Subject/Citizen' in Eduardo Cadava, Peter Connor and

Jean-Luc Nancy (eds), *Who Comes After the Subject*, Routledge, London 1991.

6. Ernesto Laclau, *Politics and Ideology in Marxist Theory*, Verso, London 1979.

7. Stuart Hall, 'Gramsci and Us', *Marxism Today*, June 1987, pp16-21.

8. Michael Freeden, 'The Ideology of New Labour', *Political Quarterly*, 1999, Vol. 69, No.2.

9. Stephen Driver and Luke Martell, *New Labour: The Politics of Post-Thatcherism*, Polity, Cambridge 1997.

10. John Gray, 'After Social Democracy', Geoff Mulgan (ed), *Life After Politics*, Fontana, London 1997, p329.

11. Tony Blair, Speech to Labour Party Conference, Brighton 1997, p7.

12. Ian Hargreaves and Ian Christie (eds), *Tomorrow's Politics: The Third Way and Beyond*, Demos, London 1998, pp1-10.

13. Tony Blair, 1998, *The Third Way*, op. cit., p6-7.

14. Giddens, 1998, *The Third* Way, op. cit., p37.

15. *Ibid.*, pp99-101.

16. *Ibid.*, p64.

17. Perri 6, 'Governance by Culture', Geoff Mulgan (ed), *Life After Politics*, Fontana, London 1997, p273.

18. Anthony Giddens, 'The Social Investment State', Ian Hargreaves and Ian Christie (eds), *Tomorrow's Politics: The Third Way and Beyond*, Demos, London, p25.

19. Nikolas Rose, 'Inventiveness in Politics', *Economy and Society*, Vol. 28 (3), 1999, pp 477-478.

20. *Ibid.*, p476.

21. Tony Blair, *Socialism*, London, Fabian Society, 1994, pp4-5.

22. *Ibid.*, p5.

23. Tony Blair, Speech to Labour Party Conference, Blackpool 1994, p11.

24. Tony Blair, Speech to Labour Party Conference, Brighton 1995, p6.

25. Tony Blair, Speech to Labour Party Conference, Blackpool 1996.

26. Tony Blair, 1998, *The Third Way*, op. cit., p6-7.

27. Chantal Mouffe, 'Politics Without Adversary', *Soundings* 9, 1998. See also Alan Finlayson, 'Tony Blair and the Jargon of Modernisation', *Soundings* 10, Lawrence and Wishart, London 1998.

28. Michael Rustin, 'Editorial', *Soundings* 8, Lawrence and Wishart, London 1998.

29. Ian Hargreaves and Ian Christie, 1998, *Tomorrow's Politics*, op. cit., p1.

30. Charles Leadbeater, *Living on Thin Air: The New Economy*, London, Viking, 1999.

31. Stuart Hall, 'The Great Moving Nowhere Show' *Marxism Today*, 1998,

pp9-14; David Held, 'The Timid Tendency', *Marxism Today*, 1998, pp24-27; Eric Hobsbawm, 'The Death of Neo-Liberalism', *Marxism Today*, 1998, pp4-8. See also Doreen Massey 'Editorial', *Soundings* 7, Lawrence and Wishart, London 1998.

32. Charles Leadbeater, 1998, *Living on Thin Air*, *op. cit.*

33. Rose, 1999, 'Inventiveness in Politics', *op. cit.*, p477.

34. Tony Blair, Speech to Labour Party Conference, Bournemouth 1999, p3-4; 11.

35. DSS, *New Ambitions for Our Country: A New Contract for Welfare*, Green Paper, Cm 3805, DSS, London 1998.

36. Ruth Levitas, *The inclusive society? Social Exclusion and New Labour*, Macmillan, Basingstoke 1998.

37. Ruth Lister, *To RIO via the Third Way*, Paper presented to ESRC Research Seminar on New Labour and the Third Way in Public Services, London, 22 April 1999.

38. Tony Blair, quoted in Levitas, 1998, *The Inclusive society?*, *op. cit.*, p6.

39. Tom Bentley, 'Learning Beyond the Classroom', in Ian Hargreaves and Ian Christie (eds), *Tomorrow's Politics: The Third Way and Beyond*, Demos, London 1998.

40. *Ibid.*, p91.

41. *Ibid.*, p92.

42. Elspeth Johnson and Rana Mitter, *Students as Citizens: Focusing and Widening Access to Higher Education*, The Fabian Society, London 1998.

43. *Ibid.*, p23.

44. Rose, 1999, 'Inventiveness in Politics', *op. cit.*

45. Karl Marx, 'The Communist Manifesto'. David McLellan (ed), *Selected Writings*, Oxford University Press, Oxford 1988, p224.

46. See Sue Fernie, *(Not) hanging on the telephone: payment systems in the new sweatshops*, Centre for Economic Performance, London School of Economics and Political Science, London 1998.

'We Have Grown to Look at the Large World As Part of Us': Modernity and the Nation in Two Indian Novels of the 1930s

ASHOK BERY

In order to rethink contemporary political and cultural identities, it is necessary to negotiate a path between two powerful forces which tug in opposite directions. On the one hand, there are the processes of globalisation and internationalisation, and on the other, there are demands for local political, cultural, religious and national affiliations, demands which often result in chauvinism and violence. It is easy to condemn these latter affiliations as atavistic and to point to the terrible consequences we see them leading to in various parts of the world. But this condemnation is too simple a reaction. For one thing, it overlooks the degree to which the pull of local affiliations can be a response to the pressure of globalisation which is often seen as being synonymous with European and North American hegemony, and as leading to an undesirable homogenising of cultures. It also underestimates the potentially beneficent aspects of such affiliations and, indeed, the human need for them. As Sunil Khilnani suggests, in discussing India: 'The demands of culture, the claims for recognition, are against large federal states, but the pressures of economics are towards interconnection and expansion of scale'.[1] The problem is to find ways of accommodating both forces.

Colonial and postcolonial societies, I suggest, can offer pointers towards this process of accommodation, and hence towards rethinking notions of identity in the kind of context outlined above. There are particular reasons why these societies might offer such pointers. They have had to negotiate the meeting of cultures in circumstances which were extremely disadvantageous to them. They were forcibly brought into contact with European modernity, and had to devise means of coping with that contact and using it creatively.

Much debate in recent postcolonial theory has been concerned precisely with the creative possibilities of the colonial encounter. Two notions which have been widely discussed in these contexts are hybridisation and transculturation. The former is perhaps most familiar from the widely disseminated work of Homi Bhabha; the latter, however, may be less well known outside postcolonial theory and Latin American Studies. Mary Louise Pratt's discussion of transculturation, in her book *Imperial Eyes*, is a readily accessible account of it:

> Ethnographers have used this term to describe how subordinated or marginal groups select and invent from materials transmitted to them by a dominant or metropolitan culture. While subjugated peoples cannot readily control what emanates from the dominant culture, they do determine to varying extents what they absorb into their own, and what they use it for.[2]

As a phenomenon of what Pratt calls the 'contact zone' ('the space of colonial encounters, the space in which peoples geographically and historically separated come into contact with each other and establish ongoing relations, usually involving conditions of coercion, radical inequality, and intractable conflict'[3]), transculturation affects both the colonising power and the colonised peoples. In practice, however, there is an asymmetry: it is the colonised who have had to grapple with the process in more urgent ways. The reasons for this lie in the imbalance of cultural and material power between the two sides, which leads to the perception of one-way traffic between coloniser and colonised. As Pratt suggests:

> While the imperial metropolis tends to understand itself as determining the periphery (in the emanating glow of the civilising mission or the cash flow of development), it habitually blinds itself to the ways in which the periphery determines the metropolis – beginning, perhaps, with the latter's obsessive need to present and re-present its peripheries and its others continually to itself.[4]

On the part of the colonised, however, there can be no such blindness. There has to be a coming to terms, a process of accommodation and negotiation. For one thing, there is the sheer physical presence of the coloniser, along with the technological and military superiority which underpins it. But perhaps more crucial for the question of cultural identity is the colonial power's claim to cultural and civilisational superiority. Macaulay's 'Minute on Indian Education' is a notorious example of this, with its arrogant assertion that 'a single shelf of a good European library was worth the whole native literature of India and Arabia'.[5]

One common way of combating views such as Macaulay's is nativism – the assertion of some kind of 'pure' pre-colonial national and cultural identity. Yet such a conception of identity – while being a necessary stage in the anti-colonial struggle – has its own limits, which include the fact that it is largely a myth and that it imposes a false homogeneity on the culture in question.[6] Different solutions have to be worked out. It is this process of developing other views that I wish to consider here by focusing on two Indian novels in English.

One important qualification is necessary before proceeding. Exclusive concentration on the colonial relationship often leads to the natives getting more than a little restive at the insinuation that this is *the* dominant factor in shaping postcolonial identities, as if their societies had no history and no cultural allegiances other than those which are fashioned by, or in the struggle against, the coloniser. On the contrary, of course, the colonial relationship is only one among many relationships postcolonial societies must negotiate. In the case of India, which is my concern here, there has been a long history of cultural interchange with the outside world. In addition, there are features such as class, gender, religion, caste, region and language, which are usually of much more pressing and everyday concern than the colonial aftermath – at least to those outside the post-independence élites.

This multiplicity within Indian society is well expressed by the novelist Nayantara Sahgal:

> So is 'colonial' the new Anno Domini by which events are to be everlastingly measured? My own awareness as a writer reaches back to x-thousand B. C., at the very end of which measureless timeless time the British came, and stayed, and left. And now they're gone, and their residue is simply one more layer added to the layer upon layer of Indian consciousness. Just one more.[7]

Both the novels I discuss here are affected by the British-Indian encounter, but both are also shaped by other forces within Indian society. In exploring how they attempt to work out versions of Indian identities amidst these multiple allegiances, it is possible to draw some lessons which may be more widely applicable. Before I move on to the novels themselves, however, it is necessary to mention a few relevant points drawn from recent debates about the nation, the state and modernity in India.

Contesting definitions of the nation have been central to political activity in India during the last two decades, decades which have seen an upsurge of exclusivist movements – Hindu nationalism in Northern and Central India and regional independence movements in, for example, Punjab and Kashmir. Partly in response to such developments, academic disciplines such as history and politics have also been deeply involved in debating the nature of Indian nationhood. In this essay I want to use perspectives arising from these debates to look at two Indian novels in English – Mulk Raj Anand's *Untouchable* (1935) and Raja Rao's *Kanthapura* (1938) – which were written during an important era in modern Indian history, a phase when Gandhi exerted a powerful influence on the nationalist movement. Gandhi or the Gandhian movement feature in both novels; and, indeed, the final form of *Untouchable* owes something to Gandhi's direct intervention.[8]

A significant theme in the debates mentioned above has been the contention between what Partha Chatterjee describes as the 'hegemonic project of nationalist modernity' and the 'numerous fragmented resistances to that normalising project'.[9] The former is associated with parts of the nationalist movement and the independent Indian state, the latter with subaltern groups such as the peasantry.

The nation-state is often seen as a product of the forces of modernisation, including modes of thought as well as social and economic processes.[10] This link between modernity and the nation has been disputed by historians such as Adrian Hastings, who argues that nation-states existed before the modern era, and hence that there is no *necessary* connection between the two (although he does not 'dispute the rapid spread of nationalist ideology and nation-creating movements' from the late eighteenth century onwards).[11] Liah Greenfeld, too, asserts that 'the emergence of nationalism predated the development of every significant component of modernisation'.[12] For my purposes, however, it is enough to say that, because of the particular historical conjunctures involved, ideas of modernity became bound up in the evolving sense of Indian nationhood. European colonialism and the development of European modernity infused each other, so that along with colonialist ideologies came ideas of modernity which shaped the nineteenth-century development of the sense of India as a nation (although, as Partha Chatterjee argues at length, these ideas did not go unchallenged).[13]

The nationalist demand for a specifically Indian history played an important role in this process.[14] Dipesh Chakrabarty suggests that, during the colonial and nationalist periods, Indian history was reconceived within the framework of a 'transition narrative, of which the overriding (if often implicit) themes are those of development, modernisation, capitalism'.[15] In this narrative, Indian history until the advent of colonialism is characterised by incompleteness and absence: the absence of a rule of law, of modernity, of capitalism. There is a significant difference between colonial and nationalist versions of the transition narrative, however: the former sees Indians as a whole as backward and as needing to be brought forward into modernity, whereas, in nationalist narratives written from the perspective of the modernising élite, it is the subaltern classes who occupy that position.

The transition narrative was underpinned by institutions such as industry, technology, law and education, so that 'to think this narrative was to think these institutions at the apex of which sat the modern state, and to think the modern or the nation state was to think a history whose theoretical subject was Europe' (Chakrabarty, p8). Indian history thus became an 'episode in the universal … march of citizenship, of the nation state, of themes of human emancipation spelled out in the discourse of the European Enlightenment and after' (p17). This narrative constructs a homogeneous story into which the histories of different nations can be incorporated.

Since the institutions mentioned above are largely in the control of a modernising élite, the perspectives of this group become identified with those of the nation as a whole. 'This "mainstream", which represents in fact a small section of the society, has … been flaunted as *the* national culture', Gyanendra Pandey argues,[16] leading to a 'totalising standpoint of a seamless nationalism' which needs to be contested:

> The dominant nationalist historiography that insists on this standpoint needs to be challenged not only because of its interested use of the categories 'national,' 'secular,' and so on. It needs to be challenged also because of its privileging of the so-called 'general' over the particular, the larger over the smaller, the 'mainstream' over the 'marginal' – because of its view of India, and all of South Asia, from Delhi alone (pp50-51).

Such homogeneity, Chakrabarty suggests, can be countered through the project of 'provincializing "Europe", the Europe that modern imperialism and (third-world) nationalism have … made universal'. This requires 'the possibility of a politics and project of alliance between the dominant metropolitan histories and the subaltern peripheral pasts' (p20), of writing 'into the history of modernity the ambivalences, contradictions, the use of force and the tragedies and the ironies that attend it' (p21) – ambivalences to which the homogenising histories deny a voice.

Attention to these ambivalences will allow the formulation of definitions of the nation which are not simply modelled on European definitions.[17] An important role in this process is played by the sections of society Pandey terms 'fragments' – the peasantry, women, disadvantaged castes, tribal peoples and various other groups: 'The "fragmentary" point of view', Pandey suggests, 'resists the drive for a shallow homogenization and struggles for other, potentially richer definitions of the "nation" ...' (pp28-29).

Aims such as resisting 'shallow homogenization' and writing ambivalences into the history of modernity seem to imply interactions between modernity and other forces; but in many of these writings there is, perhaps, an animus against modernity, the state and definitions of India centred on the (Delhi-based) state. Sunil Khilnani, in contrast, argues that there must be some room for the state, some middle way between the 'monochromy of the post-imperial imagination and ... of nationalist histories of a unified people', and the 'pointillism of the new Indian historians, ever more ingeniously trawling and re-reading the archives for examples of resistance ... to the ideas of nation and state' (p3).

These are not simply theoretical matters. A multi-ethnic, multi-religious, multi-lingual political entity such as India needs *some* 'idea of India' and some kind of state. Yet there is also, and rightly, widespread suspicion of certain definitions of India – notably the militant Hindu version – and of the collusion of state agencies with these definitions.

In theory, 'the pointillism of the new Indian historians' accepts the necessity for some notion of India. When Chakrabarty refers to an 'alliance between the dominant metropolitan histories and the subaltern peripheral pasts', he allows *some* room for the 'dominant metropolitan histories' (p20); and when Pandey criticises a 'shallow homogenization', but mentions 'other, potentially richer definitions of the "nation"', he accepts *some* definition of the nation. But what form might this definition take?

Both Khilnani and Chatterjee sketch interesting answers to this question. For Khilnani, the 'layered' nature of Indian identities is crucial. In India, he argues, 'a sense of region and nation emerged together, through parallel self-definitions', and helped create the

'distinctive, layered character of Indianness' (p153).[18] The key propo-
nent of such a definition was, in Khilnani's account, Jawaharlal Nehru,
who saw India as 'a society neither of liberal individuals nor of exclusive communities or nationalities, but of interconnected differences'
(p172). To Nehru, Khilnani suggests, India appeared as a space of
ceaseless cultural mixing, its history a celebration of the soiling effects
of cultural miscegenation and accretion: 'an ancient palimpsest on
which layer upon layer of thought and reverie had been inscribed, and
yet no succeeding layer had completely hidden or erased what had been
written previously' (p169, quoting Nehru's *The Discovery of India*).

The palimpsest included modernity, and this implied the necessity of
the state (Khilnani, p171). But Nehru also had what Khilnani describes
as a 'de-centred' conception of India: 'Indian culture was so widespread all over India that no part of the country could be called the
heart of that culture' (Nehru's *Autobiography*, quoted by Khilnani,
p170).

To these ideas of 'de-centring', the 'layer' and the 'palimpsest', I
want to add Partha Chatterjee's notion of 'confederal' histories.
Chatterjee outlines the ways in which 'Indian nationalism' came to be
synonymous with 'Hindu nationalism', and then asks: 'What … is the
place of those inhabitants of India who are excluded from this nation?'
(p110). Answers to this question have generally assumed the 'idea of a
singularity of national history [which] has inevitably led to a single
source of Indian tradition, namely, ancient Hindu civilisation' (p113).
There is, however, Chatterjee suggests, a different kind of history, as
yet vestigial, which avoids this assumption of singularity. It involves
the production of 'alternative histories for the different regions of
India'. If this were to happen:

> … the center of Indian history would not need to remain confined to
> Aryavarta ['land of the Aryans', a mythic name for India, particularly its
> northern and central regions] or, more specifically, to 'the throne of
> Delhi.' Indeed, the very centrality of Indian history would then become
> largely uncertain. The question would no longer be one of 'national' and
> 'regional' histories: the very relation between parts and the whole would
> be open for negotiation. If there is any unity in these alternative histo-
> ries, it is not national but confederal (p115).

This brings me to the threshold of my discussion of the two novels,
which I wish to explore in relation to these different ways of imagining
India – 'the national', centred on northern India and a modernising

élite, and the 'de-centred' or 'layered'. *Untouchable*, I shall suggest, can be aligned with the former, *Kanthapura* with the latter. A significant aspect of both novels is the relationship between the nation and one particular 'fragment' of Indian society, the untouchables, so this issue needs particular attention.[19]

Towards the end of *Untouchable*, Mahatma Gandhi arrives in the town of Bulashah, where the novel is set, to address a public rally. In describing the crowd as it hurries to hear Gandhi, Anand depicts a heterogeneous nation unified in a common cause:

> Men, women and children of all the different races, colours, castes and creeds, were running towards the oval. There were Hindu lallas ... Kashmiri Muhammadans ... rough Sikh rustics ... fierce-looking Pathans ... black-faced Indian Christian girls ... people from the outcastes' colony ... there was everybody going to meet the Mahatma ...[20]

Later, a member of Gandhi's audience reiterates the point by remarking: 'He has made Hindu and Mussulman one' (p150).

However, this idealised picture of the nation as a unity-in-diversity needs to be placed in the context of the whole novel, which focuses on the plight of one of the most oppressed 'fragments' of Indian society, the untouchables. It describes a day in the life of its protagonist, the sweeper Bakha, a day punctuated by the routine humiliations which untouchables suffer. For instance, when Bakha accidentally bumps into someone on the street, he is abused by a crowd and slapped by the man he touched. Later, his sister is sexually harassed by a priest, and, when she resists, is accused of defiling him. In depicting such incidents, the novel represents the exclusion of untouchables from the community of the nation.

However, it also offers the hope that eventually they will be incorporated into that community – partly through the unifying power of Gandhi, but mainly through technological progress. After Gandhi's speech, Bakha overhears a conversation between two intellectuals, a lawyer and a poet, in the course of which the poet argues that since the legal system now recognizes the equality of everyone before the courts, the 'legal and sociological basis of caste' has been removed, and the only thing sustaining the caste system is occupation. He then adds:

> When the sweepers change their profession, they will no longer remain Untouchables. And they can do that soon, for the first thing we will do when we accept the machine, will be to introduce the machine which

clears dung without anyone having to handle it – the flush system. Then the sweepers can be free from the stigma of untouchability ... (p155).

The poet suggests, in effect, that the institutions of modernity – represented here by the law and technology (the flush system) – will eradicate untouchability, and so incorporate untouchables into the nation. This idea is signalled earlier in the novel through Bakha's admiration for British soldiers and his desire to imitate their clothing. With his 'strange and exotic items of dress', the narrator comments, 'he had built up a new world, which was commendable, if for nothing else, because it represented a change from the old ossified order and the stagnating conventions of the life to which he was born. He was a pioneer in his own way ... ' (p78). His clothes are an emblem of that modernity which is given more articulate expression by the poet.

The poet's argument has another side to it, however. In embracing modernity, he says, India will not lose its soul:

> We will accept and work the machine. But we will do so consciously. We can see through the idiocy of these Europeans who deified money. They were barbarians and lost their heads in the worship of gold. We can steer clear of the pitfalls, because we have the advantage of a race-consciousness 6000 years old, a race-consciousness which accepted all the visible and invisible values. We know life. We know its secret flow. We have danced to its rhythms ... We can see things clearly. We will go the whole hog with regard to machines while they nervously fumble their way through it all. We will not become slaves to gold (p153).

The poet is clearly an embodiment of this combination of Indianness with European modernity: he is dressed in 'flowing Indian robes', unlike his companion, a supercilious Oxford-educated barrister who is wearing a 'smartly-cut English suit', yellow gloves, spats and a monocle (pp150-151).

The poet's argument bears a striking resemblance to the discourses of Indian nationalism, which, in Partha Chatterjee's analysis, distinguish between the material and the spiritual, the former being 'the domain of the "outside", of the economy and of statecraft, of science and technology', the latter 'an "inner" domain bearing the "essential" marks of cultural identity'. In the former domain, the West was superior, and its achievements had to be emulated; however, 'the greater one's success in imitating Western skills in the material domain . . . the greater the need to preserve the distinctness of one's spiritual culture'(p6). This is precisely what the poet proposes. And, because of the sympathetic way he is presented (in contrast to his arrogant and Anglicised friend), it is a view that the novel seems to endorse.

However, this vision contains difficulties, since an uncertainty between two perspectives on Indian identity runs through the novel, and this is connected to two ideas of caste and untouchability. The uncertainty is between identity as 'race-consciousness', as essence, and identity as social and historical. Paralleling this is an uncertainty about whether caste and caste-consciousness are to be located in the inner domain or the outer, in the trans-historical 'race-consciousness' or in history.

The poet's remarks about the machine suggest that caste is an historical accretion which can be swept away by technological change. Yet the novel also locates caste feelings in the 'race-consciousness'. When an army NCO offers Bakha a hockey stick, the narrator comments:

> Charat Singh's generous promise had called forth that trait of servility in Bakha which he had inherited from his forefathers … the passive contentment of the bottom dog suddenly illuminated by the prospect of fulfilment of a secret and long-cherished desire (p17).

The benefactor is described as having a 'grin which symbolised six thousand years of racial and class superiority'(p16) – the same period of time with which the poet identifies Indian 'race-consciousness'. The image used here of Bakha as a 'bottom dog' is reiterated later in the novel, when he tries to look inside a temple which he is not allowed to enter:

> He soon lost his grace in the low stoop which the dead weight of years of habitual bending cast on him. He became the humble, oppressed under-dog that he was by birth, afraid of everything, creeping slowly up, in a curiously hesitant cringing movement (p58).[21]

First, his humbleness is something he has learned ('habitual bending'); then it becomes something congenital ('the … under-dog that he was by birth'). The word 'under-dog' may seem a cliché; yet his 'hesitant cringing movement' is depicted in terms which more literally evoke the movement of stray dogs. Indeed, as Arun Mukherjee has observed, animal images are repeatedly used to describe Bakha; sometimes they convey ideas of strength, but often, as in this example, they emphasise his down-troddenness.[22] These images represent Bakha as part of the natural rather than historical and social order, and thus suggest that his characteristics are essential ones.

One view of caste and untouchability implies that they are in the trans-historical 'race-consciousness'. (In this context, the coincidence of the 6000 year period specified by the narrator in depicting Charat Singh's sense of superiority and by the poet in describing India's spiritual essence is revealing. For the implication is that caste-consciousness is indeed part of the Indianness which the poet eulogises.) The other view, however, suggests that caste is a historical institution, alterable by human action. At the end of the novel, though, this contradiction is bypassed; the optimistic vision which sees untouchability disappearing under the impact of modernity evades the intractability of the problem and the possibility that protracted ideological and political activity may be involved in eradicating it.

Furthermore, since technology, like the other institutions of a European-style modernity, is in the control of the modernising élite, this solution reduces untouchables to passivity. Bakha, as Mukherjee points out, is a 'passive recipient of others' actions and discourses'. The use of the animal images discussed above is part of this representation of passivity, this 'denial of power and agency to Bakha'.[23]

Anand's narrative method reinforces this impression by making the narrator's perspective superior to the limited consciousness of Bakha. A typical example of this is the comment about Bakha's clothes, part of which was quoted earlier: 'He was a pioneer in his own way, although he had never heard of that word, and was completely unconscious that it could be applied to him' (p78).[24] This narrative method replicates the split discussed by Chakrabarty (p18) between an active 'modernising élite' (poet/ narrator) and the passive 'yet-to-be-modernised' subaltern classes (Bakha). The novel is, therefore, embedded in the transition narrative, in the discourses of an élite nationalism which, despite its claims to preserve an essential Indianness, promotes a homogeneous view of the nation, since the layered, palimpsestic, confederal dimensions of that Indianness are never unpacked.[25]

In contrast, Raja Rao's novel, which depicts the arrival of the Gandhian movement in the South Indian village of Kanthapura and the destruction of the village after conflict with the authorities, presents a 'fragmentary point of view' and gives a complex sense of versions of the nation being debated. Rao's narrative method plays an important part here. The story of *Kanthapura* is told, in the style of an oral narrative, by an old Brahmin woman from the village.[26] Events are filtered through a particular sensibility located in a particular place and social structure; the broader world outside is seen from the vantage point of the village. This is established right from the opening paragraph of the novel, when the narrator describes how local agricultural produce is transported to the coast and thence abroad: 'There, on the blue waters, they say, our carted cardamoms and coffee get into the ships the Red-men bring, and, so they say, they go across the seven oceans into the countries where our rulers live'.[27] The words 'they say' signal the perspective of someone to whom this is rumoured knowledge, some-one who has not been far from the village.

Such hearsay contrasts with the narrator's intimate inside knowl-edge of the village, as in this description:

> Our village had four and twenty houses. Not all were big like Postmaster Suryanarayana's double-storied house by the Temple Corner. But some were really not bad to look at. Our Patwari Nanjundia had a veranda with two rooms built on the old house. He had even put glass panes to the windows, which even Postmaster Suryanarayana could not boast of. Then there were the Kannayya-House people, who had a high veranda, and though the house was I know not how many generations old, it was still as fresh and new as though it had been built only yesterday (p3).

In his famous foreword to *Kanthapura*, Rao aligns this localisation with Indian narrative traditions:

> There is no village in India, however mean, that has not a rich *sthala-purana*, or legendary history, of its own. Some god or godlike hero has passed by the village – Rama might have rested under this pipal-tree, Sita might have dried her clothes, after her bath, on this yellow stone, or the Mahatma himself, on one of his many pilgrimages through the country, might have slept in this hut … In this way the past mingles with the present, and the gods mingle with men to make the repertory of your grand-mother always bright. One such story from the contemporary annals of my village I have tried to tell (pv).

An important example of this creation of a *sthala-purana* is the story of the goddess Kenchamma who 'killed a demon … that had come to ask our young sons as food and our young women as wives' (pp1-2). According to village lore, the demon's blood is the reason why the local hill is red. Motifs from this myth are recycled through the novel: the British are repeatedly referred to as 'red-men', and the demon resur-faces in modern guise as the British owner of a coffee plantation who also takes the men as food and the women as wives – in the sense that he has a captive labour force, and exercises a *droit de seigneur* over the women. Thus contemporary events merge with legends in the evolving *sthala-purana* of the village.[28]

Gyanendra Pandey's essay on the fragment speaks of how remote Delhi can appear from other parts of India and of the need to represent that remoteness rather than adopting a Delhi-based view (p51). The Kanthapuran narrative perspective means that the idea of Delhi as centre is absent. Instead of depicting the village's struggle as an offshoot of a national narrative whose true locus is elsewhere, the novel stresses the rootedness of the local conflict in the village's topography, mythology, people and narratives. This is not to say that it offers *only* a local story; a narrative of India is outlined in the myth about Gandhi mentioned in my next paragraph. However, Rao's method does allow for a sense of the intermeshing of the regional and the national, of the 'layering' of Indian identities.

Rao also fragments the novel by multiplying perspectives and voices through embedded narratives, a common technique of oral story-telling. Inserted within the old woman's story are songs, myths, gossip, hearsay. At the beginning of the novel, Gandhi is mythologised by an itinerant storyteller as an incarnation of Siva sent to free India, the god Brahma's 'beloved daughter' (p12), from those who 'have come from across the seas and the oceans to trample on our wisdom and to spit on virtue itself'(p11). The novel is also punctuated by songs – ritualistic, work-related, political (e.g., pp3, 58, 98-99, 147, 161). At the climax of the villagers' struggle, for instance, the crowd starts singing a song which draws inspiration from a heroine of the 1857 uprising, the Rani [Queen] of Jhansi:

> O lift the flag high,
> Lift it high like in 1857 again,
> And the Lakshmi of Jhansi,
> And the Moghul of Delhi,
> Will be ours again (p174)

These narrative fragments help to create a sense of the nation's dialogic nature, of a multiplicity of histories, an effect summarised by Gyanendra Pandey:

> What the historians call a 'fragment' – a weaver's diary, a collection of poems by an unknown poet (… creation myths and women's songs, family genealogies and local traditions of history) – is of central impor-

tance in challenging the state's construction of history, in thinking other histories and marking those contested spaces through which particular unities are sought to be constituted and others broken up (p50).

Rao's method, then, contrasts with the monologic narrative perspective of Anand and with the singularity which is built into the 'hegemonic project of nationalist modernity'. This contrast between singularity and multiplicity is also evident in their depictions of caste. *Untouchable* tends to represent the upper castes' feelings of superiority in a monolithic way. Even the occasional acts of kindness by caste Hindus towards untouchables are invariably accompanied by condescension. Although Rao's narrator is a Brahmin, which means that, as in Anand's novel, the untouchables are again viewed from an external perspective, we are given more of a sense of contested positions. Thus the local Gandhian leader Moorthy's contact with untouchables arouses opposition from other members of the upper castes, including his own mother. Indeed, in the beginning, he himself is uneasy about possible pollution through such contact. Early in the novel, the narrator describes the geographical segregation of the different castes and comments: 'Of course you wouldn't expect me to go to the Pariah quarter' (p5); yet she later comes to take the presence of the untouchables as members of the community almost for granted: 'When he went up to the Promontory and blew the conch, people came – men, women, children – and the pariahs and the weavers and the potters all seemed to feel they were of one caste, one breath' (p130).

However, the picture is by no means one of idealised unity. There is the upper-caste unease I have mentioned; others resist the Gandhian movement for material reasons – a religious leader who benefits from British gifts of land, for instance, or businessmen from Bombay who buy up the villagers' property. *Kanthapura* offers a complex picture of conflicts between and within different sections of society, of the various interests at stake, and of their differing perspectives.

Kanthapura also represents the untouchables as active participants in the nationalist movement, and here it differs from Anand's novel, in which Bakha is largely passive. Yet, to borrow a phrase used about the representation of women in this novel, there is only a 'limited emancipation' for the untouchables – more limited even than that of the women.[29] Though the untouchables are shown as active, they are not – unlike the women – given a capacity to represent themselves. They remain objects rather than subjects of the narrative, since the story is recounted by a Brahmin woman.

It should be noted also that *Kanthapura* largely endorses a Gandhian perspective, and that Gandhi's ideas on caste were strongly disputed by some untouchables, notably their most important leader, B.R. Ambedkar, who said that they should 'Beware of Mr Gandhi',[30] on the grounds that Gandhi saw a reformed caste system as a valuable social arrangement. For Ambedkar, however, 'without abolition of caste there is no hope of abolition of Untouchability'.[31] This is a perspective which remains occluded within the novel. Also missing are non-Hindu perspectives. The novel is rooted in specifically Hindu mythologies, and the one Muslim character, the policeman Badé Khan, is presented unsympathetically. In pointing to these occlusions, I am not suggesting that Rao should have provided some kind of 'balance' and given voice to this or that 'fragment' of Indian society. I am merely noting that the narrative design of *Kanthapura* has particular effects.

Despite these absences, though, the novel does articulate, to varying degrees, the subjectivities of 'fragments' such as women, the peasantry and the region. In addition to these local identifications, its 'layers' include influences from the world outside India. There is room also for elements of European modernity, which becomes part of the Indian palimpsest – notably in the form of socialist ideologies. Early in the novel, for instance, one of the characters recounts a somewhat idealised and mythicised view of the Soviet Union, prompting an untouchable to comment: 'So in that country pariahs and brahmins are the same ... strange country, Mother' (p32). Towards the end, the young local Gandhian leader Moorthy, who has helped to initiate the struggle in Kanthapura, adopts a Nehruvian socialist position, arguing that 'the Mahatma is a noble person, a saint, but the English will know how to cheat him, and he will let himself be cheated' (p188). The issue, he suggests, is not just one of independence from the British; rather, 'It is the way of the masters that is wrong' (p188). For this reason he supports Jawaharlal Nehru. Weaving together ancient Hindu mythology and twentieth-century socialism, he asserts that:

> Jawaharlal is like a Bharatha [in the ancient epic *The Ramayana*, Bharatha is the loyal younger half-brother of the exiled hero Rama] to the Mahatma, and he, too, is for non-violence and he, too, is a Satyagrahi, but he says in Swaraj [self-rule, i.e., independence] there shall be neither the rich nor the poor. And he calls himself an 'equal distributionist' ... (p189).

Kanthapura, then, seems to me to align itself with the layered ways of reimagining Indian history discussed earlier, as opposed to two different unitary conceptions: 'a history whose theoretical subject was Europe', on the one hand, and the history of Aryavarta on the other. This mythic territory was important for Indian nationalism but also dangerously animates virulent forms of Hindu supremacism. Nevertheless, as was suggested earlier in this essay, some vaguer, non-exclusivist version of the notion of Aryavarta, under a different name and stripped of its Hindu and northern trappings, may well be indispensable to the viability of any Indian state, given its multiplicity of ethnic, religious and linguistic groupings.

Sunil Khilnani speaks of the 'idea of India' being constituted in a struggle to accommodate contrary pulls between a myth of national unity and India's actual diversity (pp194-5). *Kanthapura* goes some way towards a fictional representation of such a process of accommodation. In the myth about Gandhi at the beginning of the novel, the 'idea of India' is present in the form of Bharatha, the 'enslaved daughter' (p11) of the god Brahma (although this remains a Hindu myth). Yet the novel's layered perspectives, which include aspects of European modernity, contrast with *Untouchable*, which embodies the more centralised focus of the 'transition narrative' and sets up a rigid and stereotypical opposition between what is European (the material) and what is Indian (the spiritual).

Kanthapura picks out a route amongst the different forces impinging on the society it depicts – modernity, internationalism, the colonial influence, nationalism, as well as demands for local identities of various sorts. Perhaps the lessons it can offer are best summed up in the author's foreword:

> We are all instinctively bilingual, many of us writing in our own language and English. We cannot write like the English. We should not. We cannot write only as Indians. We have grown to look at the large world as part of us (pv).

The lack of any colonial rancour in that last sentence: 'We have grown to look at the large world as part of us', the refusal to retreat into insular notions of identity, the sense of ease in being both Indian *and* in some way connected to the world – these are ways of negotiating the dilemmas with which I began this essay.

NOTES

1. Sunil Khilnani, *The Idea of India*, Hamish Hamilton, London 1997, p194. Subsequent references to this book will be given in the text.

2. Mary Louise Pratt, *Imperial Eyes: Travel Writing and Transculturation*, Routledge, London 1992, p6.

3. *Ibid.*

4. *Ibid.*

5. Macaulay, 'Indian Education: Minute of the 2nd of February, 1835', in *Macaulay: Poetry and Prose*, selected by G.M. Young, Rupert Hart-Davis, London 1967, p722.

6. For a classic critique of nativism, see the chapter 'On National Culture' in Frantz Fanon's *The Wretched of the Earth*, Constance Farrington (trans), Grove Press, New York 1968, pp206-248.

7. Nayantara Sahgal, 'The Schizophrenic Imagination', in *From Commonwealth to Post-Colonial*, Anna Rutherford (ed), Dangaroo Press, Sydney, Mundelstrup and Coventry 1992, p30.

8. For Gandhi's reaction to an earlier version of *Untouchable*, see Mulk Raj Anand, 'On the Genesis of *Untouchable*: A Note', in *The Novels of Mulk Raj Anand*, R.K. Dhawan (ed), Prestige Books, Delhi 1992, pp9-12. The wider influence of Gandhi on Indian literature is discussed by, among others, Sisir Kumar Das, *A History of Indian Literature 1911-1956: Struggle for Freedom: Triumph and Tragedy*, Sahitya Akademi, New Delhi 1995, chap. 3, especially pp64-80, and K.R.S. Iyengar, *Indian Writing in English*, 5th edition, Sterling Publishers, New Delhi 1985, pp248-294.

9. Partha Chatterjee, *The Nation and its Fragments: Colonial and Postcolonial Histories*, Princeton University Press, Princeton 1993, p13.

10. For instance, Benedict Anderson, *Imagined Communities: Reflections on the Origin and Spread of Nationalism*, 1983; 2nd edition, Verso, London 1991; Ernest Gellner, *Nations and Nationalism*, Blackwell, Oxford 1983; Eric Hobsbawm, *Nations and Nationalism since 1780*, Cambridge University Press, Cambridge 1990. For a survey of the debate on nationalism and modernity, see Anthony D. Smith, *Nationalism and Modernism: A Critical Survey of Recent Theories of Nations and Nationalism*, Routledge, London 1998.

11. Adrian Hastings, *The Construction of Nationhood: Ethnicity, Religion and Nationalism*, Cambridge University Press, Cambridge 1997, p11.

12. Liah Greenfeld, *Nationalism: Five Roads to Modernity*, Harvard University Press, Cambridge, Mass. 1992, p21.

13. The argument that the sense of India developed in the nineteenth century has been made by Sudipta Kaviraj, 'The Imaginary Institution of India', in *Subaltern Studies VII: Writings on South Asian History and Society*, Partha Chatterjee and Gyanendra Pandey (eds), Oxford University Press, Delhi 1993, p1, and Khilnani, *Idea of India*, pp154-155. The challenge to European ideas of modernity is one of the central themes of Chatterjee's

The Nation and its Fragments.

14. On the development of Indian nationalist historiography, see Chatterjee, *The Nation and its Fragments*, chaps. 4 and 5, and Ranajit Guha, *An Indian Historiography of India: A Nineteenth-Century Agenda and its Implications*, K.P. Bagchi, Calcutta 1988.

15. Dipesh Chakrabarty, 'Postcoloniality and the Artifice of History: Who Speaks for "Indian" Pasts?', *Representations* 37, Winter 1992, p4. Further references to this essay will be given in the text.

16. Gyanendra Pandey, 'In Defense of the Fragment: Writing About Hindu-Muslim Riots in India Today', *Representations* 37, Winter 1992, p28. Further references to this essay will be given in the text.

17. See Chatterjee, *Nation and its Fragments, op. cit.*, p5.

18. On the relationship between the sense of the region and the sense of the nation in India, see also Kaviraj, 'Imaginary Institution', pp22-25. The term 'layer' needs to be treated with some caution, since there is a danger of assuming that the earlier ('deeper') layers are in some way more fundamental or essential to Indian identities, a view which leads to the conception of Indianness assumed in Anand's novel. For a succinct critique of the 'layer' model applied in this sense to language, see Arvind Krishna Mehrotra's introduction to *The Oxford India Anthology of Twelve Modern Indian Poets*, Oxford University Press, Delhi 1992, pp5-6. However, Khilnani does not appear to be using the term 'layer' in this sense of depth, so I shall, on occasions, borrow it myself as a convenient term.

19. The term 'untouchable' is used infrequently today, the preferred term being 'Dalit'. However, since it figures in the title and text of Anand's novel, I continue to use it here. For a discussion of the pros and cons of the various terms which have been used to designate this group of Indian society, see Oliver Mendelsohn and Marika Vicziany, *The Untouchables: Subordination, Poverty and the State in Modern India*, Cambridge University Press, Cambridge 1998, pp2-5.

20. Mulk Raj Anand, *Untouchable*, Penguin, Harmondsworth 1935, 1940, reissued 1986, p136. Further references to the novel will be given in the text.

21. Bakha is compared to a dog on p42 as well.

22. Arun P. Mukherjee, 'The Exclusions of Postcolonial Theory and Mulk Raj Anand's "Untouchable": A Case Study', *Ariel*, 22, no. 3, July 1991, p37. The use of animal imagery is noted also by Susie Tharu, 'Decoding Anand's Humanism', *Kunapipi* 4, no. 2, 1982, p37.

23. Mukherjee, 'Exclusions', *op. cit.*, pp37, 38. Bakha's passivity is also noted by Teresa Hubel, *Whose India? The Independence Struggle in British and*

Indian Fiction and History, Leicester University Press, London 1996, pp174-175.

24. For another, more extended, example, see pp94-95. The distance between the writer or narrator of *Untouchable* and the people and places represented in the novel is commented on by Mukherjee, 'Exclusions', *op. cit.* p36, Hubel, *Whose India?*, *op. cit.* p170, and Tharu, 'Decoding Anand's Humanism', *op. cit.* pp32-36.

25. Suresht Renjen Bald argues that 'paternalistic élitism' is a feature of both Anand's novels and his political ideas. See his essay 'Politics of a Revolutionary Elite: A Study of Mulk Raj Anand's Novels', *Modern Asian Studies* 8, 1974, pp473-489. Bald develops this view in his book *Novelists and Political Consciousness: Literary Expression of Indian Nationalism 1919-1947*, Chanakya Publications, Delhi 1982, chap. 5, especially pp115-126, 131-134. He also suggests (pp1-6) that there were forces producing élitism in writers of Anand's generation generally. Bald stresses the Leninist provenance of Anand's élitism.

26. For a discussion of the narrator of *Kanthapura*, see Meenakshi Mukherjee, *The Twice Born Fiction: Themes and Techniques of the Indian Novel in English*, Heinemann, New Delhi 1971, pp38-40.

27. Raja Rao, *Kanthapura*, 1938; Oxford University Press, Delhi (1938) 1989, p1. Further references to the novel will be given in the text.

28. For further discussion of *Kanthapura* as a *sthala-purana*, see Mukherjee, *Twice Born Fiction*, *op. cit.* pp144-147.

29. See Senath W. Perera, 'Towards a Limited Emancipation: Women in Raja Rao's "Kanthapura" ', *Ariel* 23, no. 4, October 1992, pp99-110.

30. B.R. Ambedkar, *What Congress and Gandhi Have Done to the Untouchables*, 2nd edition, Thacker and Co., Bombay 1946, p250. Although this book appeared after the two novels discussed here, Ambedkar's conflict with Gandhi preceded the publication of the novels. For an account of Ambedkar's views and his disagreements with Gandhi, see Mendelsohn and Vicziany, *The Untouchables*, *op. cit.* pp100-117. Ambedkar is also discussed by Mukherjee, 'Exclusions', *op. cit.*, pp39-41 and Hubel, *Whose India?*, *op. cit.* chapter 5, especially pp149-150, 156-161, 177-178

31. Ambedkar, *What Congress and Gandhi*, *op. cit.* p271.

Getting Some Distance On The News: Simon Armitage, Douglas Oliver and the WTO

PETER MIDDLETON

Douglas Oliver died in April 2000. I would like to dedicate this essay to his memory.

What part does the daily influx of news play in the political lives of those of us who are not full-time professional politicians with other more direct sources of political information? One immediate answer is that it presents us with the task of sorting the material by degrees of relevance to our existing political commitments (to an environmental campaign, party membership, union work or more dispersed activities, including jobs). We then need to respond to some of what we have heard, probably by adjusting the plans and actions entailed by those commitments in conjunction with the groups with which we work. Put as abstractly as this it sounds reasonable enough. Looked at more closely, the daily life of news is much more cacophonous, disorienting, and cognitively fuzzy. There is so much news (who could read all the newspapers – or even one from end to end – and listen to the radio and television reports, then click on their websites to see if anything was missed?), and it is contradictory and discontinuous, spinning with ideological bias. So much news, so little time. And this is only half the story. Responding to the news from within our contingent circumstances is also part of the problem. One of the most vivid accounts of the problem is set out by the poet Douglas Oliver in a retrospective preface to a sequence called *The Diagram Poems* (1979). At the time he is writing about, Oliver had a professional interest in the news as well as a more ordinary political interest, but this only makes him exceptionally aware of the problem of the news: what can the political subject do with it?

> If any urban guerillas tried not to deserve the label 'terrorist' it was the Tupamaros in Uruguay, savagely put down by the military governments of the 1970s … We used to get their stories on the English Desk night shift at Agence France-Presse in Paris; they would be wired through by AFP's local stringer, translated into French and English by the subs, and the next you knew the story would be sold on the streets of news-voracious Tokyo: orchestrated by the Spanish-speaking Tupamaros for maximum heroic effect, transformed into a French news story, into an English news story's very different rhetoric, and finally into the columns, say, of the *Asabi Shimbun*, in whatever rhetoric the Japanese use. At HQ you were in the middle of the news-making, but were not a pure element of transmission. You were a little drunk from a visit to 'Les Finances' on a corner of the Bourse, an all-night bar … back upstairs in the large foreign-service room, you'd look at the Uruguay copy, try to understand happenings thousands of miles away, and simultaneously might be thinking in a maudlin way about a son who'd died two years before, or about the difficulty of political judgement. This too entered the occasion of the story for you.[1]

This prefatory account of a largely forgotten Latin American revolutionary movement is a vivid instance of the dilemma of all political subjects in contemporary Western democracies. Politics demands judgement, and judgement always operates under what might seem to the political theorist imperfect, and potentially correctable, conditions. Whatever your proximity to events, their publicity always arrives already interpreted by news organisations whose journalists are struggling with incomprehension and distraction, and it occurs in material forms and national rhetorics which diagram the information into simplified abstraction, only to be further mediated by the recipient's weaknesses of cognition, failures of memory, interruptive moods, centrifugal emotions, and anomic bodily states. But can such tensions be neutralised into an ideal objective receptivity?

I shall argue that any viable contemporary politics must begin by recognising the conditions under which citizens make political decisions and contribute to policy-forming public debates. This need not mean an acceptance of the imperfections of the news media themselves, nor a licence for self-indulgence. Improving the reliability, quantity, and scope of the news would help create more democratic public spheres. Education, concentration, a willingness to listen and, above all, an attentiveness to distant news stories are ethical tasks for the citizen who takes political responsibility seriously. But the muddle of daily life in history will not go away, and we need therefore to reconsider the conditions that it imposes on our political engagement. One starting point might be that political subjects need some distance from the deluge of new history that they are dealing with all the time, a modulated distance of the kind Theodor Adorno opposed to positivism:

> Only at a remove from life can the mental life exist, and truly engage the empirical. While thought relates to facts and moves by criticizing them, its movement depends no less on the maintenance of distance ... Essential to it is an element of exaggeration, of over-shooting the object, of self-detachment from the weight of the factual, so that instead of merely reproducing being it can, at once rigorous and free, determine it. ... The unbarbaric side of philosophy is its tacit awareness of the element of irresponsibility, of blitheness springing from the volatility of thought, which forever escapes what it judges.[2]

He is careful to avoid the charge that this is a form of superior detachment, or a method that will inevitably yield more profound insights than a factual record, saying that this distance does not insulate the thinker; it is a 'zone of tension' in which what matters most is the 'delicacy and fragility of thinking'. Rigorous thought is not usually represented in this manner, as an uncertain, tentative edging along the limits of articulation with attention to meanings glimpsed poetically beyond strict referentiality. Adorno is talking about political philosophy but his idea of distance might help approach this question of how to re-imagine a radical engagement with the news, not least because his formulation of the negativities of distance so strongly suggests certain cultural practices, such as poetry.

Ezra Pound said that poetry was news that stays news. In this paper I shall explore the condition of the political subject by looking at a recent news story – the World Trade Organisation talks in Seattle – which is timely for anyone interested in the changing conditions of democracy, political information and political struggle as globalisation increases, and then at the work of two British poets, Simon Armitage and Douglas Oliver, for whom poetry is an opportunity to transform the news into the beginnings of a responsive political practice. They write with varying degrees of success about the dominance of the news in contemporary cultural memory, by acknowledging the fragility of political thought as the news mingles with the ideas, emotions, and fantasies which it elicits in its respondents. The WTO also provides a continuing reminder of the changing situation of the political subject, and of the scale of news events to which a local political response is required.

REPRESENTING POLITICS: NEWS OF THE WTO

The World Trade Organisation meeting in Seattle in late 1999, and the riots that it evoked from those who believe it practices global government without democratic accountability, surged into the headlines for a short while raising these issues. For British readers these were events happening halfway across the world, yet the deliberations might affect the growing of genetically modified (GM) crops here and otherwise alter European policy. There was both too little information (just what is this organisation and what influence does it have?) and too much (technical discussions of import regulations and sanctions). What should we do with it all, and how begin to incorporate its evidently important influence into our political thinking? The criticism that the WTO itself refuses dialogue with anyone outside its governmental representatives brings into sharp focus the wider issue of one-way information, so evident in the news media generally.

Coverage began for many newspaper readers with articles like that in *The Guardian* in November 1999. 'World trade chief tries to head off biggest protest since Vietnam' was the front page headline of an interview with Mike Moore, the new chairman of the WTO, who was busy defending its record to the news media in the knowledge that the FBI was expecting anything up to 150,000 demonstrators to arrive in Seattle.[3] Emollient words might help. This prospective news was important to anyone concerned, in the words of Douglas Oliver, with the way Britain is now 'obsessed with free markets, following the gleam of international power blocs, the EU, the WTO'.[4]

The information came in the usual tangle of technicalities, breathless awe, new names, and exoticism which is the news, although at least the print medium allowed for some complexity of presentation. Moore argued that the organisation is now much more responsive to the heterogeneous and competing demands of less wealthy countries than before, and provides a necessary set of rules for international trade which would be chaotic and would lead to dangerous conflict without them. His answers all emphasised the need for the organisation to be both democratic and representative: 'We need to develop institutions that represent the sovereign will of the people. In the end what happens at the WTO depends on sovereign governments. I get ratty when people say that it only represents the will of ruling élites'. Here in these three sentences are references to political issues which extend beyond the WTO and its organised opposition in Seattle; these are the problems of how to both theorise and negotiate effective political representation of the interests of those who struggle for representation even within their own local polities. His deft elision of any reference to institutions (including cultural institutions) which already mediate within the public sphere, and his conflation of himself with the organisation, are also reminders of how difficult it is for left-wing political campaigners to elicit the terms on which political struggle can be understood. In these sentences he first acknowledges the need to create new political structures to represent what he calls the 'sovereign will of the people', because existing forms at best represent only a partial 'sovereign will' and are in many areas of international politics simply absent; and then contradicts the invitation to nominate existing nongovernmental institutions, or create new ones, by locating such structures elsewhere. Such institutions do after all already exist: they are called 'governments'. They have meta-governmental councils, such as the WTO, which fulfill the role of representing the will of the people, even if this will is mediated through the national governments. Rhetorically, he therefore makes the WTO more than just a shiny new bloc of existing governments by proposing that it also stands for a future political system which will be fully democratic in ways in which the existing governments are not.

How does he resolve this contradiction between the two images? His display of emotion does the trick. The ratty anger at critics of the political institutions through which the WTO operates is meant to be a manifestation of that 'sovereign will of the people' which denounces the critics, not the governments, as their enemies. Representing a collective political will in words and images is difficult; political affect works better and resolves a logical contradiction. It is a strategy endemic to the media image of the political process, and one reason why such cultural practices as poetry might be relevant to a rethinking of the politics of news reception – these linguistic practices are particularly well-attuned to the nuances and implications of social affect.

Coverage began by reporting a display of pre-emptive tactical anger. A few days later the demonstrators are fulfilling the newspaper prophecies out on the streets of Seattle and displaying their own counter-affect through words and actions, which include performances of anger at injustice – attacks on global store chains and journalists. The

WTO abandons its opening ceremonies, as if these rituals now lack legitimacy, and supposedly goes straight into the negotiations, while 'black masked protestors overturn newsstands' and the police, dressed like actors from a Hollywood science fiction epic on location, in layers of black uniform, bulked out with backpacks, cables, strange guns, shields, unidentifiable gadgets, and more pockets than even the most fashionable trousers, enter the public arena of the street with pepper spray, tear gas and sting bullets. (*Guardian*, 1.12.99, p5) News media record it all, and an especially interesting assessment of the situation is attributed to Moore: 'It is difficult to maintain a dialogue if people do foolish things that disrupt the flow of information'.[5] The ambiguity of just who ought to be in 'dialogue' is deliberate. Although he must have meant the negotiations between delegates, he made it sound as if those out on the streets could participate in this political process if only they would allow the free flow of information by shutting up, although the reality was that not even journalists were allowed into the key negotiating sessions: this was a dialogue of nations.

The demonstrators were only the most visible sign of a widespread unease about this recent creation. The WTO was formed in 1995 as a more effective global regulator of trade, to succeed GATT (General Agreement on Tariffs and Trade), and from the start has attracted criticism for its lack of democratic accountability. Its power to enforce trade rules and to overrule the laws and import controls of member states has been especially worrying to many non-governmental organisations who argue that they and the people they represent are excluded from the decision-making process. In practice, it is a technocratic organisation, 'a transnational epistemic community of trade experts'.[6] The high level of expertise required to understand the negotiations, coupled with the need for secrecy during delicate diplomatic adjustments, as well as the guiding principle that the organisation is a kind of parliament for nations rather than a global citizenry, led to the neglect of any structure within the organisation for making possible dialogue between the organisation and either individuals or NGOs such as environmental or aid movements.

Even countries that might have seemed likely allies of the new social movements resist their increased participation because they fear that, if such groups are allowed a voice in negotiations, that voice may well speak in favour of the North (from which almost all the campaigns begin), and may create a potential opening for powerful business interests to demand their own forms of representation. Even commentators who perceive a democratic deficit in the WTO believe that a fundamental issue is therefore the democratic nature of the social movements themselves. Marc Williams writes:

> If social movement organisations are to constitute an alternative to the interests of state and capital, then they must develop intra-organisational and inter-organisational accountability. Specifically, the nodal points of the movements which lobby the WTO directly need to establish mechanisms that give a voice in campaign strategies to local communities, national associations, and members of the movement lacking in the skills or finance to send representatives to Geneva.[7]

Williams doesn't see these as insuperable obstacles; nor does he think they are easy to achieve. The new conditions necessary for global democracy to emerge remain largely unarticulated and unimagined.

Obviously the campaigners did not expect to be granted access to the delegates and the decision-making process in Seattle if only they would settle for dialogue; at best they could hope to open discussions with their own political representatives in their own states and countries. But both sides know this. What is revealing about Moore's response is that he stigmatises the demonstrators not as anti-democratic but as obstacles to the flow of information. Information and its distribution are the pivotal issues. We can only guess what he means by information, but it seems likely that he means the pure flow of information about issues under negotiation that ought to be transmitted without any foolish interruptions, through the news media to their readers, viewers and listeners, and he is dismayed that instead of reporting on the gains for low-wage economies or access to world markets, the journalists will be interested only in riot attacks on Starbucks. Moore presupposes that possession of information is tantamount to democratic participation, but the actions of the protestors suggest that more than mere receptivity is needed. The protesters want their own representations of global politics to find their way into that same flow of news, providing a context for newsworthy images of smashed windows, so that we newspaper readers will see the slogan 'This organic farmer opposes the WTO', and hear some fragments of their response.[7] It will be dialogue of a kind.

Moore assumes that the flow of information through the news media is sufficient for democracy, and anything that inhibits it undermines the political process. Let us examine this familiar and seemingly reasonable idea in more detail. Stanley Cavell offers a good starting point, when he makes a basic point about the danger of political anaesthesia due to information overload: 'It seems that the more total our access to information becomes, the more complete becomes our ignorance of why it is given us, over what it means, over whom to believe, and over what fruitful action we could take on its basis'.[8] Is this the fault of the media themselves? It might seem that the one thing uniting both the WTO and the demonstrators was belief in the theory of news as information; they only differed as to what constituted the needful information. We readily imagine that more information, better news media, more informed reporting and more journalistic integrity, greater governmental commitment to an informed citizenry and legislation for freedom of information, would of themselves create a better politics. Or does our relation to the news really work in this way? Can it not also disenfranchise us with its contextless immensity and fractured presentation, however informed we might be about the fine detail of such negotiations as those at the WTO? Perhaps Moore was right for the wrong reasons, and the protestors were interrupting and transmuting the flow of WTO information for reasons that might bear further investigation.

Let's take the WTO reports, as they extended across the newspapers, as a further step towards considering the condition of the political subject interpellated by the news. When the WTO talks were concluding I tried to gather a wider picture of how events had been reported in the British press, and found that there was so much other news that I could not find any references to the WTO talks in Seattle in many of the newspapers now that the demonstrations had been scaled down. It seemed that the demonstrators had been broadly correct in their assessment of what was needed to gain media attention. Babies are being 'butchered' without their parents' permission in the *Daily Mail*.[9] *The Sun* reports that William Hague has been 'humiliated' after sacking a minister by pager for his refusal to uphold the shadow cabinet position of support for the law against 'promoting homosexuality', and compounds the humiliation by giving the story the smallest possible space opposite its page three image of Jennifer Lopez.[10] Nelson Mandela and Princess Diana are chosen by *Daily Mirror* readers as the 'most inspirational man and woman of the millennium' – although they have to compete with other inspirational figures in the same issue: a thirteen year-old boy who is the father of twins, Eamon Holmes who cried on morning television at the sight of his children, and a man who jumped off a statue of Jesus outside Rio de Janeiro ('I will remember it a lifetime ... there was a religious element and I really felt moved ... I will never experience anything like it again').[11] More grief and inspiration for the reader to experience follows a few pages later in a story in which Russia figures briefly as the background to the tragic romance of Mikhail Gorbachev's grief for his wife Raisa. At the bottom of the second column this story mentions in passing that 'he oversaw the dismantling of communism', and later that he may have new political ambitions, but ends with the man in mourning: 'something, something in the eyes, is gone' (p23). What is recent Russian history compared to this story of loss? I look in vain in the tabloids for any reference to the concluding stages of the WTO talks.

At least the broadsheets kept the story going, although in their reports too there is a similar dissonance and sensationalism. The *Financial Times* reports that EU ministers had reversed a decision by EU commissioners to collaborate with a WTO working-party on biotechnology because the ministers suspected that it would be used to 'ride roughshod over member states' policies in a very sensitive area'.[12] Their columnist Philip Stephens calls the demonstrators 'confused', although he conceded that they had some justification for sharing a general confusion due to the way no-one can 'see the lines of account-ability in the new system'.[13] *The Independent* manages to talk to a few protestors, and report their views. One calls himself an 'art criminal', and another, an environmental activist, Julie Pike, speaks lucidly about the dangers of lifting all logging restrictions in the Northwest and turn-ing the 'region into one big commodity the corporations can make money out of'.[14] The *Guardian*'s main interest is now in the cleverness of their reporter who is illicitly inside the WTO talks in Seattle and can therefore report from 'the secret world of the deal makers'.[15] The odd thing about this secret world is that it uses the language and theory of the open society, a liberalism that we might recognise from John Rawls or Jürgen Habermas. Our clandestine reporter beachcombs some of the contextless detritus of dialogue washed up in his dark corner: 'our only objective is to launch negotiations [EU] ... countries are concerned about civil society ... we can resolve those issues [Japan] ... investment should be in the next round ... a modest and humble approach [Korea] ... no consensus exists [Hong Kong/China] ... important not to prejudge the issues ... agreement must be reached at a certain point ... listen to civil society [USA] ... real confusion in many of our countries following the [failure] of the MAI negotiations' [Australia]. These opaque utterances are further occluded by the jour-nalist's extended portraits of sleepy, amorous, pretentious and gum-chewing delegates, fighting off yawns and boredom. On later pages are familiarly emotive headlines and reports of the WTO speaking of 'outrage as EU cedes regulation of GM foods ... embarrassing diplomatic siege ... regulation of trade in biotechnology ... soften the blow to EU members ... the strength of feeling of European ministers ... consumer outrage ... biosafety protocol ... predicted political outrage'. The broadsheet newspapers thankfully return to what they clearly perceive as their job of providing a good range of emotional variety for consumption, perhaps not as rich as the *Daily Mirror*, but enough to sustain this remote and abstract fare.

The Guardian also reports that marchers were no longer fighting 'running battles with the police'; instead they were marching to the chant of 'this is what democracy looks like'. Their gesture towards the WTO (where presumably the delegates were exchanging their ritual citations from Western political theory as they divided up the future wealth of trade amongst the most powerful nations) is intriguing, but we might wonder whether what democracy 'looks like' is more what this entire event 'looks like' to us, as we receive the newspaper and television reports, than some more abstract or symbolic image of a nation or a parliament. The news in tabloids and broadsheets projects a series of narratives, images and affects with which readers are encouraged to cathect, identify and opinionate, imagining themselves at the helm of the WTO, a graffiti attack, Russia, South Africa, the Conservative Party, the monarchy, breakfast television, or simply Public Opinion condemning human dissection. The WTO's own reports and competing newspaper stories typify the volume of information we call the news: its complexity and incompleteness, its turbulent flow, and above all the difficulty of even beginning to work out what it means, whom to believe and what political action is called for.

Coverage didn't really begin with the news of Mike Moore's anticipation of demonstrations against the WTO. Every encounter with the news is a new beginning from imperfect conditions of care and distortion, and our politics must take account of these imperfections. It is sometimes the 'foolish things', those that don't just go with the flow of information, but impede, reconfigure, translate or re-imagine it, which offer some of the most useful insights into our changing political condition within global capitalism and the new cultures of information. My examples will be textual distortions of the news produced by poets, whose very medium seems marginal and interruptive of discursive clarity. Poems written in response to the news would seem indeed 'foolish things' even without the fantasies and affects they are infused with. I shall argue that such poetries explore the implications of the stream of news for future political activism in ways that we should not ignore.

Since readers will be expecting it, let me make the obvious pun: these foolish things, poems on the politics of news, do remind us of the collective 'you' of possible public spheres. In its tiny way, this predictable textual play on the WTO director's words points to the kinds of creative appropriation of the news that have the power to extend public spheres enough to include what otherwise might remain outside altogether.

THE POLITICAL FOOLISHNESS OF POETRY
The company running the Millennium Dome recently commissioned the well-known poet Simon Armitage, who is published by the leading commercial publisher of poetry, Faber and Faber, to write a millennium poem. The result was a long sequence, *Killing Time* (1999), about the most newsworthy events of 1999 and by implication, how living within the public culture of news makes demands on our political and moral imagination. He chose the topic because ours is an:

> age of cynicism, material goods, and communication and information ... My gut feeling is that news is just as much about what we don't know is going on, what doesn't find its way into our living room. We use the news as a barometer of the world, and it tells how we're to meant to feel that day. But there are issues of selection, presentation, authorial judgement. News is business, and it ends as entertainment. Sometimes I find that stomach-churning.[16]

The poetry is almost as global as the WTO. It re-echoes certain major news stories ranging from war to trivia – Kosovo, the Paddington rail crash, the eclipse, the circumnavigation of the globe by a hot-air balloon, and the Colorado high school shootings – in poems whose common mood is a persistently disenchanted vision of the world, despite the insistent comedy. The implicit question throughout the poems is what to do with the levelling juxtaposition of news stories about fatal accidents, wars and trivia. One strategy is to elicit from these news stories lost opportunities for alternative visions of the future. The world-record hot air balloon ride becomes an almost Deleuzian vision (or perhaps this is really a WTO vision of the world): a deterritorialisation based on the detachment of elevated vision, freed from the allegedly murderous impulses of nationalisms fuelled by border disputes. Most stories, the poetry implies, don't even offer such opportunities for imagining heroic transformation, because the media have so saturated the social imaginary with their own vision of iconic figures representing the sovereign emotiveness of the people, that if we try to imagine Shakespeare in our world he would be 'making /an arse of himself for Children in Need', and a Hitler would be appearing on the Oprah Winfrey show.[17] What is needed is a politics capable of projecting social transformations with a force similar to those of the poetic imagination represented by the *whimsy* Armitage uses to neutralise the discourse of atrocity. Whimsy is his distancing technique. In the most compelling poem in this volume, he retells the story of the boys who took their guns to murder classmates in the Colorado high school: here they take flowers instead, and the only trace of their actual violence is a fierce insistence that even those who don't want their gifts of flowers must accept them. Political redemption is imagined as an act of remetaphorising the news along poetic lines.

Armitage's poetry is proud to be foolish and to celebrate poetry's fictions as a better form of faction, and is all too aware of a readerly suspicion of seriousness in poetry, evident in a reviewer of Douglas Oliver's poems in the *Penguin Modern Poets 10*, who condemns the poems as 'patronising': 'We know we're awful, and Africa is brilliant, and that when Africa isn't brilliant it's our fault – so why write poems about it? … One has the sense before embarking on every next poem in this selection, that once more, the poet is about to tell you something important – about society, politics, the way the world is ordered, run by villains and filled with injustice'.[18] Armitage appears to share the belief that poets ought not to attempt to speak with the same authority as the news, by assuming that poetry is capable of a responsive intelligence equal to its political informations. Distance is better thought of as fooling about.

Armitage treats the news media as part of a general moral failure of humankind that fosters stupidity and at times, atrocity. The penultimate poem begins with an itemisation of the species and fates of many of the birds displaced or destroyed by the war in the Balkans, before introducing a figure which represents the political journalist who gave us news of Kosovo and Bosnia, the 'lyrebird', which behaves like a journalist's tape-recorder. A series of five stanzas lists the noises of war and violence the bird has emulated, before adding another mysterious sound, 'a background drawl', a 'babble of white noise' that is slowly revealed to be the combined effect of all the colours of the spectrum of news reports, creating a white 'radiation'.[19] This interesting metaphoric logic which parallels the loss of cultural difference in a homogenised Western modernity with the merger of colours of the spectrum in white light, is undeveloped.

The poetic humour disarms the resistance of reviewers to serious engagement with politics and history by disowning responsibility for what is said, but there is a price for this, both in the limited development of metaphoric logics and, more importantly still, in the lack of reflection on its own terms of engagement with history; Simon Armitage doesn't let the poem reflect on its conditions of reception, and on why the news elicits whimsical Ovidian metamorphoses of guns into flowers. Satirical gibes at media practice help him disavow any connection between the news and the poetry by representing him as no more than a reader of the news who is external to it. Poetry speaks for some purer, more unenchanted condition than the media's enthrallment to the contingencies of history can – a condition in which time and memory are given full recognition, because poetry is assumed to elude the public sphere of television and newspaper. The poet does not see himself as another kind of reporter. This is unconvincing in Armitage's case, not simply because the poem became the basis of a television documentary about millenium Britain, but also because the poetry revels in its own illocutionary power to influence public culture with its jokes, clever rhymes and accessible narrative vocabularies.

This discussion of Armitage's poetry helps make plain a problem with any attempt to think of the news in terms of singular readers and authors. One critic of Habermas's theories of the origins of the public sphere, Benjamin Lee, argues that the idea of society as waiting to be read belongs to the eighteenth century bourgeois public sphere and has little relevance today: 'This ideology explicitly represents the roles of authors and readers as the starting point for constructing a public whose boundaries are coterminous with the citizenry'.[20] This prompts Lee to speculate whether 'a theory of communicative action based on an essentially dyadic speaker-hearer model of speech acts [can] be adequate for the mixed, large-scale communicative modes characteristic of modern societies' (p409). It will be clear by now that I do not want to jettison reading and textuality in order to better represent the new communications, although I agree with Lee's description of this complex heterogeneity of discursive practices in which our political subjectivity is negotiated. I shall go on to show that it can be possible to imagine public spheres through certain literary practices whose textuality questions this dyad and responds to the diversity of discursive politics. Lee's reservations do apply to Armitage's entertainment poetry, however, and suggest that we need to question the relation between his poetic practice, especially its self-representation as reading, and the striking images of a polity that sits in front of the television unsure whether this is a game show, war – 'and on satellite TV we watch a game-show host/ disguised as an anchorman for CNN' – or golf (not Gulf) because we misheard the vowel – 'although these are the opening shots of operation Desert Fox,/ not the Ryder Cup,/ we have men on the fairway pointing at divots and cranes' (p5).

Cavell offers an extension of Adorno's idea of exaggeration as intellectual distance from co-optation by ideology and science, which suggests how the poetics of reading the news might be extended to better represent the new public spheres of news production and reception. Cavell is interested in how we participate in political process by reflecting on demands for our consent and participation within a democracy, which is why he writes the aside cited earlier about the difficulty of knowing how to respond to the excess of news. He finds in Ralph Waldo Emerson the idea of 'aversive thinking', which he glosses as 'an incessant conversion or refiguration of society's incessant demands for his consent' and at the same time 'to mean that his writing must accordingly be the object of aversion to society's consciousness, to what it might read in him'.[21] The idea is that social and individual improvement demand a certain kind of self-consciousness that will both acknowledge its complicity and resist it, and in the process will make possible the transformations of human existence that democracy's idealism still faintly projects. Emerson wrote that 'in every work of genius we recognize our own rejected thoughts' and find that 'they come back to us with a certain alienated majesty'.[22] This could also apply to our relation to the news: its social self-consciousness presents everything from alienated majesty to alienated atrocity, and the task for the political subject is to work through this alienation without either resignation or denial. Armitage doesn't recognise his own complicity as thinker and political subject in this alienation of worlds already transformed by the *poeisis* of the media. His poetry is not nearly as aversive as it thinks.

'IN THE MIDDLE OF THE NEWS MAKING'

Douglas Oliver is a poet whose work *is* strongly aversive, and has therefore attracted extremes of praise and dismissal, because it enacts highly cathected appropriations of the news and its images of politics, and thereby proposes radical reinventions of political activism. His retrospective preface to *The Diagram Poems*, cited earlier (p180), suggests why and how his interest developed in this direction, and why his poetry might be an interesting guide to these issues. It is his attention to the 'occasion' of the news, the constituents of this swirling babble of political judgement, professional interpretation, mourning and alcohol, without simply pushing clear and condemning it as 'white noise', that enables him to offer powerful insights into the dilemmas of the political subject.

The Diagram Poems itself is an unusually intransigent text as a result of its unwillingness to simplify or resolve its contradictions. It displays doodles or diagrams opposite the poems, as well as an italicised commentary on the guerilla actions that inspired the poem, but offers little in the way of the allegorical or symbolic reading of these events that a reader might expect (although it invites the reader to try). The diagrams are both analytic jottings made while events were taking place, in order to think through the story of the guerilla band's movements from bank to bank while they were happening, and tracks of unconscious fantasy. A series of looping lines that chart the changing directions of the vehicles form a face in the second diagram, and in another the plotting of a bank raid mutates first into a Goya-esque drawing of a policeman holding up a stick figure as if to contemplate or even eat it, and then into an adjustable spanner threatening to crush a stick man who is holding its jaws open. The diagrams have become part of the publication of the poem because references to their detail pervade it, making unusually visible the stages of secondary revision. The result of all this is a poetry which risks balance, objectivity, pertinence and even good taste, but exemplifies more thoroughly than any other poetry I know, the contemporary political and cultural dilemma of political information.

Commentators have sometimes recognised what Oliver is doing, but not always with approval, because they want to draw the line somewhere to protect the free flow of information from the babble of creative interventions, however well-intentioned. Oliver freely admits the role of fantasies about the news in the composition of the poem: 'I made notes ... letting fantasy deepen till something in me – no matter what – pierced the screen of words and answered to the urgency of Operation Pando'.[23] For one reviewer of The Diagram Poems this went too far. Jeremy Harding objected to foolish fantasising about contemporary politics in a revealing metaphor that enacts a transference by which Oliver becomes the aggressor because his imagination consumes the news story like one of Goya's giants, 'The danger here is that elements of the real, once seized on and dragged back to the lair, begin to decompose unrecognisably in the dank atmosphere of Oliver's moral habitat, which he shares with a pride of hungry categories: grace, hope, love, courage, innocence, and so on'.[24] This inappropriate judgement does reveal that Oliver's strategy can be perceived as a powerful one, even by an unsympathetic reader, since the poet becomes a predator capable of seizing hold of reality and sequestering it. What we want to see is whether or not this process can be represented more favourably in terms of our wider discussion about news, political subjects and public spheres.

Let me trace some of the transformations at work in the poems, noting that the text never loses sight of the dialectics of the poet's intermediation between events in Uruguay and newspaper readers in the West. The first poem is based as much on the shapes in the diagram as on the story itself, so the two circles in his heuristic diagram indicating the fire station and the police station become 'two spectacle lenses', and the knots indicating the arrivals and departures from the four banks they robbed resemble four apples, and are referred to as apples by the text. In the second poem a certain Sgt Olivera becomes 'Sergeant My Namesake', indicating how the poet comprehends this as a field of possible identifications. The fourth poem 'Central' introduces a new element from the author's world, memories of his son who died in infancy, whom he imagines phoning from the telephone exchange that is cut off by the guerillas. Tom tells his father to ring his mother and warns that communication will be cut off, not by death but by the guerillas' act of disconnecting the telephone exchange. The poem then circles into a metapoetic loop:

> It's the end of the line and here's a ..."
> (Still Tom's voice, the past ahead of me, but fading. I'd
> better put that down to feeling and feeling's
> part of my work.) "Yes it is part ... Don't put down
> the receiver ..." (fading) "... the ear hears with feeling ..."
> (fading, cut dead).[25]

The boy hears the inner thought indicated by the bracket, although the sentence reads as if it were a later interpolation, and agrees that emotion is a necessary part of attention to politics. Words and events double and redouble their meaning. The telephone receiver becomes the father, the journalist, the political subject, the receiver of information. The dead phone line is also a reminder of his son's death. The poet's imagined participation in these remote events in Uruguay constructs a field of imagined messages for him, culminating in the message from a guerilla commander telling him that he should 'obey/ the voices that come from long distance, obey sound and feeling' (p114). What I find striking is the depiction of the generation of affect that permeates the press, as we saw in the WTO reporting (and its absences). Here the poem announces that it will follow the sounds of its language and the fellow feelings of its expression knowing that this will transmute the news without knowing where it will end.

Anxiety about the ethics of these appropriations takes over the final poem. The authorial voice pulls back from the speculations, fantasies and identifications, wondering what right it has to use any of this material at all as a vehicle of expression. The stories that 'came to me at night in a busy newsroom' cannot be claimed as the poet's own, 'for I little own this poem; it is nothing/ without the original movements', nor does the poem have any right to take this news story and 'jig it into shapes'.[26] The tentative justification in answer to these doubts, is not the pressure of personal need, nor the public availability of such information for anyone to use as they please, like copyright-free images in a computer graphics programme, but the ethical demand for wider recognition of the culminating violence and injustice of the guerilla actions themselves. All this comedy of political activism in the manner of Bonnie and Clyde suddenly turns nasty in a brutal murder of most of the guerillas, and this elicits a concluding reflection on political responsibility:

> We cannot ask the prisoners to forgive
> our foreign nations
> but we may hope the dead can kiss
> for us the face of innocence in the rushing dark
> and grace and courage arrive calmly in us (p126).

This only partially answers to the poem's occasion, and nothing else is said about why these foreign nations which include our own should need to be forgiven, except that the entire poem's attempt to use the news for its own purposes, just as Armitage used the Colorado shootings for a flight of botanical fantasy, admits a comparison between such poetic expropriation and other more direct forms of economic exploitation (which Armitage's poetry represses). The musings of the poet in Oliver's narrative sequence show that the news is never pure, just as the poem is never pure; it is always carrying the freight of our losses and hopes, our dead and our promises.

Oliver's admission of exaggeration, over-shooting and self-detachment into his volatile picture of the primary process of the journalist as news salesman shows why ordinary remedies for the insufficiency or suppression of information are not sufficient on their own. More effective political organisation and more information more freely available need to be accompanied by transformations of the condition of political communication. Political events happen at speed and cannot be fully analysed until much later; political subjects will read the news as events in their own worlds and as narratives coloured by their own mourning, elation, anxiety, fear and joy. All political subjects will be working through their desires and memories as they work out their political judgements. The question is how to remain politically aware and capable of participation in public culture, or rather, how political discourse and political activism can work with these conditions rather than always hoping that a pure transmission of political knowledge will somehow happen this time, and that a purely political subject will respond solely with objectivity and rationality.

WRITING AND THE PUBLIC SPHERE

This emphasis on 'news' as one of the arenas in which politics takes place, deliberately gives the more abstract concept of public spheres a textual and affective visibility, although at the cost of some dissonance with the standard theorising of the public sphere. It emphasises both the passivity of the subject consuming the news, a situation explored in the poems by Armitage and Oliver, and then poses the question of what constitutes an adequate intellectual response. The terms in which this question is posed are different from those ordinarily understood, raising the possibility that an innovative radical politics may benefit from paying more attention to the distances and tensions of this initial stage of reception and engagement they so vividly depict, especially as the global complexity of democratic politics and its information rapidly increase.

With these poetries and the problem of news in mind, we should therefore briefly turn to existing theories of public spheres and public culture, to follow up the implications of our findings, for our opening questions about news and political activism. At first sight this move would seem difficult, because theorists of the public sphere have been reluctant to investigate the role of such foolishnesses as poetry and fiction in the workings of public spheres, despite Habermas's recognition of the contribution of eighteenth century novels to the emergence of the coffee house culture and its creation of something that could be called public opinion. The suspicion of exaggerated claims by Romantics (to be unacknowledged legislators – can a legislator legislate without recognition, they would wonder) and avant-garde writers who thought revolutions against the supposed laws of literary form would overturn the legitimacy of the law that founded the oppressive state, was compounded with fear that aestheticisation of politics always leads to totalitarianism. The study of Literature has been largely divided between those who treat literary texts as autonomous, almost Platonic, forms (at the level of a specific text) rather than iterative practices embedded in history and ethnography and those, more recently in the ascendant, whose theory, while showing the work of language, desire and power in the construction of texts and their subjectivities, intends to develop persuasive accounts of the location of sociality, intersubjectivities, and cultural memory in texts. Consequently, there has been little theoretical discussion of the significance of literary work for such questions as the relation of the news to the political subject, and the best work has been done as investigations of specific historical conjunctures. Political theories of public culture remain an uninvestigated resource for literary and even some cultural studies.

Maria Pia Lara's recent and important study of the contribution of feminist writing to public spheres in America, *Moral Textures* (1998), is a sign that things are changing.[27] She argues that aesthetic practices are an important part of the struggle to extend public spheres to those previously excluded on grounds of gender or race. These literary, performative, visual and musical practices are politically significant 'because the cultural contestation of meaning is a struggle in which every social movement is intensively engaged' (p169). Her own case studies of feminist practice in the past decades, and her citation of Houston Baker, Jr's belief that the first step in black politics towards the reconstruction of public spheres was the 'creative agency' that produced songs and texts which were 'conversions of wish into politics', lead her to a specific analysis of just how these aesthetic practices have worked (p166). Although she largely ignores non-narrative and poetic textualities, her discussion makes it possible to formulate the public radii of the poetic foolishness about politics in the poetries of Armitage and Oliver with greater acuity.

Lara concentrates on the autobiographical narratives of feminist writers as the key agents of transformation of both access and, more importantly, the structures, especially the moral norms, of these public spheres. This is not as restrictive as it might be, since both poets we are discussing write semi-autobiographically, and because she herself extends the category by arguing that feminist narratives are not, as sometimes they are caricatured, celebrations of an essential human identity, but 'fragmentary and, as historical textures, they are woven into the symbolic and cultural orders' so that 'this creation of individualities contains an intersubjective core born of the networks of linguistically mediated interactions' (p88). This would enable her to include many texts which are not ordinarily thought of as conventional, personal narratives. Their authenticity is, according to Lara, both the sign of a process of self-realisation and also a performance of identity that requires the recognition of a public culture, and this recognition is best understood as dialogue or negotiation, rather than simply a single moment of identification. Their effectiveness depends upon what Habermas and others have called 'illocutionary force'.

J.L. Austin's idea of illocutionary force was an attempt to describe certain kinds of utterance 'such as informing, ordering, warning, undertaking, &c., i.e. utterances which have a certain (conventional) force'.[28] The utterance is not just a comment on some state of affairs, whether external or internal; it also acts on others, makes demands on them, calls for an adjustment of intersubjective relations. It is not the same as a statement that affects someone (bad news for example), nor the kind of declaration that opens a new shopping centre, although Austin admits that hard and fast distinctions are elusive. These distinctions suggested to Habermas that illocution was the key to understanding how political opinion is developed. Speakers use illocutionary force to persuade their listeners of the rightness of what they say, and ideally this action does not try to manipulate the listener as if the speech were some kind of magnetic force that would act directly on the will of the subject, but works within a mutuality of will between persons:

> ... reaching a rationally motivated understanding *with* the hearer, an understanding that comes about on the basis of a criticizable validity claim. We can understand the illocutionary components of assertions and confessions as the linguistic representations of claims to the validity of the corresponding assertoric or expressive sentences.[29]

Criticism of Habermas usually focuses on either the cognitivism of this process or its apparent reliance on ideal conditions unlikely to be achieved in this world, such as an absence of differences of power. Such reservations, though, can miss the direction of Habermas's interest in the conditions which make communication possible, which point to the way in which social agreement is reached, to whether it is coercive or participatory. This is why it remains important to him that the basic model of co-ordinated action should avoid too much contamination with both affect and textuality.

Textuality and affect have been important to the women's movement, as Lara notes. Feminist writers' novels and autobiographies were crucial to their political effectiveness:

> My implicit claim is that women achieved knowledge through narrative, but these narratives in turn have transformed our notions of justice and democracy. This knowledge is developed first in what is now known as the 'counterpublics'; second, in the varieties of different roles played by women in the public sphere; and, third, by the projections of new narratives about the past into a utopian future which, above all, recovers a self-reflexive process.[30]

Feminists had to show that existing guiding political concepts of justice and the good, of public and private, and even those old metaphysical abstractions, universal and particular, were narrowly defined by male interests and needed to be reconfigured if they were adequately to include women. Fictions with a strong illocutionary force helped them to do this.

The head of the WTO accused the demonstrators of obstructing communication, but as Lara points out, such obstruction may be an attempt to command the medium itself: 'As long as groups needing to be heard or accepted do not first conquer channels of communication to call attention to the way they have been treated, nothing will be solved'. Talk of conquering is slightly misleading, as I think she realises elsewhere in more moderate formulations, and it is more accurate to think of a public sphere as intersecting communications networks that will always produce a partially cacophonous convergence of informations. Illocutionary force is needed in order to be heard amongst the myriad others: 'Public space is the arena where all discourses have to compete for the acceptance of a new interpretation criticizing previous ways in which people understood themselves'(152).

And illocutionary force is precisely what both Armitage and Oliver are pursuing. The mutation of guns into flowers displays just such force, as does, in a halting, but more powerful way, the mutation of Tupamaro guerilla raids into diagrams. The question then is what exactly does this illocutionary force look like when closely examined? To what extent does it incorporate Adorno's distance or Cavell's aversive thinking? Is there a certain confusion built in to the concept, as

Benjamin Lee argues, because it presumes a face-to-face encounter? Lee thinks that we cannot use the face-to-face dialogue as the paradigm of political life, because communication takes place in other forms which are not reducible to it. Speech acts are not interchangeable with textuality, and it may be impossible to find one single paradigm of linguistic interaction: 'There may be no general model of communication under which specific modes may be subsumed or which can serve as a standpoint of a critique'.[31] His reservations do however show why attending to the combination of reading and writing as response, which is evident in the poetry and in the demonstrations, and giving the concept of illocutionary force a more extended significance as a way of mapping the activities of the zone of tensions, might clarify the problem of the news. This is recognised by some of Oliver's poetry, especially the major works that followed *The Diagram Poems*. A useful concept of illocutionary force must mean more than simply motivating a single other subject. It must include more extended influence in both space and time and be more intersubjective, more reflexive about its transferential and counter-transferential potential. Some idea of what might be involved can be found in Oliver's poem *The Infant and the Pearl* (1985).[32] This extended meditation on the elusive problem of how to find the necessary critical distance from the news while remaining politically committed, shows that fact and fiction are interdependent.

AVERSIVE NARRATIVES OF POLITICAL ACTION

In two major poems written during the 1980s Oliver depicted first Thatcher's Britain and then Reaganite America in poems which elicited remarkable praise and criticism. *The Infant and the Pearl* (1985) narrates a dream journey by car and on foot through the devastated post-Beveridge landscape where the old giants of deprivation still roam, using the anachronistic metrical scheme of the medieval poem *Pearl*. The Premier, 'whose self serially/ repeated, televised, pearlised, and reported/ ten times, tampered with immediacy', turns out to be 'one of my own dream's creations', and the poem investigates the complicities between political ideologies and the fantasies of the citizens (my copy of Hugo Young's biography of Margaret Thatcher has this blue television image on its cover – her use of the medium was determining) (p4). The chauffeur of the dream car that carries the narrator through the landscape devastated by monetarism, laughs when the narrator asks whether the blue image of Margaret Thatcher in the car is a simulacrum or the actuality: 'We save the actual for believers. You'll have to behave/ as if all responses are real' (p8). It is this recognition that makes the poem such a significant meditation on the condition of the contemporary political subject.

The poet Peter Riley said he could not 'avoid the feeling that this is the poem for which we have had to wait sixty-five years' since the false dawn of Eliot's *The Waste Land*, which failed because 'Eliot's false objectivity denied authorial responsibility'.[33] (The playwright Howard Brenton also compared the impact of Oliver's next long poem, *Penniless Politics* (1991)[34] to *The Waste Land* and said that it set the 'political agenda for the next 20 years').[35] A somewhat hostile reviewer of *The Infant and the Pearl*, Adam Thorpe, notices this authorial intervention but thinks of it as narcissism, especially what he calls the 'annoying self-reference' to Oliver's own dead child.

The divided views about Oliver's project help explain his relative neglect compared to a poet like Simon Armitage and more importantly they point up the tensions aroused when a writer intervenes in the public sphere by reworking the news as poetry without keeping poet and poetry free of the supposed contaminations of history, news and politics. Oliver himself is very aware of these difficulties. John Kerrigan reports that Oliver explained to him that the prosody in *The Infant and the Pearl* 'would carry the dignity even at times when I jettisoned dignity', and comments that the resulting 'sophisticated comedy' results from 'offsetting what is boorish in the dreamer with rhymed elaboration'.[36] Many readers are not prepared to make this distinction, which tells us something important about the ways in which poetry is now read, as well as illuminating the workings of the public spheres in which the news is produced and consumed.

The Infant and the Pearl begins with fantasies prompted by news of contemporary politics similar to those in *Killing Time* and *The Diagram Poems*, notably the televisual Prime-Minister. It then goes well beyond these with more potent fantasies of himself actually participating in politics as journalist and MP and, most strikingly of all, by the radical imaginative act of taking a medieval poetic masterpiece and asking what its translation into contemporary terms would reveal about the political sphere imagined by the British government and its media in the 1980s. It is especially effective at identifying that consolatory fantasy which readily permeates our responses to the news (recall how *The Mirror* momentarily put us at the helm of Russia, and *The Guardian* made us a participant in the WTO proceedings), of putting the world right by our own special efforts, as in Armitage's balloon poem.

It starts as a dream of a muse-like figure – a woman like Petrarch's Laura – leaving the narrator. Her name is Rosine, and she is based on the central figure of the medieval poem, but here she becomes a many-sided projection of the contradictoriness of current social images of femininity: alienated masculinities, Thatcher's media images, feminism and labour politics, traditional images of mother and muse – the admission of the unresolved tensions at work in this overdetermina-tion are part of the poem's strength. The dream narrator is wearing his father's dressing gown, as if dressed in authority borrowed from his father, and is unable to detain the muse and what she represents because of the intrusive image of Thatcher. Then he dreams of a land-scape of hills dominated by a powerful city, and climbs into a Bentley which he suspects is carrying the Prime Minister, only to discover that she has been transmuted into a 'grainy blue-grey like television' (p7). The driver explains that they have invented what is called 'adjustable futurity' (p8), which enables them to measure an individual's desires for the future and then generate a three-dimensional image of the leader which matches them. Keith Joseph is in the front seat looking like Adam Smith and explaining that misery and poverty are inevitable and it is a waste of national resources to try and alleviate them. A stockbroker explains that the Brixton riots of 1981 'were a left-wing ameliorist's/ feeblest hour' – throwing money at racial inequality only worsens the situation (p10). Then he drives past the five giants that Ernest Beveridge said dominated the landscape of Britain. Want, Squalor, and Idleness are soon passed, but the fourth, Ignorance, imagined as a 'mongol' child, will recur later in the dream in the guise of the poet's dead son: 'the pearl seed of her Socialism was this subnor-mal infant' (p18). This is all recognisable satire for anyone who remembers those years, but what follows begins to complicate the simple oppositions between good and bad.

The dreamer begins to imagine ways in which he could resist Conservative ideology and redeem the nation. After the ride he becomes a reporter writing about the spectacle of Royalty, and then is transformed into an MP by this vision of the infant, 'proud that Parliament/ had seduced me' (p19). He gives a speech which exposes the class war behind Tory government, saying: 'We must switch/ to expansion, power-sharing with the potent/ multi-nationals, a new package/ of nationalisation' (p23). Then Rosine makes her own speech, which attacks left-extremism as well as Thatcherite policies: 'your unfunded promises could prove falser than/ the false pearl of the premier's policy' (p24). She is dismissive of 'internecine leftist sycophancy', saying that this helps keep the Tories in power. Calling the narrator and his fellow Labour MPs 'economic dreamers' carries special force in this dream poem, and is a reminder that the poem is a zone in which politics and the news are re-imagined. She advocates a politics of the centre, and dismisses extremes of idealism, sounding at fifteen years distance like a Blairite *avant la lettre*. The narrator's response is to realise that the Margaret Thatcher he had attacked was an invention, 'the adman's/ lying image' (p28).

The narrator's father also appears late in the dream, demanding that his son temper his political radicalism with his memories of childhood and his own history. His son's politics is made up of 'blindness and pearly roses' (p30). The father makes a crucial point about the self-understanding of a polity: 'a nation must know its own ignorance', which might function as a general summary of our discussion so far (p33). The poem's allegorical treatment of this insight is both awkward and poignant. The narrator finds himself inside the cliff of glass holding the figure of *Ignorance* in his arms. He sees a dirty window and old woman sitting there, ravaged by poverty and disease, that he recognises as Rosine, and as he does the infant in his arms becomes anguished as if believing that Rosine is his mother. He lets the infant go to the mother and she is then transformed back into a young Madonna with child, but she rounds on him and others like him, saying that 'right in the ideal's inner sanctum you prefer/ a sort of commercial for Christ or for/ the politics of set-apart poverty', whereas the gutter visible beyond the window is not hers but the poverty that surrounds the narrator's own culture (p34). Rosine also speaks via television, as if she too has become news.

One answer to our opening question might have been that we psychoanalyse both our individual fantasies and the social fantasies that swirl through the news, as a way of comprehending the emotional investments so evident in all contemporary reporting and of organising our responses to it. Oliver's poem flirts with this idea and then complicates it. It certainly offers the royal road to the unconscious, but it then shows just how much history can be seen along the way, even from the Bentley of Conservative ideology. Its very form is a reminder that Freud's dreamwork has a long genealogy in which textuality and poetics play a part. Together with my earlier discussion of the press treatment of the WTO story, the poems of Armitage and Oliver suggest that we still need to think through the implications of Adorno's call for intellectual distance. Distance is a zone in which all kinds of potentially confusing ideas and desires are in play. In this paper I have tried to show that imaginative distortions of contemporary historical and political events might sometimes be able to lead us deeper into their full implications for our politics, because they enable us to factor in our own individual and shared fantasies, affects and beliefs in ways which the sensationalism and cartoonish emotions of both tabloids and broadsheets, not to mention television, rarely achieve. There is a cultural work of politics to be done. It need not take the form of poetry. Music, visual art, performance, as well as inventive forms of reporting and comment, might all work in this way. Otherwise the scale and chaos of political information will continue to hinder the aversive thinking and acting that is badly needed.

NOTES

1. Douglas Oliver, 'night shift', intoduction to revised version of *The Diagram Poems*, in *Kind*, Allardyce, Barnett publishers, London 1987, pp101-102. *The Diagram poems* were first published by Ferry Press in 1979. The later edition contains a considerable amount of framing, explanatory material not in the first edition. The first edition, which has a larger format, is better able to give the diagrams their full force.
2. Theodor Adorno, *Minima Moralia: Reflections from a Damaged Life*, E.F.N. Jephcott (trans), Verso, London [1951] 1974, pp126-127.
3. Larry Elliott, 'World Trade Chief Tries to Head off Biggest Protest Since Vietnam', *The Guardian*, 25.11.99, p1.
4. Douglas Oliver, 'Our Family is Full of Problems', from *A Salvo for Africa*, in *Penguin Modern Poets Volume 10: Douglas Oliver, Denise Riley, Iain Sinclair*, Penguin, Harmondsworth 1996, p3.
5. Larry Elliott and John Vidal, 'Battle of the Seattle Streets', *The Guardian*, 1.12.99, p1.
6. Tony McGrew, 'The World Trade Organization: Technocracy or Banana Republic?', in Annie Taylor and Caroline Thomas (eds), *Global Trade and Global Social Issues*, Routledge, London 1999, pp197-216, p200.
7. Marc Williams, 'The World Trade Organization, Social Movements and "Democracy"', in Taylor and Thomas, *op. cit.*, pp151-169, p163.
8. Stanley Cavell, *Conditions Handsome and Unhandsome: The Constitution of Emersonian Perfectionism*, University of Chicago Press, Chicago 1990, p129.
9. 'The Organ Snatchers', *Daily Mail*, 4.12.99, p4.
10. 'Hague Humiliated', *The Sun*, 4.12.99, p2.
11. 'Masters of the Millennium', *The Mirror*, 4.12.99, pp11, 7, 7, 3.

12. 'Europeans Block Biotech Move', *Financial Times* 3.12.99, p13.

13. *Financial Times*, 3.12.99, p19.

14. *The Independent*, 3.12.99, p17.

15. 'Secret World of WTO Deal Makers', *The Guardian*, 3.12.99, p1.

16. Quoted in Robert Potts, 'Mean Time', *The Guardian* 15.12.99, G2 p6.

17. *Op. cit.*, p40.

18. Martin Stannard, in, *Tears in the Fence* 20, Spring 1998, p71.

19. *Op. cit.*, p50.

20. Benjamin Lee, 'Textuality, Mediation, and Public Discourse', in Craig Calhoun (ed), *Habermas and the Public Sphere*, The MIT Press, Cambridge, Mass 1992, pp402-420, p408.

21. Cavell, *op. cit.*, p37.

22. *Ibid.*, p57

23. Oliver, *op. cit.*, pp102-103.

24. Jeremy Harding, 'Small Presses, Big Themes', *TLS*, December 18-24, p1394.

25. Oliver, *op. cit.*, 'Central', p113.

26. Oliver, *op. cit.*, 'The Diagonal is Diagonal', pp125-126.

27. Maria Pia Lara, *Moral Textures: Feminist Narratives in the Public Sphere*, Polity Press, Cambridge 1998.

28. J.L. Austin, *How to Do Things With Words*, J.O.Urmson and Marina Sbisa (ed), Oxford University Press, Oxford [1962]) 1975, p109.

29. Jürgen Habermas, *The Theory of Communicative Action Vol.2: Lifeworld and System: A Critique of Functionalist Reason* Thomas McCarthy (trans), Polity Press, Cambridge [1981]1987, p69.

30. Lara, *op. cit.*, p71.

31. Lee, *op. cit.*, p414.

32. Douglas Oliver, *The Infant and the Pearl*, in *Three Variations on the Theme of Harm: Selected Poetry and Prose*, Paladin, London [1985] 1990. There have been several editions, as is characteristic of small press editions. The poem was also included in *Kind*, Agneau 2 Allardyce, Barnett Publishers, London 1987, an important collection of Oliver's work.

33. Peter Riley, 'Visionary Politics', *PN Review* 13/3, 1986, p93.

34. Douglas Oliver, *Penniless Politics: A Satirical Poem*, Bloodaxe Books, Newcastle Upon Tyne [1991] 1994.

35. Howard Brenton, 'Poetic Passport to a New Era', *The Guardian*, 7.4.1992, p21.

36. John Kerrigan, 'Mrs Thatcher's *Pearl*', in Piero Boitani and Anna Tosti (eds), *The Body and the Soul in Medieval Literature*, D.S.Brewer, Cambridge 1999, pp181-199, p194.

Self, Community and History in the Postcolonial novel since 1945

STUART MURRAY

In many ways, 'post-war' is the original of all the 'posts' that clog the methodologies of the Humanities at the turn of the century. As a some-time forgotten parent to the contemporary variety of postcolonialisms, post-modernisms, and indeed the whole concept of the post-subject, the postwar's emphasis on a better and brighter future following 1945 was the key note of revision and change that animates many of the cultural debates of the present. Historically, the founding of the United Nations, and especially the momentous era of de-colonisation between 1955 and 1970, ushered in not only a substantial number of new nations (in these fifteen years after 1955, the total membership of the UN doubled to 126, nearly all the new states having recently de-colonised), but inaugurated the most seminal of this century's various proclamations of the new world order.[1]

First and foremostly, the subject as conceived of in this process was a political subject, the agent of self-determination at the heart of the de-colonising process. The nature of postcolonial political subjecthood would, of course, become contested terrain as the initial optimism of independence hardened into the realities of world politics, especially in the 1960s and 1970s. But the process was not only political. Side by side with this change of subjecthood was the huge outpouring of cultural, particularly literary, expression that sought to provide the new nations not only with an official state identity, but also with a home in thought. The rise of the postcolonial novel since 1945, especially in Africa, Asia and the Caribbean, those areas which saw the bulk of postwar de-colonisation, has been the most remarkable feature of contemporary writing in English. In the work of major writers such as Chinua Achebe, V.S. Naipaul and Ngugi wa Thiong'o, and moving through to a subsequent generation that includes Salman Rushdie, Margaret Atwood and Michael Ondaatje, the postcolonial novel has negotiated – represented, analysed, celebrated, criticised – the key changes in the relationship of subject to independent community and to history. This has been more than simply a case of recording the details of the new place – an easy realism that inscribes the tones and texture of postcolonial life. Inherent in the project of postcolonial writing since 1945 has of course been the need to capture in prose cultural activities and forms that had so far been absent from novels written in English up to that point, but also to confront and come to terms with the considerable weight of European portrayals of colonial space in the modern era from the eighteenth to the early twentieth century.

Again the analogy with the political process is apt. The expansion of the United Nations offered no guarantee that the longstanding prejudices built into the colonial process would dissipate. 'After all' noted one British observer at the UN when it was proposed that new members should serve a probation period before being allowed to vote on resolutions, 'children do not have the vote anywhere'.[2] For the postcolonial novelist faced with the heritage of writing in English, the situation as perceived by others would not be dissimilar.

In terms of writing subjectivity, the authors who are the focus of this study sought to place (and often re-place) the subject in an examination of local conditions. Given the misrepresentation of many colonial spaces in earlier writing in English, these novelists fought to move from having postcolonial subjects consume images of themselves to helping them produce such images. The Trinidadian novelist V.S. Naipaul, writing in 1964, noted that, as a child reading the set texts of a colonial education, all literature was rendered external:

> To us, without a mythology, all literatures were foreign. Trinidad was small, remote and unimportant, and we knew we could not hope to read in books of the life we saw about us. Books came from afar; they could offer only fantasy.
>
> To open a book was to make an instant adjustment ... I needed to be able to adapt. All of Dickens's descriptions of London I rejected; and though I might retain Mr Micawber and the others in the clothes the illustrator gave them, I gave them faces and voices of people I knew and set them in buildings and streets I knew. The process of adaptation was automatic and continuous. Dickens's rain and drizzle I turned into tropical downpours; the snow and fog I accepted as conventions of books. Anything – like an illustration – which embarrassed me by proving how

weird my own reaction was, anything which sought to remove the characters from the make-up world in which I set them, I rejected.[3]

Naipaul's observation here is not just of the blank page that he felt
Trinidad to be with regard to the possibility of creative writing, it is
also a statement of the adaptation, the negotiations and personalising,
that often characterised the postcolonial reading process. When chan-
nelled into writing, this adaptation would produce new forms of the
novel, and would offer new versions of opinions normalised during the
colonial era. The particular questions the novelists discussed here
sought to engage with include reworkings of historical representation,
especially the power and prejudices of the representations during the
colonial period. But they also include a sharp focus on the workings of
the new post-colony in the years immediately following independence,
often a period when the promise of liberation turned into the abuses of
neo-colonialism. For a Nigerian novelist like Achebe writing in the
1960s, the dilemma was that he was often forced to concentrate on the
worst aspects of both the old and the new, seeking to confirm the legitimacy of the new state and explain how a colonial history created the
conditions of its existence, but then compelled to attack the independent regime as it perpetuated the injustices of the previous
administration. For his part, Naipaul's work of the 1960s and 1970s is
a serious critique of both the political and psychological make up of the
new postcolonial states.

Equally, though, not all postcolonial writers in this period felt that
the tie of Empire was the overriding feature that, by necessity,
governed their creative output. To do so would be to extend the power
of the colonial into a form of total, saturating coverage of all that came
after it. As Arun Mukherjee has observed with regard to Indian writers, such an argument can leave 'only one modality, one discursive
position. We are forever forced to interrogate European discourses ...
[Yet] our cultural productions are created in response to our own
needs, and we have many more needs than constantly to "parody the
imperialists"'.[4] For all the obvious gestures towards the colonial past
then, especially strong in the immediate decade after de-colonisation, it
is rather the multiple intersections between the colonial and the
postcolonial, by those who cared deeply about the relationship and
those who could live within its constructions but pay them little heed,
that became the subject of postcolonial fiction.

In the last twenty years or so, one of the major trajectories within
these histories has been the analysis of migrancy and movement by a

subsequent generation of postcolonial novelists. These writers, often not the product (as intellectuals) of the moment of independence, construct subjectivity in terms different to those of the 1950s and 1960s. In place of the focus on community and history often conveyed in near essential terms, evidenced by the concentration on landscapes or reworked accounts of culture contact for example, comes a portrayal of figures between cultures, and of narratives riddled with fantasy as much with historical accuracy, with provisionality as much as with the statement of self-determination. The journey between the two types of fiction, the latter borrowing from and working off the former even as it challenges some of its assumptions, is the already considerable legacy of the postcolonial novel. In what follows I want to chart some of these themes in the major postcolonial novels since 1945, starting with an overview of the subject as conceived of by colonial discourse, before moving into the challenge to this image that immediate postwar postcolonial writing produced, and the extension of these ideas, especially in relation to the political subject, into the contemporary novel.

In his journal entry for 6th May 1770, James Cook, on the first of his *Endeavour* voyages to the Pacific, noted, as best he could, the characteristics of the Australian aborigines he had encountered:

> The Natives do not appear numerous neither do they seem to live in large bodies but dispersed in small parties along the water side; those I saw were about as tall as Europeans, of a very dark brown colour but not black, nor had they wooly frizzled hair, but black and lank much like ours. No sort of clothing or ornaments were ever seen by any of us upon any one of them or about any of their hut ... However we could know very little of their customs as we were never able to form any conversations with them, they had not so much as touch'd the things we had left in their hutts on purpose for them to take away. During our stay in this harbour I caused the English Colours to be displayed ashore every day and an inscription to be cut upon one of the trees near the watering place, seting forth the Ship's name, date &c.[5]

Cook's comments came near the end of a voyage that had earlier seen the crew encounter other cultures in Tierra del Fuego, Tahiti and New Zealand, so the ethnology on display in these observations had been a feature of the exploration as a whole. What is of interest here is Cook's attempts to begin a classification of the aborigines along lines of rationality and empirical proof. Physique, customs and habits became the building blocks of the late eighteenth-century approach to the discussion of other subjects and their social formation, and part of Cook's frustration is that here (unlike Tahiti in particular) there is no dialogue with the aborigines. As clearly as Cook tries to signal himself and his own culture with the trappings of nation, indexes of Admiral authority and the details of the ship, he receives no exchange in return.

It is crucial to note that, for all the disappointment which Cook registers here, his approach is manifestly different to previous attempts to inscribe the subjectivity and culture of the aborigines. William Dampier's journal of his 1699 voyage to Australia and the South Seas, later published in 1729 as *A Voyage to New Holland*, had provided somewhat different conclusions:

> The Inhabitants of this Country are the miserablest People in the world. The Hodmadods of Monomatapa, though a nasty People, yet for Wealth are Gentlemen to these; who have no Houses and skin Garments, Sheep, Poultry and fruits of the Earth, Ostrich Eggs, etc. as the Hodmadods have: and setting aside their Humane shape, they differ but little from brutes.[6]

Although thwarted, Cook's attempted ethnology contains a completely different outlook on non-European subjectivity than that of Dampier (his noting of the lack of aboriginal 'wooly frizzled hair' is a direct rejoinder to a point made in the earlier text). In his own journal, Cook sought to deal directly with the conclusions that could be drawn from this study of other cultures: 'From what I have said of the Natives of New-Holland they may appear to some to be the most wretched people upon earth', he wrote as the *Endeavour* left Australia, 'but in reality they are far more happier than we Europeans; being wholly unacquainted not only with the superfluous but the necessary Conveniences so much sought after in Europe, they are happy in not knowing the use of them'.[7] Even as he granted the aborigines a legitimate culture, then, Cook began to be drawn in to the other great fascination for late eighteenth-century Europe, of the Pacific in particular, that of the pastoral paradise of the South Seas and the simplicity and virtue of the noble savage who lived there.

The crucial *modern* inscription of the colonial subject dated more or less from this point – the exploration of the 1770s and Cook's final proof of the non-existence of the great Southern Land, the possibility of which had animated imaginative geographers, and the hacks who had peddled exploration narratives, for centuries. Cook's blend of scientific rationality and cultural projection juxtaposed the ordering of the non-European world, be it the botany practised by Joseph Banks aboard the *Endeavour* or the wider development of natural history, with the imaginative construction of other peoples in narrative terms. The official journals of exploration, and the many bastardised copies of them that circulated around the major European cities, often adding monsters and savage cannibalism into the sometimes tame affairs of culture contact, were hugely popular to the reading public of the time.[8] Fact and fiction could, and did, overlap as the blank spaces of the globe became fewer and fewer.

The complexity of the exploration period's gaze on non-European spaces continued into the nineteenth century, as colonialism consolidated and solidified the hold Europe had on both the representation and the political and legal regulation of other peoples. Crucial to an understanding of the differences between the late eighteenth century and the portrayal of this subjecthood some sixty years later, however, was the rise in the idea of utilitarianism which saw the plasticity of thought present in much of the earlier period's writing harden into a greater degree of empiricism and prejudice as the trajectory of European expansion came to claim more and more of the world. This is not to imply that colonial discourse in the Victorian period was *only* prejudiced, however, pitting European power systems against a misrepresented colonial subject. As Bart Moore-Gilbert has noted, colonial attitudes were a 'process of cultural negotiations in constant conflict and evolution', and Ania Loomba has written that while 'a binary opposition between coloniser and colonised is an idea that has enormous force and power' in the thinking through of colonial and postcolonial relations, the subjects involved in such relations were and are 'complex, mixed-up products of diverse colonial histories'.[9] Nevertheless, while the late nineteenth century in particular produced colonial activities that can be seen to speak of a confused randomness *and* a vision of the world within a model of global power, the heady era of expansionist Europe with its jingoistic nationalism, its development of quasi-scientific notions of race, and, crucially, its economic exploitation, often identified the colonial subject as inferior and in clear need of government, guidance and regulation.

In terms of writing, the representation of this inferiority took hybrid forms. The great multi-volume dictionaries and histories of the nineteenth century codified the growing relationship inherent in the colonial moment, transforming utterly, and frequently negating altogether, any sense of pre-contact indigenous history. The exploration narrative, such as that of Cook, became the travel narrative of the nineteenth century where the Enlightenment sentiments of the former became what has been termed the 'planetary consciousness' of the latter.[10] Writing became one of the vehicles of a wider colonial complexity. In descriptions of landscapes and peoples in particular, travel writing helped underwrite expansionist control, especially in Africa, Asia and the Caribbean. In literary narratives, as Edward Said has so eloquently shown, the nineteenth-century novel in particular became crucially aligned with the wider arc of empire. Few of the major examples of nineteenth-century fiction are actually set in colonial spaces, but it is precisely this absence, this consignment to the outer edges and beyond of the narrative, that constituted an account of the role of the colonies in the European imagination.[11] In English literature, the Caribbean slave plantation that is absent from, but finances, the world of Jane Austen's *Mansfield Park* (1816), the criminal Magwitch, who derives the money from Australia by which he can act as Pip's patron in Charles Dickens's *Great Expectations* (1861), or the mad Caribbean creole Bertha, pushed to the furthest reaches of that icon of nineteenth-century capitalistic solidity, the big house, in Charlotte Bronte's *Jane Eyre* (1847), all testified to the notion of colonial space as a place where, along with the accumulation of capital, fear, desire and the perverse might act as the motors of the English imagination.

For the postcolonial novelist seeking to redress the misrepresentation of the colonial era, it was this twin characterisation, non-Europe both as a ruled and regulated zone *and* a space for the abstractions of the fantastic and the imaginary, that appeared to provide a total sense of imaginative mapping. The idea that the colonies were both codified and structured, and yet open to the seemingly random play of the creative mind, made the rewriting of self and historical community often tortuous. In English writing, the novels of the late nineteenth and early twentieth centuries, coinciding with the high point of empire and just after, display an ambiguity and complexity on these issues that points to a real sense of schizophrenia in the representation of colonial reality. In Joseph Conrad's *Heart of Darkness* (1899), both the landscape and the Africans are inscrutable and unknowable. The inability to *see* – whether through the dense vegetation, or into the characters of the Africans encountered – is one of the chief fears that plagues Marlow, the novel's narrator. He counters such fear with a classically Victorian attention to detail, to the navigation and the physical care of the boat on which he travels, and to the beauty of the order of the printed page, just as he has celebrated the map, displaying the range of the British empire in Africa, which is present in the company offices before his departure. Yet the novel which describes the black fireman on board the steamer as 'a dog in a parody of breeches and a feather hat, walking on his hind legs', also characterises colonialism as 'robbery with violence, aggravated murder on a great scale'.[12] Conrad's portrayal of the mercenary merchants of Africa's trading companies is intense in its criticisms of contemporary colonial activity.

In a similar way E.M. Forster's 1924 novel, *A Passage to India*, often a savage critique of all those involved in the colonial encounter in India, can portray the country as a space that the mind cannot properly conceive, and yet also point to its regulation through English law. Both in the scenes at the Marabar caves, and in the portrayal of the landscape more widely, India is seen to be 'never defined. She is not a promise, only an appeal', a space no one set of ideas can command. In an alternative image, however, Forster portrays India as a series of concentric circles radiating out from the courthouse at Chandrapore, from those involved with the law, through clients looking for lawyers and pleaders, to those ignorant and uncaring of court procedures, civility and the effect of law diminishing as the building is left behind. In a similar, though less ambiguous, image Rudyard Kipling once talked of 'lesser breeds without the law' in a characterisation of colonial Indians.[13]

The writing of empire between 1875 and 1914 in particular is often called 'colonial literature', coinciding with the high point of the European empires.[14] It was the writing of this period (and beyond, into the 1920s) that presented the greatest complexity in its portrayal of the colonial subject, as empire both reached its zenith and, in its bloated excess, immediately began its demise. The subjects in this literature could be degenerate and exotic, unknowable and yet stereotypically threatening, irredeemable and yet capable of reinvigorating a Europe (seemingly) blunted by modernity. For the first generation of post 1945 postcolonial novelists, growing up at the end of this period, it was this layered representation that offered a confused and confusing version of their selves. They saw a spectrum that ranged from idealised patronising at one end to outright racist prejudice at the other. To reinstate their sense of selfhood and community, and to reclaim a history banished from the new written accounts following culture contact, would require dealing with the full range of issues the previous 170 years had created.

The writers of the first postcolonial texts after 1945 employed a number of strategies and subjects. Some sought self-consciously to produce national epics often based on reflections upon landscape, like

Wilson Harris's first four novels, later grouped as *The Guyana Quartet* (1960-63), or Patrick White in *Voss* (1957).[15] In other cases the act of independence itself created an energy in the writing community. Indian novelists writing in English such as Bhabani Bhattacharya, Khushwant Singh, Khwaja Ahmad Abbas and Kamala Markandaya, whether in India or abroad, produced fiction that focused directly on the emergence of the new nation or portrayed details of the new community, either allegorically or using a contemporary setting.[16] In west Africa, the incredible fabular novels of Nigerian writer Amos Tutuola – *The Palm-Wine Drinkard* (1952), *My Life in the Bush of Ghosts* (1954), *Simbi and the Stayr of the Dark Jungle* (1955) and *The Brave African Huntress* (1958) – produced a raging debate about the 'difference' of African writing in English, and its ultimate worth. Equally, the novels of Cyprian Ekwensi, especially *When Love Whispers* (1948) and *People of the City* (1954), highlighted the possibility of a popular west African literature.[17]

It is hardly surprising, however, to find that many of the concerns of the earliest post-1945 postcolonial novels are political. The drive for political independence was one that was, by and large, supported by intellectuals, artists and writers across the postcolonial world. In some cases, writers themselves became part of the government, such as the Congelese author Henri Lopes. Even without such stark connections the moment of independence became, for many writers, the first chapter in the new story of place. It was thus an obvious subject, both in itself and in the way the new politics contrasted with the old colonial system of government. Many of the novels of the 1950s, whether written in the ex-colonies or by an emigrant generation moving to the former capitals of empire in Europe, focus on the ramifications of new political liberation.

V.S. Naipaul was one of the generation of Caribbean writers, including Harris, George Lamming, Sam Selvon and Andrew Salkey, who left the region for London during this period. Like his contemporaries, almost all Naipaul's early fiction is set not in the new home in which he found himself, but in the place he had left. His earliest writing forms a cycle, dealing with the Indian community in Trinidad, that progresses from *The Mystic Masseur* (1957), through *The Suffrage of Elvira* (1958) and *Miguel Street* (1959) to culminate in *A House for Mr. Biswas* (1961), the novel that established his international reputation. Naipaul was not so concerned with confronting the colonial portrayal of the Caribbean as with analysing its effects in the present in his home island.

The Mystic Masseur uses the run up to the Trinidadian election of

1946, which marked the establishment of the universal adult franchise, as the backdrop to Naipaul's analysis of individual action within the new community. In both this novel and *The Suffrage of Elvira*, which deals with the 1950 election that furthered self-government, Naipaul charts the emergence of national politics in the wake of the demise of traditional Hindu society. But for Naipaul neither system commands respect, rather both are simply a cover for individuals concerned with self advancement and personal gain. Hindu Trinidad was a product of the colonial importation of Indian labour to the post-emancipation Caribbean, to cover the work that was required in rural areas now that slaves could no longer be used. The new post-independence national politics was composed of borrowed rhetoric and forms. For Naipaul, both are distortions that become meaningless when placed in their new context. They invite only abuse and greed. Naipaul's mode for these novels is comic, but there is no disguising the cynicism behind his detailing of the rise of Pundit Ganesh, the masseur in the title of the first novel, from fake faith healer to national politician and an ultimate MBE. Ganesh succeeds not simply because of his own cunning strategies, but because he gives the people what they want. For Naipaul, it is the wider society that is still unformed and not ready for independence.

Naipaul's irony was well placed. The figures in *The Mystic Masseur* combine characteristics of actual politicians in Trinidad in the late 1940s, notably Albert Gomes and Arthur Cipriani. The comment on the actuality of postcolonial politics was meant to be recognised. Naipaul could not bring himself to celebrate the coming of independence, for all his knowledge of the misrepresentation of his home island in the colonial era. By setting his first two novels in the transition period between the end of colonial rule and the start of real self-government, Naipaul drew attention to the problems inherent in political self-determination. *The Mystic Masseur* and *The Suffrage of Elvira* differ significantly from a novel like Jamaican writer V.S. Reid's 1949 *New Day*, which views local elections as a stepping stone towards full independence and carries a distinctly nationalist sense of postcolonial possibility. For Naipaul, being true to his community and showing it for what it was meant, in his mind, analysing a place that was unmade and incapable of fully accepting the responsibilities of democratic independence. Though no other writer of this period is as extreme as Naipaul in such a view, this cynicism about politics, and especially the betrayal of the people by the new nationalist leaders when they achieve power, was a feature of emigrant Caribbean writing. The neo-colonial Mr Slime, an ex-teacher turned politician, is the vehicle for a similar thematic in Lamming's 1953 novel *In the Castle of My Skin*.

Naipaul's writing on postcolonial politics took another, more disillusioned, turn during the late 1960s and 1970s, but in the immediate post-independence period of a decade previously it was the work of Chinua Achebe in his first four novels that spoke tellingly of the hopes and fears of society following the transfer of power at the end of empire. Achebe was interested, in a way Naipaul was not, with the full force of the colonial legacy, its residual set of assumptions and prejudices. In *Things Fall Apart* (1958), *No Longer at Ease* (1960), *Arrow of God* (1964) and *A Man of the People* (1966), Achebe moves between the historical moments of turn-of-the-century culture contact in Nigeria and the immediacy of post-independence to portray the hugely complex nature of the new community. Although a generation of undergraduates have read it as the defining novel of culture clash and the colonial moment, *Things Fall Apart*, when set in the context of Achebe's next three novels, becomes increasingly revealing about the divisions within the local independent community and the problems facing the individual subject. The suicide of Okonkwo, the novel's central protagonist, points as much to the inability of the Igbo people to develop a sustained, coherent response to the British presence as it does to the incursion of European forms of religion, military technology and bureaucratic administration.

This, for Achebe, was the key tussle. In the Nigeria that achieved its independence in 1960, he saw a society pulled in different, often contradictory, directions. The need to modernise and become part of a global pattern of markets was paramount, but, by necessity it sat with the strong presence of traditional values and the hangover of a colonial sense of worth. In *No Longer at Ease*, set in the contemporary Nigeria of independence, Achebe tellingly opens the novel with the trial of Obi Okonkwo, the central protagonist, for bribery. Obi is educated, he has studied in Britain, and holds a junior government position. He is, in effect, the new Nigeria. Achebe is at pains to display how his fall could have occurred, seeking to explain in personal and psychological terms the difficulties of the new nation. Obi's subjecthood is stretched between the formal demands of his home community, which paid for his study abroad and loads him with expectations, and the reality of the more liberal world he inhabits in Lagos. In the same way as an earlier section of the novel portrays the dual inheritance handed to him by his parents (his father has an obsession with the European world of print and 'never destroyed a piece of paper', his mother is associated with coco-yames, kola nuts and the trappings of a more traditional life), Obi is forced to negotiate Nigeria's modernity, which asks that he both uphold the value system of a mainly rural, clan-based community, and be part of an increasingly capitalistic, urban national outlook. Achebe's deft characterisation means that Obi is aware of the tension inherent in this position, but never quite aware enough fully to articulate and analyse it. The novel is also adept at stressing the extension of Obi's dilemma into a greater social sphere. Driving from the city centre to the predominantly white suburb of Ikoyi, Obi recognises the stark divisions that have become integral to the new Nigeria:

> Going from the Lagos mainland to Ikoyi on a Saturday night was like going from a bazaar to a funeral. And the vast Lagos cemetery which separated the two places helped to deepen this feeling. For all its luxurious bungalows and flats and its extensive greenery, Ikoyi was like a graveyard. It had no corporate life – at any rate for the Africans who lived there. They had not always lived there, of course. It was once a European reserve. But things had changed and some Africans in 'European posts' had been given houses in Ikoyi. Obi Okonkwo, for example, lived there, and as he drove from Lagos to his flat he was struck again by these two cities in one. It always reminded him of twin kernels separated by a thin wall in a palm-nut shell. Sometimes one kernel was shiny-black and alive, the other powdery-white and dead.[18]

This passage deals with the internal ramifications of independence even as it also enters Obi's own musings. The image of the split palm-nut shell is, for Achebe, a stark demonstration of the irreconcilable pressures on Obi and the schizoid practicalities of contemporary Nigerian existence. And, as we have known since the first page of the novel, Obi succumbs to the complexities of his position.

Achebe's fiction does not, however, universally allocate blame upon his wayward characters. In the case of Obi, as with the protagonists of both *Arrow of God* and *A Man of the People*, personal failings are exacerbated by, especially, the political system which contextualises them. In *Arrow of God*, Achebe returns to the late colonial relationship of the first decades of the twentieth century, but his focus is still very much on the nature of the conflict within the local community as its people respond to British administration. 'It troubles me' one character remarks in the novel in reference to this conflict, 'because it looks like the saying of our ancestors that when brothers fight to death a stranger inherits their father's estate'.[19] The 'fighting of the brothers' in the Nigeria of the 1960s was the political struggle that seemed to many to be the betrayal of the promise of self-government, and to usher in neo-colonial corruption and ethnic intolerance. These are some of the issues of *A Man of the People*, where Achebe sets the young idealism of Odili Samalu, a Europeanised schoolteacher and would-be intellectual, against the political pragmatism of Chief Micha Nanga, a self-serving minister in the new independent government. Nanga is ostensibly the 'man of the people' of the title, but as Achebe charts the narrowing distance between him and Odili (Odili is seduced by the prospect of power, and his politics appear to develop mostly from a desire to extend personal relationships), the differences that might appear to exist between the two come into question. The politics of independence, Achebe suggests, exist in a world of selfish gain in which any individual might become lost.

A Man of the People has as its historical context the Nigerian electoral campaign of late 1964, when the period between October and December saw a rise in factional violence and corruption that marked the full force of the new nation's political instability. Achebe's ultimate pessimism lies in the fact that the coup that removes Nanga and his government at the end of the novel simply ushers in nameless and faceless generals who, it seems, will perpetuate the misrule. In addition, Achebe was more prescient than he knew. The novel in fact anticipated an actual coup which took place in Lagos during the very month in 1966 when *A Man of the People* was published.

The downbeat expression found in Naipaul and Achebe became more prevalent than any celebration of the postcolonial condition as the 1960s turned into the 1970s. Criticism of post-independent administrations and politics were frequent in novels as different as Wole Soyinka's *The Interpreters* (1965) and Ediriwira Sarachchandra's *Curfew and a Full Moon* (1978), from Nigeria and Sri Lanka respectively. They took place even as, like Achebe in *Things Fall Apart* and *Arrow of God*, postcolonial novelists sought to rework the misrepresentation of the historical past in colonial fiction. The central claim of the writers – of the right to tell their own stories – was still of paramount importance, but often as not those stories were of the dysfunctional present, and not achieved liberation.

Naipaul's novels turned from his focus on Trinidad to settings notionally fictional, though clearly based on the new nations of the Caribbean or of Africa. In *The Mimic Men* (1967), *Guerrillas* (1975) and *A Bend in the River* (1979), Naipaul extends his cynicism about postcolonial politics to become a virtual pathology of place, where sickness, decay and personal disillusionment pervade all aspects of existence. As Ralph Singh, ex-politician and narrator of *The Mimic Men*, notes on his fall from government power on the Caribbean island of Isabella: 'We pretended to be real, to be learning, to be preparing ourselves for life, we mimic men of the New World, one unknown corner of it, with all its reminders of the corruption that came so quickly to the new'.[20] For Naipaul, postcolonial political selfhood had become, as the 1960s turned into the 1970s, either the inappropriate borrowed rhetoric of racial struggle or the peripheral power invested in a small player, and loser, in the global economy. None of his characters can act out of a belief in a better future.

Other writers developed different concerns. In terms of the promotion of political ideology, the most significant polemical work during the period was that produced by Ngugi wa Thiong'o in Kenya. In *A Grain of Wheat* (1967) and *Petals of Blood* (1977) Ngugi offers a sustained Marxist attack on the neo-colonialism of post-independence Kenya. In *Petals of Blood* the inhabitants of Ilmorog, a rural village which enshrines notions of peasant virtue for Ngugi, undertake an epic trek to Nairobi to inform their political representatives of the extent of drought in the interior. Instead of being met with concern, and instead of prompting the workings of democratic government, the villagers become subject to abuse and the settlement itself becomes the object of a cynical political and cultural nationalism which overdevelops the region with an excess of capitalistic investment. The novel sees the village transformed by business interests into New Ilmorog, stripping away all community values and leaving only exploitation and oppression. For Ngugi, such abuse can only be met with the concentrated response of Marxism, and *Petals of Blood* ends with the stirring of the worker's struggle against the employers of New Ilmorog. No novelist of the post-independent period enshrined the intellectual commitment to Marxist liberation more than Ngugi, and his influence as a writer of the left can be seen in a later novelist like Nigerian author Festus Iyayi, in novels such as *Violence* (1979) and *The Contract* (1982).[21]

The political subject in postcolonial fiction increasingly became a subject of gendered politics. Jean Rhys's anger at the misrepresentation of the Caribbean creole in *Jane Eyre* led to her reworking of the canonical text in *Wide Sargasso Sea* (1966). The mute and savage Bertha of Bronte's novel is, as Antoinette, given back her own story. In Africa, Flora Nwapa and Buchi Emecheta from the west and Bessie Head from the south point to the detailed gendered patterns of the post-colony. In the work of the two former writers especially, in novels such as Nwapa's *Never Again* (1975) and *Women Are Different* (1981) and

Emecheta's *The Joys of Motherhood* (1979), the challenge posed by female characters to the dominant male power structures is in itself a comment on the political structures of the communities in question. In settler colonies, the early novels of Rhodesian/Zimbabwean writer Doris Lessing attack the colonial psyche in gender and political terms, while Nadine Gordimer's novels offer a sustained and changing commentary on South African apartheid.[22] Possibly the most forceful congruence of the issue of postcolonial identity politics and gender comes in Margaret Atwood's 1972 novel *Surfacing*. Atwood's unnamed protagonist, on a return visit to the Canadian wilderness to search for her missing father, begins a retreat from a world increasingly seen to be dominated by both patriarchal concerns and the heritage of a colonial conquest that now manifests itself in the new guise of American power over Canada. Her literal plunge into the landscape at the novel's end, in order to surface as a new, more appropriate, subject, concludes a commanding comment on the link between postcolonial and gendered power systems.

The subject emerging at the end of *Surfacing* is one conceived of in essential terms. The novel's portrayal of the landscape is one of a literal agent of cleansing, and the feminism and Canadian nationalism that run through the text are equally seen as being rooted in the landscape. For Atwood, at this stage of her writing, the soil is real soil, and identity necessarily made secure. It is not metaphorical, not hybrid.

By the 1980s, however, many postcolonial novelists were rejecting the notion of an essential identity, and portraying the issues surrounding subjectivity and politics in a more fractured and fluid manner. In part the reasons for this were historical and demographic. The novels of the 1950s and 1960s had achieved the necessary first stage of inscribing postcolonial life. The culture was now on the page and, to some degree, later novelists could look on the work of writers such as Achebe or Ngugi more as a legacy than as a recording of contemporary concerns. Equally, the turbulent era of independence had gone and was now replaced by complex political and cultural movements between the ex-colonies and the former imperial centres. In addition, a generation of writers born in Europe of parents who had made initial migrations in the 1950s and 1960s added a further layer to the kind of fiction now included in the category of the postcolonial. Fiction made its own demands too. The work of earlier writers from South America, magic realists from Jose Luis Borges to Gabriel Garcia Marquez, offered forms and methods that seemed more of use in explaining the migrancy and in-between nature of the postcolonial subject in the

1980s and 1990s. The new nature of lived experience demanded new vehicles of expression.

The most prominent novelist of this new orthodoxy is Salman Rushdie, and the key texts (especially with regard to politics) are *Midnight's Children* (1981), *Shame* (1983) and *The Satanic Verses* (1988). Rushdie's method in his novels is to write on a epic scale, injecting fantasy into the history and politics of India, Pakistan and Britain (respectively for the three above novels) and lacing the whole with satire, myth, humour and a shimmering parodic intensity that deliberately confuses narrative structures and character development. Saleem Sinai, the narrator of *Midnight's Children*, born on the exact second of Indian independence, is physically disintegrating as he recounts his narrative, redolent of Rushdie's fear that the communalism of India will tear apart the secular idea of its foundation. To further this, Saleem is twinned with his nemesis and opposite, Shiva, born at the same moment, and Rushdie balances Saleem's struggle to partake in a positive construction of India with the chaos and destruction Shiva brings. The novel's account of Indira Gandhi's suspension of civil rights during the Indian Emergency of 1975-77 is a sustained piece of political criticism, even as it is contextualised by Rushdie's word play and fabular fantasy. Equally, the central characters of *Shame* are thinly veiled recreations of Zia-ul-Haq and Zulfikar Ali Bhutto and his daughter Benazir, and the novel's account of politics led to it being banned in Pakistan.

Rushdie has himself identified the issue of migrancy as the key leitmotif of his work, and considers his own subjectivity in terms of his movement between the cultures in which he has lived.[23] It is *The Satanic Verses* that contains Rushdie's most flamboyant attempt to convey these multiplicities. The novel ranges from the tension-filled streets of racialised Britain, across the poverty and religion of the Indian subcontinent, to a fictionalised account of the rise of Islam and the prophet Muhammed, all contained within the twinned stories of Gibreel Farishta, a star of Indian religious film, and Saladin Chamcha, a London based radio and stage actor. The novel's opening, when both characters, in conversation, fall from a burning plane, is possibly the period's most graphic and arresting image of movement and migrancy.

Rushdie's novels are not simply international eclecticism. For all their similarities with the questioning of narrative form that characterises contemporary writing worldwide, they are also connected to an Indian tradition of experimental fiction that includes G.V. Desani's *All About H. Hatterr* (1951), Raja Rao's *The Cat and Shakespeare* (1965) and Madhavaiah Anantanarayanan's *The Silver Pilgrimage* (1961). In particular, Rushdie's major work of the 1980s sought to deal with social and political issues, especially those of ethnic and cultural prejudice. In this, his fiction as metaphysics is oriented around community issues in a way that is typical of the contemporary postcolonial novel. Similar interrogations can be found in Ben Okri from Nigeria, Peter Carey from Australia and Zulfikar Ghose in Pakistan, as well as Robert Kroetsch and Michael Ondaatje in Canada.[24]

Ondaatje shares Rushdie's mobility. Born in Sri Lanka of Dutch origin, he moved to Canada via schooling in Britain. In his 1987 novel *In the Skin of a Lion*, Ondaatje seeks to rewrite the history of Toronto, undermining the notion of the community as the product of great men and lofty institutions, and instead stressing the role of immigrant workers in the literal construction of the city's landscape. Eschewing the received wisdom of Canada as a nation formulated around French and English cultures, Ondaatje's workers are Serbs, Finns and Macedonians, and even Patrick Lewis, one of the central characters who is actually born in Canada, is described as being 'an immigrant to the city'.[25] Ondaatje's choice of John Berger's assertion that 'never again will a single story be told as if it were the only one' as an epigraph for the novel, neatly sums up his project, and the novel itself balances between poetry and prose, print and images, in its non linear drive. His 1992 *The English Patient* continues such concerns, with a central character stripped of skin, memory and therefore identity, and a landscape of shifting desert sand that is the perfect metaphor for Ondaatje's sense of place.[26]

The sense of a liminality of place in this later fiction no way makes the communities concerned less political. In part, the work of Rushdie, Ondaatje and others can now also be seen in the light of the end of the Cold War, and the breakdown of binary political divisions. In the same way that the new political subjects of the postcolonial world are pulled between ethnic groupings, national affiliations and the global nature of a world driven by capitalism, so their literary representation enacts multiplicities of narratives and codes. Often the desire for the accurate presentation of self and community in this later fiction shares the outlook of those writers some thirty years earlier. Whilst writers such as Rushdie and Ondaatje might be seen to constitute a new orthodoxy in the contemporary novel, it would be wrong to represent their style of writing as the only expression of the present-day postcolonial subject. In 1987, Achebe returned with *Anthills of the Savannahs*, his first novel in over twenty years and an account of a period between coups in the Republic of Kanga, a thinly veiled Nigeria. Achebe's concerns here are still similar to those of *A Man of the People*, in the same way that Nigeria's political instability has progressed apace from the 1960s to the 1990s. The form of the more recent fiction may be more fluid, and the writing may seem more secure and indeed enormously vital in its innovation, but it is worth noting that the dysfunctional society, and the individual trapped within it, is still often the subject matter of postcolonial fiction.

NOTES

1. See Evan Luard, *A History of the United Nations, Volume 2: The Age of De-colonization, 1955-1965*, Macmillan, Basingstoke 1989. See also Raymond F. Betts, *Decolonization*, Routledge, London and New York 1998.

2. Quoted in Edwin Tetlow, *The United Nations: The First 25 Years*, Peter Owen, London 1970, p100.

3. V.S. Naipaul, 'Jasmine', *Times Literary Supplement*, 4 June 1964. Reprinted in *The Overcrowded Baracoon and other essays*, Andr™ Deutsch, London 1972, pp23-29.

4. Arun Mukherjee, 'Who's Post colonialism and who's Post-modernism?', *World Literatures Written in English*, 30, 2, 1990. Quoted in Judie Newman, *The Ballistic Bard: Post-colonial Fictions*, Arnold, London and New York 1995, p4.

5. J.C. Beaglehole (ed), *The Journals of Captain James Cook on His Voyages of Discovery. The Voyage of the Endeavour, 1768-1771* Hakluyt Press, Cambridge 1955, p312.

6. Dampier, quoted in Bernard Smith, *European Vision and the South Pacific: 1768-1850*, OUP, Oxford 1960, p126. On pp125-127, Smith discusses the differences between Dampier and Cook.

7. *The Voyage of the Endeavour*, *op. cit.*, p399. Interestingly, this section was omitted by John Hawkesworth when he came to collect a number of the key late eighteenth-century voyage narratives in a single volume, *An Account of the Voyages Undertaken by Order of His Present Majesty for Making Discoveries in the Southern Hemisphere*, 3 vols. W. Strahan and T. Cadell, London 1773, possibly because of the nature of the analogy Cook draws.

8. See Philp Edwards, *The Story of the Voyage: Sea Narratives in Eighteenth-Centry England*, CUP, Cambridge 1994. For a specific account of how the voyage narratives shadowed the development of eighteenth-century fiction, see Leonard J. Davis, 'The Facts of Events and the Events of Facts: New World Explorers and the Early Novel', *The Eighteenth Century: Theory and Interpretation*, 32, 3, 1991, pp240-255.

9. Bart Moore-Gilbert, *Writing India, 1757-1990*, MUP, Manchester 1996, p23. Ania Loomba, *Colonialism/Postcolonialism*, Routledge, London and New York 1998, pp182-183.

10. Mary Louise Pratt, *Imperial Eyes: Travel Writing and Transculturation*, Routledge, London and New York, 1992, p5.

11. See, in particular, *Culture and Imperialism*, Chatto & Windus, London 1993.

12. Joseph Conrad, *Heart of Darkness*, Penguin, London and Harmondsworth 1985, p70 and p31.

13. E.M. Forster, *A Passage to India*, Everyman, London 1942, p121 & p29.

14. The dates are mainly used by historians. See, for example, Eric Hobsbawn's, *The Age of Empire, 1875-1914*, Weidenfeld & Nicolson, London 1987. In her anthology of the literature of the period, Elleke Boehmer extends both dates to allow for greater coverage. See Boehmer, *Empire Writing: An Anthology of Colonial Literature, 1870-1918*, OUP, Oxford 1998. For a collection of poetry arranged around similar themes, see Chris Brooks and Peter Faulkner (eds), *The White Man's Burden: An Anthology of British Poetry of the Empire*, Exeter University Press, Exeter 1996.

15. The four novels in *The Guyana Quartet* are: *Palace of the Peacock* (1960), *The Far Journey of Oudin* (1961), *The Whole Armour* (1962) and *The Secret Ladder* (1963). Even though the settler colony Dominions of Australia, New Zealand, Canada and South Africa had achieved self-government earlier than 1945, many of the key postcolonial concerns of self-worth and legitimacy emerge in fiction from these countries after the war. In part this was due to infrastructural events, like the growth of local publishing (as opposed to having to publish fiction in London), but it was also connected to the wider feeling that accompanied the accelerated loss of empire.

16. For Bhattacharya, see *So Many Hungers!* (1947), *Music for Mohini* (1952) and *He Who Rides a Tiger* (1954). For Singh, see *Train to Pakistan* (1956). For Abbas, see *Inquilab: A Novel of Indian Revolution* (1955), and the earlier *Tomorrow is Ours: A Novel of the India of Today* (1943). For Markandaya, see *Nectar in a Sieve* (1954) and *Some Inner Fury* (1955).

17. For the debate surrounding Tutuola, see Bernth Lindfors (ed), *Critical Perspectives on Amos Tutuola* Heinemann, London 1975. For the emergence of a popular literature in Nigeria, sometimes called 'Onitsha Market' writing, see Emmanuel Obiechina, *An African Popular Literature: A Study of the Onitsha Market Pamphlets* CUP, Cambridge 1973.

18. Chinua Achebe, *The African Trilogy*, Picador, London 1988, p187. Achebe's first three novels have subsequently been published together in this single volume.

19. Achebe, *The African Trilogy*, *op. cit.*, p545.

20. Naipaul, *The Mimic Men*, André Deutsch, London 1967, p175.

21. Both Ngugi and Iyayi spent periods studying and working in the Soviet Union. Ngugi's Marxist concerns continue in his later fiction, such as the 1987 novel *Matigari*. He also has produced a significant number of essays on the necessity of political commitment in writing. See especially *Writers in Politics: A Re-Engagement with issues of Literature and Society*, Heinemann, London 1981, and *Decolonising the Mind: the Politics of Language in African Literature*, Currey, London 1986.

22. See especially the first four novels of Lessing's Martha Quest series, *Martha Quest* (1952), *A Proper Marriage* (1954), *A Ripple from the Storm* (1958) and *Landlocked* (1965). For Gordimer, see *A World of Strangers* (1958), *Occasion for Loving* (1963), *A Guest of Honor* (1970) and *Burger's Daughter* (1979) in particular.

23. See the essays contained in *Imaginary Homelands: Essays and Criticism 1981-1991* Granta, London 1991.

24. See, Okri, *The Famished Road* (1991), Carey, *Illywhacker* (1985) and *Oscar and Lucinda* (1988), Ghose, *Figures of Enchantment* (1986).

25. Ondaatje, *In the Skin of a Lion*, Picador, London 1988, p53.

26. Like Rushdie, Ondaatje looks back to immediate postwar novels in his fiction. *The English Patient* is indebted both to Malcom Lowry's *Under the Volcano* (1947) and Paul Bowles' *The Sheltering Sky* (1949).

The Complex 'I'

PAUL CILLIERS AND TANYA DE VILLIERS

WHY COMPLEXITY?

A theory of the subject does not only determine how we think about ourselves, but also determines the way in which we behave towards others. When we talk about the subject, therefore, we are not busy only with some technical philosophical discourse, but with an ethical one as well. The realisation that we cannot maintain a clear distinction between purely rational issues on the one hand, and ethical ones, on the other, is one of the most valuable insights gained by a critique of modernity. A rejection of the instrumental and 'objective' rationality proposed by many modernists should therefore not lead to a relativist postmodernism, but to one in which the notion of responsibility is central.

Jean-Francois Lyotard characterises as *modern* any discourse that legitimates itself with reference to what he calls a *meta-discourse*.[1] *Postmodernism* can therefore be understood as incredulity towards these meta-narratives. This incredulity is not merely the result of a disruptive impulse on the part of contemporary theorists, a wilful undermining of the rules of legitimation necessary to reach consensus on our knowledge of the world, but is the result rather of the realisation that a meta-discourse, in attempting to provide unified descriptions of the world, cannot do justice to the complexities of the things described.

The term 'postmodern' has unfortunately acquired so many different connotations, many of them pejorative, that it is difficult to use the word meaningfully without a host of qualifications. One way of dealing with this problem is to emphasise that modernism's most telling weakness was the way in which it oversimplified the world. One can then develop a critique of modernity from the perspective of complexity theory which does not make use of too much postmodern jargon.

That will be our central approach in this discussion of what the self could be. In the process we will also make use of a number of ideas from deconstruction. It will be shown that the two perspectives – one from complexity and the other from deconstruction – supplement each other in a very useful fashion. The discussion will commence, however, with a look at more traditional theories of the self.

A CARTESIAN VIEW

One of the most important examples of a meta-narrative of the self remains that of Descartes. His argument rests on the claim that the only thing of which anyone can be certain is the mind and the ability to think, a capacity which operates independently of the senses and of emotions. Descartes's argument is important because it established a dominant discourse on the subject, one which cannot be ignored, despite the fact that it is meeting with increasing resistance.

In keeping with the emerging tradition of his day, Descartes wanted to discover 'only one thing that is certain and indubitable',[2] something which Stephen Toulmin refers to as the 'primitive elements in experience' which were to be available to any reflexive thinker in all cultures at all times.[3] Descartes and his successors were concerned with developing a formal theory of the subject, one with universal validity. The assumption of universality makes it unproblematic for him to start with his own existence as paradigm example – existence would be a universal attribute of all selves, 'certain and indubitable'. Yet he is not entirely clear on what this entails:

> But what is a man? Shall I say a rational animal? Assuredly not; for it would be necessary forthwith to inquire into what is meant by animal, and what by rational, and thus, from a single question, I should insensibly glide into others, and these more difficult than the first; nor do I now possess enough of leisure to warrant me in wasting my time amid subtleties of this sort. I prefer here to attend to the thoughts that sprung up of themselves in my mind, and were inspired by my own nature alone, when I applied myself to the consideration of what I was.[4]

The Enlightenment ideal consisted partly in framing questions in a purely 'rational' manner that would render them independent of context. The results of these 'rational' arguments could then be applied in other contexts as well.[5] For Descartes it is adequate to focus only on those thoughts which are inherent to his own nature and thus do not have their origin in anything other than his own mind. Only these thoughts would be independent of context. His conception of the self is that of an essential mind, able to register (albeit with a degree of suspicion) and act upon the world, but not of a mind *formed* by the world. This is the timeless, permanent structure of the self that does not change in a contingent world. The constitution of his mind is not even dependent on the body in which it resides. Indeed, it possesses independent faculties that are capable of being deceived by the rest of his body, especially his senses and imaginations.[6]

The mind (understanding) is not initially aware of its essential nature and only becomes aware of its susceptibility to deception upon reflecting on its own nature. It has to be 'retained within the limits of truth'.[7] For Descartes mental life encompasses rational calculation, intuitive ideas, intellectual deliberations and sensory inputs and the subject cannot accept responsibility for the emotions that interfere with or influence these calculations and inferences.[8]

The mind's ability to think is its essence, a fixed and universal attribute. This essence is inherent to the mind and sufficient to know it with.[9] From here, it is not difficult to see that Descartes's thought leads to a solipsism. An individual is trapped inside his own head and reflects upon images of the external world that reach his mind. The accounts of other people cannot be trusted or considered when forming a cognitive picture of the world. Descartes does not inquire into how it is possible for thoughts not to be inspired by anything beyond his own nature, to 'spring up by themselves' in his mind. Where does his own nature come from? What do his thoughts consist of? Is his true nature completely divorced from the environment in which he finds himself?

Zygmunt Bauman's description of modernity as 'a long march to prison'[10] can also be applied to the Cartesian understanding of the subject. Bauman asserts that the modernist approach to the world arose from the (shocking) realisation that there is no order *inherent* to the world; everything is contingent. In order for events to be regular, repeatable and predictable (in other words independent of context), order needs to be *imposed* onto the chaotic natural world. The same goes for the subject. Descartes wants to know what about himself is certain and indubitable; and in order for him to reach his answer (that is his mind), he has to disregard 'subtleties'; he has to become measurable, containable and knowable. Bauman asserts that modernity managed to order the world by 'obsessively legislating, defining, structuring, segregating, classifying, recording and universalising'[11] so that it could reflect universal and absolute standards of truth. Descartes's treatment of the subject also incorporates this strategy of structuring, classifying and universalising. He insists on elucidating the nature of the essential mind, independently from the contingencies that the corporeal body is subject to. His attempt to impose order onto the mind leads directly to the dichotomy between mind and body, and to the severing of the relationship between the self and the world. This view of the self is more than a little restrictive; we are caught in the prisons of our skulls. The Cartesian understanding of the subject leads us to disregard much of what it means to be human in the world. It also leads us to undervalue the relationships between selves. At the heart of this formal approach thus lies an insensitivity to the way in which the subject is constituted by ethical and political interaction. This issue will receive more attention in the final section, but let us first examine a more contemporary view which appears to stress freedom.

The Sartrean view of the self is one in which 'we will to exist at the same time as we fashion our image',[12] but does it escape the idea of the subject as an autonomous entity, an essential unity which ultimately has the ability to determine what it wants to be? Sartre declares his position so: 'Man is nothing else but that which he makes of himself...[he] is, before all else, something which propels itself toward a future and is aware that it is doing so...[b]efore that projection of the self nothing exists; not even in the heaven of intelligence: man will only attain existence when he is what he purposes to be'.[13]

Whilst the idea of freedom from determinism – including the fact that the ultimate responsibility for what man is lies with man – is an attractive one, it is not altogether certain that this ultimate freedom is possible. The ability to choose your own image, and to exist at one and the same time, presupposes an autonomous 'you' that can be distinguished over and above existence in a contingent world. This would compel Sartre to say that a person can 'make' herself in complete independence from the circumstances that she finds herself in.[14] Although Sartre denies a universal human essence or nature, he presupposes a subject with the universal ability freely to determine itself and its existence.

Both Descartes and Sartre are certain of one thing: that there is a world 'out there', external to and independent of the world 'in here'. In both cases the subject is clearly designated and is cordoned off from the world. Descartes's *cogito* and Sartre's man will have a universal structure, no matter where and when in the world they find themselves. Both these accounts of the subject lead to a number of questions: Where do subjects come from? What constitutes them? Are subjects with an immobile, essential nature able to deal with the contingencies of their environment? How does the environment affect them? Descartes purposely rejects the complexities (the subtleties) of his subject matter in order to discover what is essential to the subject. If we were to argue that it is these very complexities that constitute the subject, it becomes impossible to talk about an essential mind, or a completely autonomous subject.

We wish to argue for such a complex view of the self, a rich perspective on what constitutes the self, but also a perspective that takes seriously the limits imposed on the self. Before we do that, it may be useful briefly to examine another approach to the self, that of traditional analytic philosophy.

AN ANALYTICAL VIEW OF IDENTITY

As a point of departure for our discussion of the standard debate on personal identity in contemporary analytical philosophy, we will rely on the discussion and critique offered by Stefaan Cuypers.[15] He focuses on two approaches to identity within this tradition: the bundle theory (which draws upon 'logical atomism') and the ego theory (which has an origin in 'Cartesian atomism'). He argues that these positions overlap since both rely on a foundationalist theory of knowledge which privileges *present* experience. The 'I' is an object of direct knowledge while external objects can only be known indirectly. (The 'I' here is taken to mean the mind only. The first person's body is seen as part of the rest of the external world.) The identity of the person is considered in isolation and nothing but the first person's mind can be relevant to the construction of her identity. Atomistic identity is non-bodily identity; the mind is linked only contingently to a particular body.

These theories rely on a perceptual theory of self-knowledge. Knowing oneself is to observe one's own mind and its contents. Ontologically these theories rely on both an external and internal (psychological) world and these consist of separate particulars or atoms. Atoms are indivisible and stand in external relation to one another. The self is either a spiritual atom (the Cartesian ego) or a collection of mental atoms (a bundle of experiences). Cuypers criticises these two theories by showing that the perceptual model of self-knowledge, on which the two theories rely, is radically inadequate.[16]

Cuypers's critique is based on the argument that the problem of personal identity rests on an intellectual illusion. The standard debate on personal identity (in the analytic tradition) seems to accept philosophical atomism,[17] something which leads to epistemological foundationalism. If the perceptual model of self-knowledge is untenable, then the atomistic idea of the self as object of introspective knowledge becomes impossible. Cuypers asserts that his epistemological criticism makes it impossible to interpret the problem of identity as the problem of the self-identity of the first person and that it also casts doubt upon the idea of the ontological separateness of selves and experiences.[18]

Within the bounds of analytic philosophy Cuypers postulates a person as 'a bodily, public and dynamic agent who engages with other persons and the world'.[19] He believes that this conception of the person does not go far enough because it does not transgress 'the bounds of descriptive metaphysics'. There is nothing wrong with trying to render our experiences intelligible through postulating non-experiential metaphysical principles. He calls upon the 'psychophysical personalism of the Aristotelian-Thomistic view,' where an existing substance, as an 'active self communicating presence, cannot *be* without *being* related in some way.'[20] Along the lines of this 'Aristotelian-Thomistic validatory anthropology', Cuypers develops a non-atomistic view of personal identity. Because a person is a substantial psychophysical unity, personal identity has bodily identity as an essential aspect. A person manifests and communicates himself or herself to a community of other beings; s/he constitutes a web of relations around herself or himself. In this web of relations a being exists in her- or himself toward others.

According to Cuypers the bodily aspect of personal identity depends upon the spacio-temporal continuity of a personal body, but this does not exclude a non-bodily personal identity.

> Although bodily identity essentially realises (earthly) personal identity, the latter is not reducible to the former. As Rodin's statue of 'The Thinker' is constituted by a particular lump of bronze without being identical to it, so a person is constituted by a particular human organism without being identical to it. In other words, bodily identity is a necessary but not sufficient condition of personal identity.[21]

Cuypers asserts that personal identity comprises of an agential identity over and above bodily identity: a person is a dynamic, self-communicative agent in relation to a public world. An agent needs the powers of intellect, will and memory. These are self-consciously exercised and make agential identity subjective; 'a person is continuously and immediately present to himself'.[22] This self-presence occurs in a unitary spacio-temporal framework, a personal body. 'In sum, personal identity as agential identity essentially consists in the narrative unity of the actions of a rational and moral agent in a social setting within a historical condition.'[23]

Cuypers's argument helps us to make some important advances. He is sensitive to specific historical conditions and to the importance of the ethical dimension. However, an approach informed by complexity theory would also have a number of important differences. Cuypers views a person as a logical unity with a bodily identity which does not exclude a 'non-bodily identity'. He adheres to a distinction between the body – with its functions of intellect, will, and memory – and a separate, non-bodily identity that is fully present to itself, which can present itself as an agent in social relationships. Is this position really that different from Descartes's *cogito*? It seems that Cuypers does not manage to move much beyond 'philosophical atomism'. He still distinguishes between an external world, which the self experiences and acts upon, and an 'in here' with an essential, separate identity (even though it is dependent upon its spatio-temporal body). In order to develop an understanding of the self that is relational through and through, a brief introduction to the theory of complex systems is required.

WHAT IS A COMPLEX SYSTEM?

The burden of the argument so far has been to show that traditional theories of the self are too rigid. Starting from essentialist features or distinctions fails to capture the complexity of the self and leads to an impoverished account of what it means to be human. An approach which views the self as a complex system would, we hope, overcome some of these problems.

Talking about a complex system requires that we take into account how constituents of this complex system interact amongst themselves, as well as with the environment that the system functions in.[24] A complex system has a large number of components whose working and interactions as a whole cannot be analysed precisely. Any analysis will have to impose limits on the description of the system, and will therefore distort aspects of the system. Examples of complex systems are usually living or social systems: the brain, for example, or living organisms, language, the economy. What follows is a brief and general description of the characteristics of a complex system.[25] The implications of this for the self will be returned to later.

i)   A complex system consists of a large number of elements which by themselves could be simple.

ii) The elements of a complex system are in dynamic interaction. This interaction need not necessarily be physical; but could also be thought of in terms of transference of information.

iii) The interactions between elements are rich, where every element can influence many other elements in the system. The behaviour of the system is not determined by the exact number of interactions associated with specific elements.

iv) The interactions between them are non-linear. Small causes can have large results (and *vice versa*).

v) The interactions occur over a short range, but can have long-range influence, mediated by other components. The influence interactions can have can be suppressed, enhanced or modulated along the way.

vi) There are many loops and feedback paths in the system – the effect of any activity can feed back onto itself.

vii) Complex systems are open systems. They interact with their environment and it often becomes difficult to define the borders of a system. The limits of a system are usually imposed on it by our description of it, not by some natural feature of the system. This is referred to as the problem of framing.

viii) Complex systems operate under conditions far from equilibrium. Equilibrium is another word for death.

ix) Complex systems have a history. They evolve through time and their past is co-responsible for their present behaviour.

x) Each element of the system is ignorant of behaviour of the rest of the system, or of the system as a whole – it can only respond to information available to it locally.

A complex system is not merely a passive reflection of its environment, nor does it control the environment. The relationship between the two involves a dialectic that is neither active nor passive.[26] The environment is usually complex in itself, and in order to cope, a complex system needs to be able to do two things: it needs to be able to store information about its environment, (memory) and it needs to be able to adapt its structure to changes around it. This means that a complex system needs to gather information about its environment. This information cannot be a random collection of elements; it has to be meaningful to be to the system's advantage. Interesting philosophical questions can be raised at this point: How does this meaning come about? Is it inherent to the environment, waiting to be comprehended by the system, or does the environment have no meaning, save for that which the system confers upon it?

The environment in which a complex system functions changes continually and for this reason the system cannot behave in a rigid manner. It needs to be adaptable in order to cope with changes. Specific adaptations cannot be programmed into the system, nor can the system act according to inherent or *a priori* principles which do not take the external world into account. In order to deal with contingencies, the system has to be able to organise *itself*. This self-organisation relationally incorporates the history of the system (memory) and elements external to it. What is important here is that there is no central control, the network acts upon the relation between memory and external information to satisfy the constraints under which it operates.[27] Thus the structure of the system cannot be determined completely by the environment in which it finds itself, nor is the environment important merely to the extent that it serves the purposes of the system. Meaning, for a specific system in a specific context, is the result of a process, and this process is dialectical (involving elements from 'inside' and 'outside' the system) as well as historical (previous states of the system are vitally important). The way in which a complex system cannot be clearly demarcated from its environment has obvious implications for our understanding of the self, an idea to which we shall return.

The information that the system stores cannot be random, it needs to be useful for the survival and success of the system. The meaning this information has cannot be explained simply in terms of correspondence to some objective set of conditions in the world. If it merely mirrors the world around it, the system will have no separate identity that can be recognised. The system needs to interact with its environment, it needs to interpret what it sees in terms of its specific history. The relationships already established among the structural components of the system provide a framework that confers 'meaning' upon what is perceived. Such 'meaning' then, is in the world, but not *determined* by the world. This again has implications for how we understand ourselves in the world.

We cannot separately analyse each constituent of a system in the hope that we will capture the essence of the system. Because the characteristics of the system are established in the relationships between the components, we destroy such characteristics (often called 'emergent properties') when we divide the system up. Since emergent properties are the result of the interactions in the system, they cannot be predicted by an examination of the individual. Furthermore, the non-linearity of the interactions means that we cannot replace one set of interactions with another, simpler set of interactions. The law of superposition does not hold. This leads us to an important conclusion: a complex system cannot be broken into its constituent parts, nor can it be replaced by a simpler system, without losing its vital characteristics. From this we can deduce that formal, *a priori* models of complex systems (like the self) will not fully capture their nature.[28]

Before we offer a more detailed examination of the implications of the theory of complex systems, in order to further our understanding of the self, we will present some insights from the work of Derrida. It is illuminating to compare the affinities between deconstruction and complexity.

DECONSTRUCTION AND COMPLEXITY

In a recent interview Derrida asserts: ' ... a pure identity which is identical to itself is simultaneously identical to death'.[29] This statement, which may seem ambiguous at first glance, can be given content in terms of our discussion of complex systems. A complex system can only exist, and transform itself, if there is a flow of energy and information through the system. A system survives (and also flourishes) in terms of tensions, anticipations and investments that may or may not mature.[30] When it reaches a state of equilibrium, it ceases to exist. These tensions are exactly the kind of thing that deconstruction zooms in on – not to destroy or eliminate them, but to tease them out, to transform them. Deconstruction and complexity are both notions that cannot do without some form of engagement. Meaning is a result of engagement.

The relationship between deconstruction and complexity can be made in a more general way with reference to Saussure's model of language. This model describes language as a system of signs which obtain their meaning through their relationships with all the other signs in the system. These relations are rich, non-linear (they are relationships of difference) and there are many feedback loops. It is not surprising that language can be described in terms of complexity. It is also interesting to follow how Derrida's elaboration of Saussure's model helps us to develop our understanding of complex phenomena.[31]

The traditional way of viewing language, one to which Saussure also adhered, is to take spoken language as the pure case. It occurs in a context where meaning seems to be *present* as a result of the illusion that the person who is being addressed can at any time, at least in principle, interrupt the conversation and ask for an explanation or clarification. Someone reading a written text does not have this certainty. A written text is the representation of the words that would have been spoken. With the writer of the text absent, the reader is left to interpret the text as accurately as possible, but there is always room for misunderstanding. Derrida argues that written language provides us with a better understanding of language, and that we should see speech as a kind of writing.

Meaning is never present in an unmediated form, but has to be reconstructed. The spoken word is, like the written one, a material form which needs to be interpreted, and which gains its meaning from its differences from other material forms. We cannot conceive of meaning outside these conditions (as, for example, an *a priori* essence, or as an ideal representation). This dynamic would not only pertain to language as such, but to anything that can be given meaning. It is in this sense that our interpretation of the world, and of ourselves, are textual events. We, as subjects, become who we are, have meaning, in terms of a set of relationships with others. In Derrida's terms, 'the assemblage to be proposed has the complex structure of a weaving, an interlacing which permits the different threads and different lines of meaning – or of force – to go off again in different directions, just as it is always ready to tie itself up with others'.[32]

A text's meaning cannot be exhausted, nor can it be controlled or prescribed. Meaning is not *present* in the text itself, it lies in the relationships between elements in the system of which it forms a part. Derrida calls the relationship between any two elements in a system a *trace*. A myriad of traces work to generate a pattern of meaning which they constrain, but cannot fix.[33] Any trace can contribute to a different meaning in a different context since there will be a different *collection* of traces when the context changes. One can also see traces as that in which the history of the system is sedimented. To establish a meaning in a given instance is to alter the traces, and this will influence future interpretations. Meaning cannot be static.

It is useful to explain the way in which traces interact in order to constitute meaning in terms of Derrida's notion of *différance*.[34] In French this word corresponds phonetically to the word *difference* and in this manner encompasses three meanings, namely 'to differ', 'difference' and 'to defer'. Traces are different from one another, and in the interaction between these differences meaning is generated. But meaning is not static or final, it is always deferred. The process in which meaning is generated is suspended somewhere between active and passive. The sign is produced by the system, but at the same time the meaning that is generated for it through the process of *différance* reverberates through the system, influencing other signs. The characteristics of the system are not inherent to it, but are the result of the process of *différance*.[35]

Meanings are constituted in a context, in a discourse. There are many contexts which do not have an absolute centre and which cannot be exhaustively defined. 'A context can always and continuously be extended in all directions'.[36] The limits to the text with which one is working are continually shifting. Samuel Ijsseling makes the point that these limits are chosen (he calls this deciding the undecidable) and in choosing to demarcate or frame a text we are making an ethical and political decision, a point to which we shall return.

From the perspective of deconstruction we can therefore conclude that the self is constituted in a network of meanings and it cannot be separated from its context. The self is the effect of a kind of textuality.[37] We have seen, in accordance with Derrida's conception of trace and *différance*, that identity cannot be pure, it cannot be present to itself: 'It is only on the basis of *différance* and its "history" that we can allegedly know who and where "we" are, and what the limits of an "era" might be'.[38] The self can only be a pure, unified entity when it does not exist by virtue of its relation to other elements, when it does not change and ceases to be part of a dynamic system – when it is dead. Derrida's claim that 'there has never been, never will be a unique word, a master-name'[39] can, in the light of our discussion, be reformulated to the following: There has never been, never will be a unique self, a master identity. A person is not the origin of her identity, nor can she have complete control over it.[40] Can we then be more specific about what identity is? We will return to complexity theory with this question.

THE SELF AS COMPLEX SYSTEM

We have quoted Cuypers as saying that a person's identity is not identical to her or his bodily identity. Rodin's 'The Thinker' is constituted by a lump of bronze, but is not identical to it. By using a statue as a point of comparison, Cuypers raises a few interesting issues. A statue implies a sculptor. If identity can be thought of as analogous to a statue, an external agent would be implied: someone or something that forms a self which is dependent upon, but not identical to, the body in which it resides. Now this has something in common with our argument thus far: the self is dependent upon its world/environment and cannot be separated from the body. What does not sit well is firstly the idea of the self as something created, a finished product, cast in bronze; and secondly the idea of a separate bodily and personal identity. We have argued that a complex system needs to be able to adjust to its environment if it is to survive, and that contingent circumstances and a specific historicity make up the environment. It would be preferable to develop an idea of identity that is dynamic and does not depend on an external agent for defining its nature.

Derrida asserts that: '*Différance* is no more static than it is genetic, no more structural than historical'.[41] What he says about *différance* is also true for the self. To think of the way that we perceive the world in terms of receiving (particles of) information about it, through our senses, and ordering these perceptions into a coherent whole, and then acting upon them as an abstract subject, is to disregard our own historicity and our own interaction with the world that we perceive. Our 'intellect, will and memory' (to return to Cuypers's argument) do not serve only to provide us with a spacio-temporal conceptual framework by means of which we order the world, they participate in and change that world. At the same time, the self has to operate within the structures and constraints provided by the environment. In the process we both partic-ipate in and create a world too diverse and complex to grasp or describe fully.

Part of this argument is that we cannot be born pre-programmed with an inherent idea of what it means to be human and of how we have to be in order to get on in the world, nor with a fixed idea of what the world itself is. These ideas have to be developed through an engage-ment with the world. To be able to deal with the contingencies that form part of daily life we have to be able to act upon information we are exposed to and adjust our ideas accordingly. It would seem more feasible to think of the self as a dynamic process, continually needing to adapt and change in response to its interaction with the world, while being influenced by its history through memory. This process can be given content by taking a more detailed look at how the different char-acteristics of complex systems (discussed above) manifest themselves in the self.

i)   If we think of the self as something that is constituted in a system of differences, then it must consist of a large number of elements. The self is not a singular thing, but divided in itself. This is not a schizophrenic understanding, but one that wants to give a voice to all the different, sometimes contradictory, aspects of personhood. What is more, all the innumerable traces in the textual field (the world and ourselves) contribute towards identity. The traces that make up our view of ourselves and the world include everything that we are exposed to: other people, conversations, books, our education, our material circumstances, state of bodily health, our childhood memories and future prospects, everything. These things do not contribute to the self in a deterministic way, they interact and merge. We cannot identify all these components, and then fit them into a coherent whole in order to provide an exact description of the self.

ii) Traces gain their meaning from the textual field in which they operate and are empty (meaningless) if they do not interact. A self cannot be meaningful in isolation. The self is constituted by its relationships to others and the world. Our environment (context) is continually shifting and changing and we need to adjust the sense we make of it and of ourselves. We interact with others and with the world and these relationships are never static. No person can be understood independently from their context and different aspects of the self can be relevant in different contexts.

iii) The interactions between traces are rich. People and things which contribute to our conception of self can be numerous and divergent and we interact with them continuously.

iv) Some influences have a profound effect on the self; others may pass without much of a ripple. The influence that something has on us is not only determined by the size of the cause, our context and history also contribute to the outcome. Some people and events may therefore be a bigger factor in a person's identity than others (e.g. family members as opposed to shop assistants). Another way of making this point is to say that the interactions that constitute the self are non-linear.

v) We can only respond to the influences available locally. Interactions thus have a fairly short range. Our sense of self comes from things and people we have seen and are exposed to. However, stories, songs, books, artworks, news broadcasts and travel mean that this exposure is not limited to our immediate environment, but rather to a kind of 'first-hand' encounter with texts that fall within our cultural orientation or our field of interest. Much of how you think about yourself and the world is contingent on your spatial and temporal location.

vi) There are many loops in the interactions with others and the world. Many of our actions feed back on themselves. We have seen in the earlier discussion of *différance* that every instance of ascribing meaning (interpretation) is to alter other possible meanings. When we ascribe meaning to the world we interact with it. The world we are born into is not determined. Against our spatio-temporal background, education and economic means, we are able to choose some of the texts that we are exposed to. Our choice of literature or friends for example will be constrained by our view of the world and ourselves, and will also feed back upon this view. The way that we perceive things might be confirmed or called into question by texts we encounter. The world is not merely the origin of meaning, we participate in our world and change it. In some instances we may have more control over this than in others. The effects of some of our interaction with the world can be unexpected and unpredictable.

vii) The self is an open system. It is impossible to point to some precise boundary where 'we' stop and where the world begins. To confine the self to the prison of the skull is a gross oversimplification.

viii) The self is never in a state of equilibrium, our interaction with the world is dynamic. As our environment changes, we adapt. We are constantly reflecting and acting. We do sometimes long for a peaceful state in which no demands are made upon us. Freud refers to this as the death-drive.

ix) The self is greatly influenced by its history. The history and context of a person co-determines their identity. No two people have histories or contexts that are identical. Even if two people had very similar backgrounds, a host of other factors would contribute towards their view of themselves and the world. In a way the self is nothing more than the sedimentation of its history in memory.

x) You can not be aware of your whole self. Nor are you consciously aware of your complete history as a series of distinct events that chronologically make up your personal narrative. We are only conscious of parts of the self at any given moment. Much of what makes us what we are is not available to consciousness.

To summarise, the self is not a complete and coherent entity present to itself. It is constituted through the complex interaction amongst a host of factors, the significance of which cannot be pinpointed. Our sense of self is the result of transient patterns in this network of traces. Consciousness is an emergent property of this network, not a central control system that 'causes' the experience of the self. Let us turn to this issue in a little more detail.

WHAT IS IDENTITY?

Viewing the self as relational makes for a more flexible way of understanding how we come to be who we are. Yet it is still possible to talk about someone's identity or beliefs in a meaningful way. By arguing that identity cannot be fixed we are not suggesting that identity is fragmented and arbitrary. A dynamic, open system cannot be discussed in isolation from the different discourses of which it forms a part, which influence and constrain it. Returning to the analogy of the text, we can describe this in the following way: texts exist in a contextual field, in a network of meaning. They refer to each other and they rely on each other. They bear a likeness to one another, but also distinguish themselves from one another. In short, texts are *intertextual* events. Because of this intertextuality, texts can be quoted in other texts, recited, reproduced, commented on, interpreted, clarified, improved, summarised, amplified, supplemented, condensed.[42] A text comes into being in an already existing network and this network places constraints upon its possibilities. The self is not fragmented into a multiplicity of selves, it is distributed over a network of traces, in which it can be identified, but never exhausted.

A complex system is not chaotic; it has structure, even if this structure is continuously transformed. Just as words cannot have meaning if they are not repeatable or iterable,[43] the structures in a complex system must be identifiable. Transformation cannot be other than the transformation of something specific into something which can be recognised as a new form of the previous structure. There is thus no contradiction involved if we deny an essentialist understanding of the self, but still talk of someone's 'identity'. However, this identity cannot be separated from its embeddedness in social conditions, and will therefore always have a political dimension. It is to this aspect that we turn in conclusion.

THE POLITICAL SELF

Elizabeth Wilson addresses an objection frequently raised against postmodernist theories, and against deconstruction in particular, namely that these theories do not offer a positive project.[44] Critics accuse them of being more concerned with negative criticism of Enlightenment or modernist projects than with offering any suggestions as to alternatives. In Wilson's words: 'These critical theories are deemed dangerously apolitical'.[45] Wilson answers this criticism by asserting that it is possible to say that deconstruction *exceeds* such classical concerns as a positive project. 'What this means is that rather than negating, excluding, or preventing classical political and epistemological projects, deconstruction is engaged in an examination of the conditions that make such projects possible and the implications and effects of their operations'.[46] This claim is also relevant when talking about the self. The modernist or essentialist understanding of the self works with the notion of a subject that is pre-formed, that first exists, and can then engage in a number of activities, including political ones. The understanding of the self we propose is constituted through social interaction, and is therefore already a political thing.

An understanding of the self as political through and through cuts in two directions. In the first place, it argues that a 'neutral and objective' view of the self does violence to the subject in question. It disregards crucial components of what makes up a person. It leads to a kind of 'colonisation' of subjects: 'we know what a subject is, therefore we know what you really are, and therefore we know how to treat you'. These violations do not only affect the others in question, but ultimately also those who do the violating. Such an approach leads to a disregard of difference, to a social homogenisation, and therefore to an impoverished environment. Since we can only come to be in the social environment, a poorer or less complex environment will deprive those in it of certain possibilities. A fostering of difference will have the opposite result.

In the second place, an emphasis on the political nature of the subject reminds us of the inevitability of political involvement. We are formed by our social interventions (or lack of them), and others are shaped in the same way. We are not completed subjects that have to make political decisions; we come to be through those decisions. The choice to abstain from certain actions is also a political choice.

This kind of argument can also be made from the perspective of complexity theory. We cannot give a complete, formal description of a complex system in terms of a finite set of rational principles. This means that when we deal with complex things, like human subjects, we cannot get by with calculation only. We have to make use of frameworks and assumptions. Since there are no meta-rules which supply these frameworks, we have to make choices based on values, rather than on rational knowledge or the outcome of calculations. Another way to formulate this is to say that we are always in the realm of ethics. Since we cannot shift the responsibility for our decisions onto some procedure, we have to assume that responsibility. Accepting the responsibility for our choices, and for how they affect others, is not a burden we have to bear, it is what makes us who we are.

NOTES

1. Jean-François Lyotard, *The Postmodern Condition: a Report on Knowledge*, University of Minneapolis Press 1988, ppxxiii-xxiv.
2. René Descartes, *A Discourse on Method. Meditations and Principles*, Everyman's Library, London 1978, p85.
3. Stephen Toulmin, *Cosmopolis The Hidden Agenda of Modernity*, The Free Press, New York 1990, pp14-20.
4. René Descartes, *op. cit.*, pp86-87.
5. Stephen Toulmin, *op. cit.*, pp21-24.
6. Descartes insists that the imagination and the senses do not belong to the mind (intellect) and cannot comprehend the world correctly:

   ... it is now manifest to me that bodies themselves are not properly perceived by the senses nor by the faculty of imagination, but by the intellect alone; and since they are not perceived because they are seen and touched, but only because they are understood [or rightly comprehended by thought], I readily discover that there is nothing more clearly apprehended than my own mind (René Descartes, *op. cit.*, p94).

7. Descartes paints a picture of a mind which is naturally wilful and wayward and which needs to be constrained:

   But I see clearly what is the state of the case. My mind is apt to wander, and will not yet submit to be restrained within the limits of truth. Let us therefore leave the mind to itself once more , and, according to it every kind of liberty [permit it to consider the objects that appear to it from without], in order that, having afterwards withdrawn from it from these gently and opportunely [and fixed it on the consideration of its being and properties it finds in itself], it may then be the more easily controlled' (René Descartes, *op. cit.*, p90).

8. Stephen Toulmin, *op. cit.*, p40.
9. In fact, the world and the rest of the body can be disregarded as superfluous and cumbersome: 'And there are besides so many other things in the mind itself that contribute to the illustration of its nature, that those dependent on the body, to which I have here referred, scarcely merit to be taken into account' (René Descartes, *op. cit.*, p94).
10. Zygmunt Bauman, *Intimations of Postmodernity*, Routledge, London 1992, pxvii.
11. *Ibid.*, pxiv.
12. Jean-Paul Sartre, *Existentialism and Humanism*, Methuen, London 1946, p29.
13. *Ibid.*, p28.
14. Sartre concedes that historical situations are variable and place limitations upon the subject, but argues that the necessities of living in the world do

not vary. One needs to labour and die in the world. These limitations 'are lived and are nothing if man does not live them' (Jean-Paul Sartre, *op. cit.*, p46). By 'lived' Sartre means that man freely determines his existence in relation to these limitations.

15. Stefaan Cuypers, 'Philosophical Atomism and the Metaphysics of Personal Identity', *International Philosophical Quarterly*. Vol. xxxviii, no. 4, issue no. 152, December 1998.

16. In his attempt to do this, Cuypers argues that introspection cannot be modelled on external perception, as is the case in the perceptual model of self-knowledge. In his own words: 'the use of the pronoun "I" is *identification free*.' (Stefaan Cuypers, *op. cit.*, p355). The self cannot be interpreted as an object. Similarly, he argues, the analogy between introspection and perception cannot be sustained in the light of the causal relation that exists between the phenomenological character of the perceived object and its perception. Introspection has no object.

17. Cuypers explains philosophical atomism as picturing 'the self as a non-bodily, private and static object with which the first person is intimately acquainted', *op. cit.*, p354.

18. This will be a key issue in the discussion of a complex view of the self and we will argue that Cuypers does not manage to overcome this separateness adequately.

19. Cuypers, *op. cit.*, p364. From complexity we will argue that a subject can neither be 'complete' nor can it be a 'logical unity'. Within a complex view it is equally impossible to distinguish with finality between separate bodily and non-bodily identities.

20. *Ibid.*, p365.

21. *Ibid.*, p366.

22. *Ibid.*, p367.

23. *Ibid.*

24. When talking about the self, the term 'environment' refers to the myriad of influences that the self is exposed to everyday: other people, the media, objects that it encounters, its own history, memories, perceptions, physical sensations etc.

25. For more detail, see chapter one in Paul Cilliers, *Complexity and Postmodernism: understanding complex systems*, Routledge, London and New York 1998.

26. This dynamic is captured best by Derrida's notion of *différance*.

27. This point will be elaborated upon in order to argue that a complex system (and identity) cannot be seen as an arbitrary construct.

28. Such models can be helpful in developing ideas, as long as we are aware of their limitations. It is exactly in these murky waters – that of the status of

formal models – that research into artificial intelligence has been floundering.

29. Jacques Derrida, 'Die tragiese, die onmoontlike en die demokrasie. 'n Onderhoud met Jacques Derrida', *Fragmente*, No.3, 1999, pp35-61. This interview with Jacques Derrida was published in Afrikaans in the South African philosophical journal, *Fragmente*. The translation is ours.

30. The Freudian contribution to the understanding of the self will not be elaborated upon, but should be clear from statements like these.

31. See Cilliers, *Complexity and Postmodernism*, pp37-47 for a more detailed discussion of Derrida's elaboration of Saussure's language theory, and its implications for complexity theory.

32. Jacques Derrida, *Margins of Philosophy*, University of Chicago Press, 1986, p3.

33. 'A text presupposes an extremely complex textual field that branches off in space and time in all directions, and to which a text points to and relies on' (Ijsseling Samuel, 'Derrida on Text and Context', in Boileau and John (eds), *Tradition and Renewal*, Louvain Philosophical Studies 5, Leuven University Press, Leuven 1992, p21).

34. See Cilliers, *Complexity and Postmodernism*, pp43-46 for a more complete discussion of this important concept.

35. 'Since language, which Saussure says is a classification, has not fallen from the sky, its differences have been produced, are produced effects, but they are effects which do not find their cause in a subject or substance, in a thing in general, a being that is somewhere present, thereby eluding the play of différance' (Jacques Derrida, *op. cit.*, p11).

36. Ijsseling Samuel, *op. cit.*

37. 'Thus one comes to posit presence – and specifically consciousness, the being beside itself of consciousness no longer as the absolutely central form of Being but as a "determination" and as an "effect"' (Jacques Derrida, *op. cit.*, p16).

38. *Ibid*, p7.

39. *Ibid.*, p27.

40. Samuel Ijsseling, *op. cit.*, p21.

41. Jacques Derrida, *op. cit.*, p16.

42. Samuel Ijsseling, *op. cit.*, p26.

43. *Ibid.*, p25.

44. Elizabeth A. Wilson, *Neural Geographies, Feminism and the Microstructure of Cognition*, Routledge, London 1998, p21.

45. *Ibid.*

46. *Ibid.*, p22.

The Feeling State and the Emotionally Literate Self

JAMES PARK

The second millennium rattled to a close with many policy-makers and business leaders chanting a common mantra. Made up of words like 'passion', 'commitment', 'creativity' and 'resourcefulness', their formulations variously articulated the hope that these qualities would provide the keys to a prosperous economy, a successful business sector, an inclusive society or a vibrant democracy. The hunt was on for strategies that would stimulate their manifestation in employees, for example, as well as in citizens and school pupils. In one instance, when he took over as CEO of British Airways, Bob Ayling declared his intention to cut out layers of management and to devolve responsibilities throughout the company as a way of promoting 'initiative, creativity and trust'. And at the Department for Education and Employment, proposals put forward in the early part of 1999 for restructuring the teaching profession were justified by the promise that they would provide all young people with 'the opportunity to become creative, innovative and capable of leadership'.[1]

Underlying this mantra was a belief that the current pace of social, technological and corporate change needs to call forth a new level of responsiveness in individuals. Unless people have the ability rapidly to read the way situations are shifting, to take advantage of new opportunities as they arise and generally to shift as the world changes around them, they will be left behind in whatever race they find themselves.

The same considerations were apparent in thinking about organisations, in both the public and the private sectors. High levels of flexibility and sensitivity were seen as being required to meet the changing desires of clients and customers. Managers need to be able continuously to gather up, from those engaged with customers and clients at the front line of the marketplace, the knowledge that they hold. This requires ideas to flow upwards, downwards and sideways so as to ensure that all the information available is brought to bear on the decisions that are taken. All organisations need to become 'learning organisations', and all individuals need to become part of this learning process.[2]

Such thinking presents a considerable challenge to the 'traditional' way of doing things, because those who hold the information often operate a long way down the hierarchy from those who have the power and the responsibility. As Martin Sorrell, chairman of the major advertising group WPP, put it to an interviewer from the American business magazine *Fast Company*: 'The people at the so-called "bottom" of an organisation know more about what's going on than the people at the top. The people in the trenches are the ones in the best position to make critical decisions. It's up to leaders to give those people the freedom and the resources they need to make those decisions'.[3]

Today's managers, therefore, are increasingly required to think about how they can ensure that their people are empowered to make decisions sensitive to information they pick up from customers and clients, and are not merely working from scripts and delivering the basics, but are developing connections to people based upon some level of empathy. Managers need also to ensure that everyone involved in the organisation is committed to realising a shared vision of its future, and that the company's culture is one which draws out people's best efforts and stimulates their imaginations. Evidence to support this argument for the importance of attending to the human dimension in business comes from many quarters. For example, when an economist and a psychologist monitored, over a period of eight years, the profitability of 100 manufacturing businesses in Britain, they identified a firm's ability to engage the commitment and motivation of employees as having a more significant impact on subsequent performance than managerial emphasis on quality, technological sophistication or emphasis on research and development. 'Organisations,' they wrote:

> ... are not simply buildings or products or cultures or traditions. They are all of these things, but fundamentally they are groups of human beings working together (more or less) to achieve often overlapping and sometimes shared goals. It is the management of their human needs, the release of their creativity, the co-ordination of their efforts and the creation of co-operative and effective communities which determines their productivity.[4]

It might seem, therefore, as if arguments are being mustered which present a strong economic and business argument for a fundamental transformation in the way people are valued and related to within organisations.

THE PARTNERSHIP ARGUMENT

This gathering evidence behind these arguments has provoked the emergence of a second mantra, this time comprising words like 'partnership', 'collaboration' and 'community'. Where only recently the managerial strategies most commonly propounded relied upon the idea that you could cajole people into high performance by setting them competitively against each other, and setting them high targets, there is now a greater tendency to recognise the advantages that flow from also ensuring that people pool ideas, support each other, learn together. The challenge is in finding ways to maintain a creative tension between the forces of competition and collaboration.

The currency of this second mantra flows through business and the public sector into the way in which the present Labour Government proposed its plans for constitutional reform. Speaking before the election that brought him to the premiership, Tony Blair promised 'a new relationship between government and people; a relationship which sees the public as legitimate stakeholders in the running of the country'. Once in office, the Department for Environment, Transport and the Regions published guidelines that local authorities should follow in experimenting with fresh ways of enabling citizens to make 'an effective contribution on an equal basis', thereby contributing to the evolution of 'a new brand of involved and responsible citizenship'.

Contained in the second mantra is a belief in the need to develop other processes which will channel the resources of knowledge and intelligence held throughout any organisation or community towards positive change. Somewhere in the idea of partnership is an ideology waiting to get out, one that will replace dogmatic confidence in the virtues of central planning, or in the capacity of the market efficiently to channel resources towards need. As David Marquand has written: 'Governments don't and can't know enough to remake society in accordance with a grand design, since no conceivable grand design can do justice to the complexity and reflexivity of human behaviour'.[5]

THE STARTING POINT

The rhetoric contained in this double mantra has a heady feel to it. It contains the aspiration that all individuals should become empowered agents with a capacity to exercise some influence over the decisions that affect them. It conveys the apparent dawning of a realisation that people will be responsible if they are given responsibility, creative if they are allowed the freedom to create and motivated if there is some reason for them to be so. It conjures the possibility of a world where it might be possible for individuals to take real enjoyment in their work, to feel engaged in the lives of their communities and to have a sense of being united with diverse others in a common endeavour to improve their lot. The relevance of such approaches to challenging disaffection in young people, encouraging entrepreneurship in business and promoting participation in local government is patent.

And yet, the responses that flow from this insight too often involve a dismal array of tactics for destroying initiative and innovation. The rhetoric turns quickly to dust in the hurly-burly of organisational life. Managers who spout about people being a company's major asset, nevertheless end up constraining people to meaningless targets, strait-jacketing them in cumbersome systems and repressing their energies with management styles that emphasis control over facilitation. As management consultant Anne Dearing has remarked, 'Leaders are saying that they want to move beyond command and control, but they revert to it when they hit trouble'.[6]

The distance between rhetoric and implementation was evident in the DfEE's Green Paper, *Teachers: Meeting the Challenge of Change,* which spoke of the need to stimulate creativity and innovation in young people. Among the measures it proposed for achieving this noble objective was a system of performance-related pay which researchers generally argued could potentially damage the sort of collaborative working which the literature on learning organisations suggests might strengthen teachers' ability to respond to the needs of young people and the demands of the classroom. Further, when a 'Listening Government' asked teachers whether they agreed with the system being proposed, over two thirds said 'No'. The DfEE, however, pushed on with the measure.

At British Airways, Bob Ayling set up various procedures to improve communication within the company, which employs around 60,000 people. Alongside a weekly newsletter, the company arranged a TV broadcast through which managers could articulate their vision of the airline, and different sections of the corporation could learn about each other. BA people were invited to feed their ideas about how service and operational efficiency could be improved through a process called 'Brainwaves'. But when employee satisfaction surveys were analysed in the middle of 1999, some 60 per cent of those who replied revealed that they did not believe any ideas they had would be listened to by management, nor did they believe that management was capable of communicating with them 'openly and honestly'.

Everyone working in British workplaces has heard similar stories of listening systems being undermined, aspirations to partnership being exploded and hope being dashed. The tales are recounted so often because of the feelings of frustration and disempowerment that they generate. The result is that even senior managers feel an enormous sense of dissatisfaction with the quality of their working lives,[7] while those citizens who are being invited to become more involved in the political process are in reality experiencing a high level of cynicism about the democratic ideal – as evidenced by the turnout at successive elections – local, referendal and European.

Such angry feelings undermine motivation and breed recalcitrance. And while such attitudes need to be met by a sensitive responsiveness that is rooted in understanding, too often they are met instead with rebukes and exhortations. Tony Blair at least conformed to this pattern when, on 6 July 1999, he addressed a group of entrepreneurs and described the 'scars on his back' which had resulted from trying to get people in the public sector to change their ways of working.

But, as Su Maddock and Glen Morgan have shown in their research into changing programmes in Health and Local Authority organisations, the most important factor that causes these altered programmes to fail is not inbuilt resistance to change – most people long for change of a certain sort – but the way in which change is implemented by senior managers. There is a tendency for managers not to consult in ways that appear meaningful, nor to put in the time required to negotiate widespread support for the measures that are proposed. 'Too often', they write, 'those staff required to be most responsive within the current "modernising" agenda are the most fearful, the most controlled and the most lacking autonomy'.[8]

THE PARADOX

Why is it that systems set up to open flows of communication end up breeding this sort of frustration? What is it that blocks the capacity of managers and policy-makers to listen or to act on the basis of what they have heard? The answer to these questions lies somewhere within one of the central paradoxes of human nature – how in infancy and to a considerable extent throughout our lives, we find our distinct individuality through our dependency on another. From childhood on, we come to know ourselves through our intimate connections with others. It is through many millions of different communications – gestural, empathetic, aural, verbal – with those who care for us or otherwise share our lives that we acquire a sense of who we are, and who we might become.[9] We find a definition of ourselves in the 'working models' of relationships with others that we build through these experiences with carers and then apply to others.[10]

As infants, it is the knowledge that someone is there for us which gives us the courage to be curious, to explore people, spaces and objects and to exercise our capacities to influence the world around us. We gain a sense of inner security through being connected to others, and this experience of being linked gives us the courage to experience ourselves as separate. To a greater or lesser extent, this remains true throughout our lives. As the American psychoanalyst Stephen Mitchell writes, 'The pursuit and maintenance of human relatedness is the basic maturational thrust in human experience'.[11]

But if our experience of relationship to others provide us with support, containment and warmth, it also exposes us to feelings of abandonment, powerlessness and loss. When the people upon whom we rely are not available to us even though we call out for them, or when they cannot attune to the expressions of our need for them, we experience a plunge into insecurity. And as we become aware of how much we rely on attention and recognition from others, we come to understand too how dangerously weak are our own capacities, how unstable is the self that we project into the world. If we rely on others for our sense of inner resolve and contentment, then discover that others whom we come across are unstable or unsatisfactory, our lives begin to feel insecure.

Trapped in such an uncomfortable place, the temptation is to deny our need of others and to insist upon our own power as independent beings. Instead of being open to what others ask of us or communicate to us, we look for ways to control, command and direct. Losing confidence in our ability to influence others through persuasion, we seek to achieve mastery of the situation through other means. Participative processes seem ideal in theory, but the reality too often feels untidy and difficult because of the emotions they provoke and the qualities they require us to display. It is tempting to persuade ourselves, against all the evidence, that we actually do have the capacities to achieve, on our own, the objectives we have set. It is because collaborative and participative processes answer to a human need, but also arouse fears that are so deeply rooted in experiences of infancy and childhood, that people tend to give off such confused and contradictory messages about them. Even while they endorse processes designed to achieve these ends, they set about undermining those same processes. And then, having convinced themselves that these processes cannot work, they have recourse to strategies based on pulling levers, issuing mandates and setting penalties for the non-delivery of targets. It is in this set of paradoxes that an explanation can be found for how New Labour can talk about encouraging consultation and partnership while at the same time pursuing highly centralised policies in education and elsewhere.

BREAKING THE CYCLE

A central challenge for modern organisations, and for society as a whole, is to find a way of breaking into this process of degeneration from participation to control. The cost to organisations, and to society, of individuals closing themselves off from an awareness of what other people are experiencing, and from their own desires for connection, is that they close off access to emotions which communicate valuable information about the people they work alongside, and what is happening in the world around us. We weaken our ability to learn and at the same time become cut off from knowledge about ourselves, what drives us, what we want to achieve. We become inflexible and one-dimensional in a world that increasingly calls upon us to be innovative, creative and resourceful.

How, though, can Managers and Ministers learn to follow the logic of their own arguments and let go of the control that at some level they know is inimical to the results they wish to achieve? One solution might be for them to acquire the level of emotional literacy – the ability to understand their own feelings sufficiently to connect to those of others – that will enable them to intercept their own self-destructive inclinations. And for this to happen, the organisations within which they work will have to find ways of fostering such qualities and dispositions.

There is currently little thinking available about how organisations, or communities, can become emotionally literate or about what they would have to do to become promoters of emotional literacy in their people. The germ of a possibility, though, might be sought in attachment theory, the body of psychological research inspired by the groundbreaking discoveries of British psychiatrist John Bowlby into how the physical and emotional availability of carers influences the 'working models' out of which individuals construct their relationships, and how these models are, in turn, handed on, or not, to their children.[12]

The tendency is for parents to offer their own children an experience of being parented that is very similar to that which they experienced. So the child of a mother whose upbringing left her feeling anxious and insecure is likely to experience a similar pattern. Some, though, break the cycle, and there is some current interest in what enables them to do so. Surveys of 'intergenerational patterns of attachment' seek to understand how cycles of dysfunctional behaviour come to be broken.

The answer seems to lie in the extent to which these 'cycle breakers' have been provided with a context that was experienced as sufficiently 'safe' to enable processes of thinking to take place that had not been possible in infancy. In this process they 'surface' painful feelings, come to see how they have been influenced by these feelings, and are able to develop a narrative which integrates the facts of their past with the feelings associated with it. What distinguishes those parents who simply repeat, and those who have been empowered to do something different, is their capacity to construct narratives that, because they link feeling to fact, present well-organised, coherent and consistent stories about the world and their place in it. This capacity to integrate the two dimensions of their mental activity enables them to become responsive, empathetic and aware, able to use all their resources to handle any situation that arises.

Like dysfunctional parents, many Managers and Ministers who can give a factual explanation of the policies they pursue, or of the style they adopt in dealing with staff and 'clients', cannot 'surface the feelings' about the history of experiences that bred these patterns. And it is equally unlikely that they will be open to others doing the surfacing for them by revealing the other side of the position they hold. As Martin Sorrell again explains: 'Let's face it: CEOs of big companies rarely get told the truth. We are surrounded by people whose job is to look after us, to make our lives easier. For the leader of a global organisation, it's all too easy to get out of touch with what's really going on'.[13]

If people are to hold on to the participative urge, to not find themselves enclosed in a bubble where they set up systems and pull at levers without any understanding of the situations they seek to influence, they need to be able to tolerate a plurality of voices, and to experience themselves as made up of pluralistic identities – contradictory, multiple and continuously in process. And if too many find themselves unable to do so, it is because nothing in their education system encouraged them to tolerate conflict – whether internal or external. It is only when our schools start enabling children to experience the plurality within themselves that a capacity to engage with the plurality in others will become widespread.

CHANGE IN EDUCATION, BUSINESS AND CITIZENSHIP

The weaknesses in the organisational structure of our businesses and of our political life reflect the focus of our education system on cognitive skills, to the exclusion of the affective dimension. The situation has been accentuated in the past decade, with the importance being allocated to exam results, league tables and the spurious standards superintended by the inspection system, and with a philosophy which assumes that the achievement of academic excellence is an activity to be distinguished from the 'wider personal and social development of young people'.[14] In reality, an education system which does not conceive its central priority to be the personal and social development of children and young people will constrict their development as thinking, learning and responsible individuals. Pupils will only become 'creative, innovative and capable of leadership' if it is recognised that education is simultaneously an emotional, a social and an intellectual process.

The starting point for creating emotionally literate schools is to equip teachers with the emotional resources they require in order to be able to acknowledge children's emotional needs, to offer them supportive relationships and to show sensitivity to the needs of individuals and groups in ways that build trusting and respectful relationships. It is only if teachers start to experience themselves as truly partners in the project of education that they will play their part in evolving an education system which equips individuals to stay out of the cycle of control. When teachers experience themselves as partners, they can bring pupils and parents into the process. When they feel that they are there to be cajoled and then rebuked for slipping up, they become recalcitrant and resentful.

An emotionally literate education system, therefore, requires the institution of processes that will enable administrative staff and teachers to explore together questions about how schools should be managed, how improvements in behaviour and academic attainment can be brought about, what the true goals of the organisation might be.

Within such a participative environment it becomes possible to experience learning as something that evolves through a group of people exploring their ideas, their feelings and the information they are given. The classroom becomes a space where, at the same time, people learn about themselves, about others and about the world of learning that is on offer to them.

One of the more bewildering aspects of our disconnected educational paradigm is that it is so often justified by allusions to what 'business' says it wants. And yet if it is true that employers have sometimes complained about the quality of school-leavers' spelling, and that they take an interest in the qualities measured by the battery of tests and exams to which students are subjected, what they really seek more of are the social and emotional qualities that have nothing to do with any of this. They want to know whether or not their potential employees can access information from others, can communicate clearly to their colleagues, can collaborate with them on evolving creative responses to challenges and can then carry through agreed strategies in decisive and effective ways.

At the same time, the hunt is on for ways to bring emotional literacy into organisations through processes that nurture it. Too often, the answer is seen to lie in training individuals and groups, rather than in trying to find ways to change the institution. How can organisations find ways to 'surface' feelings within a context of safety, opening up channels of communication between people who work alongside each other, so that those things which are kept under wraps because they are too tricky, sensitive or difficult to handle can be expressed? The argument for emotional literacy is that only creating such spaces for the pluralism within all of us will allow people to discover what is really happening within themselves as well as within their organisations.

As for citizenship, the reality is that the will fundamentally to transform the nature of the relationship between citizen and state does not exist. The mechanisms for a more open relationship get wheeled into place, but are then distorted to another purpose. 'Whitehall,' write Beetham and Weir, 'issues streams of consultation papers and official guidance which now say that meetings and hearings should become standard practice. But open consultation remains rare, opportunities for citizen initiative and participation rarer still; and consultation processes are notoriously unbalanced and unsystematic in some areas'.[15]

These structures block the feelings that wait to be expressed: with their confusions, their conflicts, their ambivalences, their yearnings. It does not draw out our capacity for dreaming and engagement, the yearning to be recognised, to have influence, to discover where one stands in relation to others. We find ourselves looking two ways and, when nobody is there to help us find the way, we withdraw into ourselves. What is absent and what is required, in business as well as in government, are processes that surface the political emotions being experienced in ways that allow them to be thought about. Whether the challenge is Kosovo, inflation, the motor car or our local park, we have complex and ambivalent feelings about them. Their difficulty makes them less thinkable. They are less thinkable to the degree that they are difficult. Therefore we need help to think about them. And yet we are less fully human, less open to experience, by the inability we have to think about them. There is a need, then, to create the spaces in which these emotions can surface; where these issues can be discussed in ways that enable us to grow in understanding, and to contribute to a growth of understanding, allowing for continuous, genuine and deep dialogue between citizens – and we are all citizens. We need space to embrace the uncertainty and confusion that we all experience so that we can move beyond it, through a politics of process, managing our anxieties and processing our dreams. Such a politics of process is also a politics of conflict, but conflict that has the potential to be always invigorating, stimulating and exciting. It contains the desire to destroy the other, but also the capacity for the other to survive, and it enables us to be recognised. At the moment the State is too timid, too frightened of us, for it to allow itself to become strong by recognising us.

NOTES

1. DfEE, *Teachers: Meeting the Challenge of Change*, 1999.
2. P. Senge, *Fifth Discipline, The Art & Practice of the Learning Organization,* Doubleday/ Currency, New York 1990.
3. W.C. Taylor, 'Whatever Happened to Globalisation', in *Fast Company*, September 1999, pp228-236.
4. M. West and M. Patters, 'The Workforce and Productivity', *New Economy*, Vol 6, March 1999, pp22-7.
5. Marquand, D., *Prospect*, June 1999.
6. A. Maitland, 'A Future Based on Sharing', in *Financial Times*, 10.6.1999.
7. Charlesworth, *Are Managers under Stress?*, The Institute of Management, London 1998.
8. S. Maddock and G. Morgan, *Conditions for Partnership*, ESRC, 1998.
9. D. Stern, *The Interpersonal World of the Infant*, Basic Books, New York 1995.
10. J. Bowlby, *A Secure Base*, Penguin, Harmondsworth 1988.
11. S. Mitchell, *Relational Concepts in Psychoanalysis: An Integration*, Harvard University Press, 1991, p289.
12. J. Holmes, *John Bowlby and Attachment Theory*, Routledge, London 1993.
13. W.C. Taylor, *op. cit.*
14. DfEE, 1999, *op. cit.*
15. D. Beetham and S. Weir, 'Auditing British Democracy', *Political Quarterly*, Vol. 70, issue 2, 1999, pp128-138.

The Life of Men: An Ethics
of the Male Self

JONATHAN RUTHERFORD

My father told me that if I wanted to be a good writer I had to find something to write about other than myself. He had not liked the auto-biographical style of my last book and was concerned about what I might do next. I told him that my generation, which had grown up in the 1960s and 1970s, was more confessional and preoccupied with the self than his own, brought up in wartime austerity. It wasn't, I argued, because we were narcissistic or plain self indulgent or spoilt and pampered (which is exactly what he thought it was although he didn't say as much), but because we were trying to make sense of our lives. We left it at that: part of our ongoing difference of opinion. But as is the way with these things his criticism left me with a niggling doubt which I couldn't shake off. I kept hearing the phrase 'me generation' chattering away at the back of my mind, reminding me of a poem by Stephen Knight which he'd entitled 'Notes for a Poem Called Me, Me, Me' after his own father had told him 'There's more to life than "Me, Me, Me"'. In any case, I thought, holding my doubt in check, my father was one to talk: had I ever known what he thought about anything?

There seems no one better to discuss the self with than a father. By which I mean no one more risky and likely to raise awkward questions. After all Freud describes the father as responsible for the making of the self. His symbolic figure heralds the arrival of language, individuation and access to culture, which breaks the infant's bond with the mother. He is the figure of otherness and difference, which is present between mother and infant from the beginning: a growing intimation in the developing mind of the infant of the existence of something more than 'the two of us'. And yet he is not so benign. Freud chooses to express the father's presence, in the discussion of the Oedipus complex, as an extremely violent intrusion which he describes metaphorically as the threat of castration: 'The complex is not simply repressed it is smashed to pieces'.[1] It is an injunction which implies: separate or die. As if the father holds the right of life and death. Not a literal death, but a denial of self-becoming and a life lived without vitality; an exclusion from the language and the law of the father.

In his essay 'Family Romances', written in 1909, Freud describes how the sexual rivalries initiated by the Oedipus complex ensure that the boy, 'has a far more intense desire to get free from ... [the father] ... than from ... [the mother]'. The conflict between father and son has become the most widely held understanding of the Oedipal drama. Freud, in his writings, can only eulogise the mother / son relationship as 'the most perfect, the most free from ambivalence of all human relationships'.[2] He reiterates the special bond between mother and son in several of his essays. Read Freud more carefully, however, and you detect a powerful ambivalence about the mother's influence. His glowing remarks do not disguise the 'terrifying impression of helplessness' he perceives in the infant's predicament of dependency on her. For Freud, it is in a mother's nature to project her thwarted ambitions onto men: 'Even marriage is not made secure until the wife has succeeded in making her husband her child as well as acting as mother to him'.[3]

The maternal body emerges in his writing as an archaic, shadowy and amorphous presence. His anxiety about her influence is compounded by his fear of the father's failure to protect his son from her. 'This helplessness lasts throughout life [and makes it] necessary to cling to the existence of a father'.[4] Freud resolves his Oedipus complex in the name of the father: the infant's attachment to the mother is repressed and her influence excluded. The self develops in language and culture under the Law of the Father. The boy becomes his father's son, but it is an ambiguous and antagonistic identification: father and son, same but different.

Same but different. I take my father's comment – that if I desire to be successful I must stop writing about myself – to be an oblique reference to his perception of me as the same as himself, but different. A difference which is not overtly acknowledged, but which is tacitly accepted by both of us as the sign of my lack, of being the one who does not measure up. Ambivalent. The one who does not have enough self, who experiences the self as something unresolved and hence the introspection, the search for a resolution to this never feeling completely 'me'. Of course, there is no resolution. It is in the nature of desire and its unending pursuit of plenitude never to achieve completion. Only in death do we finally grasp this nothing of ourselves. It is, too, the experience of finding oneself male and with a father. One feels only ever less than he, and that part of ourselves which is the experience of feeling less than our father is our continuing and unresolved need for our mother. In the sameness of father and son exists a difference which is excluded and whose absence is a defining quality of our maleness. The absence is the mother's body, or more specifically the son's need of the mother's body. The father who was once the intimation of otherness in the developing mind of the infant, is now recognised as the same, and the maternal body which was once experienced as undifferentiated sameness, is now repressed and excluded.

Taking heed of my father I will not talk about 'me'. Instead I want to discuss the difference in me which is the 'not me'. I will describe it as simple lived life, which is the life anterior to language from which the Oedipal father has freed his son, drawn him away from mother and her body: from natural life into culture, from need to desire, from emotion to reason; into the law and social contract. Son and father, who are the same in a sameness – the Law of the Father – which excludes the simple lived life of need, the body and feeling. Here we are present in our separateness, our presence before one another constituted in the absence of the mother's body. We are never sure where we belong or who we belong to. If not to her, then to each other? If not to each other then to her? We are both sons who hover together in this liminal state of proximity to our fathers, neither the same nor different; ambivalent and yet colluding in our lack; united only by the Oedipal injunction to be a man or lose face. The patrimony of disappointment.

'MERE LIFE'

In his essay 'Critique of Violence', Walter Benjamin discusses the role of sovereign violence in juridical law-making.[5] Violence, he argues, is an integral element of law-making. In the moment a law is instated violence is not deposed, a law does not become an end immune and independent from violence but one which is intimately and necessarily bound up with it. Benjamin does not address the issue, but his linking of law and violence is rooted in the relationship between men and women. In ancient Greece the labour to satisfy human needs was considered to be the work of women and slaves, and incompatible with citizenship and participation in public affairs. Man was only capable of moral conduct when freed from necessity. The labour of reproducing life was confined to the private household where force and violence were justified as the only means to master necessity. 'Violence' writes Hannah Arendt in *The Human Condition* 'is the pre-political act of liberating oneself from the necessity of life for the freedom of the world'.[6]

Freedom, legality, the political, the sphere of free and moral men, only commenced outside the walls of the household. A similar condition appears in the exercising of ancient Roman law. The father had unconditional authority over his son: *vitae necisque potestas* – right over life and death. Over his daughter or wife caught in the act of adultery he had the power to kill. It was a power confined to the domestic sphere, but his right over the life and death of his son formed the paradigm of political power and juridical law which embraced every free male citizen.[7] In both ancient Greece and Rome, the household where life itself was reproduced, which coincided with the domain of slavery, women and female sexuality, was subject to extra juridical violence. Where the relationship of blood – the father and son relationship – extended itself into the civic realm of freedom and law it too retained rights over life and death.

Benjamin, in his attempt to understand the origins of juridical power over the individual, conceptualises this relationship with the term 'mere life'. 'Mere life' describes the bearer of the link between violence and the law. It is the individual stripped of the accoutrements of identity and civic status. It is the simple lived life of the body and feeling, life-laid-bare subjected to the threat of patriarchal violence which, in its powerlessness and dispossession, can claim nothing but a right to continued existence. A right to exist is the most basic appeal which society's weakest can make when they have no civic status, no cultural identity and no political representation. A woman's place within the household, indeed within society in general, has, throughout history, been 'mere life'. For the male citizen, 'mere life' existed in his transgression of the Law of the Father, and meant banishment beyond the walls of the city to a realm where moral and legal obligations waned and violence ruled. 'Is man no more than this?' laments Shakespeare's mad King Lear. Cast out on the heath, stripped of the robes of office, Lear reflects on his downfall. 'Thou art the thing itself; unaccommodated man is no more but such a poor, bare forked animal as thou art.' It was the life of both soul and body which was excluded from sovereignty and yet, in its absence, formed the nucleus from which political power was built.

FEELINGS

I evoke my self in my desire for self-realisation, self-belief, self-affir-
mation, self sufficiency. And yet the life which is mine – 'mere life' – is
what is excluded from my self-becoming. My pursuit of my self is a
chimera. I am confronted with my own absence, the part of me which
is not me. Not the identity lived in the public realm, but an interior
idiom I lack the words to describe. Since childhood I have learnt to
discipline and mediate my body and feelings through language.
Language imposed its own schema of rational behaviour. The meaning
of myself I established was a safe distance from the inner place where I
experienced my life. I seek always to make sense of things, to understand events, ideas and behaviours and in the process rationalise them
to myself, take them in and in the same instant project this process of
reasoning back out to others as if to say: this is the reasonable man I
am. And yet in my reliance on reason I am unable always to feel what
I feel. And when I know what I feel I can't always think it. And not
being able to think it, I have no words to express it. Self-knowledge can
never be purely rational and intellectual. It has little meaning without
emotion.

In these past few years, it has often been remarked that men are, in
a metaphorical sense, having difficulty describing where they are going.
While women pursue their independence, men appear to be flailing in
the dark, unable to express or control their feelings. The emotionally
inarticulate man who does not know himself has become a pervasive
archetype in our culture. The balance of power between men and
women has shifted. The gap between private and public life has diminished. The lingua franca of masculinity – civility, duty and emotional
restraint – which once dominated public life, is under challenge from a
culture of informality and self-expression. Change is occurring in
people's intimate lives, in personal experiences of the self, of relationships, love, family, friendship, sexuality, the body and emotions. It is a
cultural revolution in which the public language which imbued men
with authority and virtue has been thrown into doubt. We are unsure
of what we feel we should think about things, and equally unsure of
what we think we should feel. How can we embark on a process of self-
knowledge if we are unable to speak of the intangible things which
connect us to others? Without the necessary words, it is difficult to
understand the feelings of love, intimacy, empathy, loyalty, fear, hatred
which bind us to others. It is as if we have language but have lost our
voices.

The nature of 'mere life' has changed with the decline of the realm of necessity and the increase of individual autonomy. In the modern exercising of power, 'mere life' is no longer defined by the symbolics of blood and necessity. It becomes co-terminous with the normative regulation of feelings and with the disciplining of body and sexuality. Michel Foucault, in his *The History of Sexuality: An Introduction*, has described how 'the ancient right to take life or let live' has been replaced in the modern period by 'a power to foster life or disallow it to the point of death'.[8] We can already witness the beginnings of this shifting nature of power in the Republic of ancient Rome when, in the first century BC, changes in Roman upper-class marriage customs weakened private patriarchal authority. Norbert Elias has described how changes in the relationship between the family household and the public sphere of the state encouraged greater egalitarianism between men and women.[9] Subsequent to these cultural changes, legislation altered the balance of power between men and women in women's favour. New love relationships and sensibilities were inaugurated. These can be illustrated by the love poems of Catullus (*circa* 84 – *circa* 54 BC), addressed to the aristocratic Clodia. Catullus falls in love with this socially superior and older woman. She grants him her favours, but then turns away from him. He continues to love her but she appears to be indifferent to him. He begins to hate her for tantalising him.

> Goodbye, my girl. Catullus from now on
> Is adamant: he has made up his mind:
> He won't beg for your favour like a bone.
> You'll feel the cold, though, you damned bitch, when men
> Leave you alone. What life will you have then?
> Who'll visit you? Who'll think you beautiful? Who'll
> Be loved by you? Parade you as his own?
> Whom will you kiss and nibble then?
> Oh fool,
> Catullus, stop this, stand firm, become stone.
> (Enough)

Catullus is ambivalent about Clodia. '*Odi et amo*', he rages at her: 'I love you and I hate you'. Such love relationships became increasingly common and brought with them a new range of emotions in men. A woman's love renders a man powerless, confronts him with his own vulnerability, in effect reduces him to a symbolic state of 'mere life'. What Elias describes as 'this rather surprising development' of greater parity between men and women led to a heightened sensitivity and self-

restraint on the part of men. This period also marked a growing preoccupation with managing the body and taking care of the self. The Stoic
philosopher Seneca (c. 4BC – AD65) wrote to his 'pupil' Lucilius, 'I see
in myself, Lucilius, not just an improvement but a transformation,
although I would not venture as yet to assure you, or even to hope, that
there is nothing left in me needing to be changed'.[10] As Foucault points
out in his book *The Care of the Self*, the concern with the cultivation
of the self – 'spend your whole life learning how to live' – was not
simply a valorisation of private individualism, but indicative of a crisis
of the subject: 'the difficulty in the manner in which the individual
could form himself as an ethic of the subject'[11] – by which Foucault
means the difficulty in finding meaning and purpose in life.

Self-reflection or inward lookingness developed in social classes and
groups where securing the necessities for living was no longer the
central function of everyday life, and where there was also a demise of
clear patterns of patriarchal and religious authority. Our modern
preoccupation with the self is consolidated in the eighteenth century
and the age of the Enlightenment. In *Emile*, published in 1760, Jean
Jacques Rousseau discusses what he means by the passions. The word
comes from *patio*, I suffer, I am worked upon. To be subject to passion
is to cease to be the sole instigator of one's actions. Passion confronts
Rousseau with the loss of self, his fear of dependency and the threat to
personal well-being which these imply. He describes Emile's first real
passion as his love for Sophie: 'Sophie you are the arbiter of my fate.
You know it well. You can make me die of pain. But do not hope to
make me forget the rights of humanity. They are more sacred to me
than yours. I will never give them up for you.' Sophie is Rousseau's
perfect imaginary wife, a coquette who is confined to the private realm
and subordinated to the abstract, rational ideas of public life. 'Women
have, or ought to have, but little liberty', he declared. Six years after the
publication of *Emile* Rousseau was exiled in England. He attempted to
assuage his fear of emotional dependency on women in his life story
The Confessions: 'I was born, a weak and ailing child; I cost my mother
her life.' His introspection, his concern with the memory of childhood,
and his search for personal fulfilment established a revolutionary fash-
ioning of the self which has formed a central feature of modern culture.
But women are destined to be the source of his anguish and disdain, or
else they remain submissive, approving spectators of his act of self
creation. In the final paragraph of *Confessions*, Rousseau wrote, 'I
concluded the reading of my *Confessions*, and everyone was silent.
Madame d'Egmont was the only person who appeared to be affected;

she trembled visibly, but she quickly recovered herself and remained silent'.

Rousseau's work marked the birth of Romanticism – a reaction against the rationalising tendencies of the Enlightenment and the anti-human, anti-aesthetic influences of commerce. Despite its revolutionary sentiments, Romanticism evolved not so much in the absence of women writers but in their exclusion. It gave birth to the modern self and our contemporary notions of identity, but it was a predominantly masculine affair with men attempting to claim personal feeling as the authentic expression of their individuality without succumbing to the sentimental emotions associated with women. No one was more affected by Rousseau's misogyny than Mary Wollstonecraft. 'What nonsense!' she retorted in *A Vindication of the Rights of Woman* (1792). By trivialising women, Rousseau merely contradicted his philosophy. Mary Wollstonecraft's feminism demanded women's rights to reason and to a public existence alongside men. Wollstonecraft's commitment to the Enlightenment principle of reason as a force of change was tempered by her recognition that emotions could not be divorced from rational thinking. They connected an individual to life itself. 'My reason obliges my feelings to be my criterion', wrote Mary in 1795, to her lover the American adventurer, Gilbert Imlay. She told him that there was no end to the pleasure inspired by beauty and sublimity: they were infinite.[12]

Four years earlier, in 1791, she had encountered William Godwin briefly at a lunch given by the radical publisher Joseph Johnson in honour of Tom Paine, the best-selling author of *The Rights of Man*. They had argued. After this inauspicious meeting, Wollstonecraft was in revolutionary Paris where she had met Imlay and given birth to their child, Fanny. Imlay abandoned them and, as her French acquaintances became caught up in the terror, Mary returned to London. In the spring of 1796 she once again met William Godwin, by now a renowned radical philosopher and novelist. He had evolved from participating in a fundamentalist puritan sect to declaring the radical individualism of his major philosophical work, *An Enquiry Concerning Political Justice*, published in 1793. Godwin believed in the pre-eminence of human moral conscience. The application of reason and persuasion would achieve the long transition to a perfect society. He wrote, in the first edition of *Political Justice*, 'Man is perfectible, or in other words susceptible of perpetual improvement'. His faith in the sure hand of rational thought was not to survive his relationship with Mary Wollstonecraft. After their second meeting they became lovers, and Mary was once again pregnant. They married on 29 March 1797 at St Pancras Church in London. Five months later she contracted septicaemia while giving birth to their daughter Mary, and died ten days later on 10 September 1797. She was thirty-eight years old.

This extraordinary, brief and intense love and loss transformed Godwin. The man who had believed in the pre-eminence of reason and language had nothing to say. 'It is impossible to represent in words the total revolution this event made in my existence. It was as if in a single moment "sun and moon were in the flat sea sunk"'.[13] He shut himself away and reread all Mary's books and papers and then, in ten weeks, he wrote a memoir of her which was published in 1798. Readers were appalled by his uncensored depiction of Mary Wollstonecraft's illicit love affairs; her questioning of the role of wedlock; his frankness describing her attempts at suicide; and his attention to the detail of her delivery and eventual death. In chapter 9, Godwin describes their 'friendship melting into love': 'I have never loved till now', he writes, portraying their early affair with the daring words 'We did not marry.' Despite their eventual marriage, ignominy was heaped on both him and on Mary's posthumous reputation. Such was the ferocity of the reaction that over one hundred years later, as women began to organise themselves into a feminist movement, the name Wollstonecraft was still associated with prostitution and moral calumny.

With two children, Fanny and Mary, to care for, Godwin began to question his devotion to the Enlightenment tradition of rationalism. In 1798, he wrote a memorandum suggesting that some of the ideas in *Political Justice* were 'defective in the circumstance of not yielding a proper attention to the empire of feeling.'[14] The Enlightenment new man could never be wholly in control of himself, society could never achieve the progress he believed in, if feeling were excluded. The abstract principle of reason alone would not move the world, nor could it fully account for the operation of power.

MODERN MALE MONSTERS

It was Mary Shelley, the daughter of William Godwin and Mary Wollstonecraft, who would provide an enduring and incisive image of the suppression of feeling and its impact on men's lives. In the summer of 1816, she and her lover Percy Shelley visited Switzerland and became neighbours of Lord Byron on the shores of Lake Geneva. Confined indoors during a period of wet weather, their conversation turned to human nature. Was man merely an instrument? The contemporary scientific ideas of a life force, galvanism and the principles of animation were discussed. Perhaps it would be possible to bring together the component parts of a creature and galvanise it into life? Byron suggested they each write a ghost story. One night, not long after, Mary suffered a terrible nightmare, out of which was born *Frankenstein*. The man Frankenstein is the obsessed believer in the progress of science and reason. In his quest for knowledge, he imagines he will discover the true meaning of life and will therefore find happiness. He locks himself away from friends and family and ignores his burgeoning love affair with his childhood friend Elizabeth. His consuming passion is to create life, but when his 'demoniacal corpse' draws breath, Frankenstein's dream of creation turns into nightmare. He sleeps fitfully and dreams of kissing his beloved Elizabeth. Suddenly she is transmogrified into his dead and rotting mother. He wakes in dread to discover the monster leaning over him. He flees in horror. When he returns the following day, the monster is gone. He attempts to forget it, but it pursues him, bringing misery and suffering to his family. Eventually Frankenstein confronts the monster in the sublime surroundings of the Alps. The monster appeals to Frankenstein's compassion: 'All men hate the wretched; how, then, must I be hated, who am miserable before all living things! Yet you, my creator, detest and spurn me, thy creature, to whom thou art bound by ties only dissoluble by the annihilation of one of us. You purpose to kill me. How dare you sport thus with life?' 'Begone!' replies Frankenstein, 'I will not hear you. There can be no community between you and me'.

Frankenstein's dream of his lover turning into the nightmare of his mother, and into the waking reality of the monster, is his repressed wish for love which returns as horror. It is the monster 'son' who breaks the taboo on the expression of feelings and openly pleads with Frankenstein for a woman's love: 'You must create a female for me with whom I can live in the interchange of those sympathies necessary for my being. This you can do, and I demand it of you as a right'. *Frankenstein* is about the human longing and need for love. Without love and emotional relationships, there is only the despair of being alone, exiled and outcast. Mary Shelley demands that human feelings be freed not simply from patriarchal domination, but also from the cold hand of rationality and science. Frankenstein and the monster are father and son, the same but different: mind against body, mastery of nature against natural life, science warring against the imagination. Frankenstein is the bearer of modern industrial society who holds the power of life and death over his creation. The monster is the son who is sacred. The Latin word *sacer* reflects the ambiguity of this term. It means both sacred and consecrated, and infamous and detestable. The father's blood right has been the foundation for exercising political and sovereign power over the female body. It has enforced women's exclusion from civic life, and it has ordained the body of the son as sacred. The son was adorned and loved as the embodiment of culture, civilisation, honour and courage. But when he betrayed his difference to his father he was cast out and stripped of his civic refinements.

With the emergence of modern political cultures, 'mere life' ceases to reside beyond the walls of the city – the destination of the outcast and dispossessed. Returning to an earlier literary convention, we note how King Lear's 'unaccommodated man' enters into the heart of male subjectivity. In *King Lear*, Shakespeare was prescient about the future in which the gap between what is public and what is private, what is 'inside' us and what is 'outside', is diminished and the distinction between the two is confused. In 1912, Freud marked his entry into old age (he was fifty-six) with a short essay entitled 'The Theme of the Three Caskets' in which he analyses the old king's relationship to his three daughters. Lear resolves to divide his kingdom between the three in proportion to the amount of love each expresses for him. Goneril and Regan exalt him; the third and youngest daughter Cordelia refuses to participate in this gaudy pretence and says only: 'Unhappy that I am, I cannot heave my heart into my mouth'. Lear disowns her and divides his kingdom between her two sisters. Yet it is Cordelia who remains loyal to him. Freud suggests that the three sisters represent: 'the three forms taken by the figure of the mother in the course of a man's life – the mother herself; the beloved one who is chosen after her pattern; and lastly the Mother Earth who receives him once more'. It is the silent one who represents death. At the end of the play, when Lear carries Cordelia's body onto the stage, he has usurped his fate. He is a dying man who refuses to die, because he cannot renounce the love of women. He needs to hear how much he is loved. And yet: 'It is in vain that an old man yearns for the love of woman as he had it first from his mother'. It is only the third daughter, the silent sister of death, who will take him in her arms.

Lear is a victim of his own sovereign power which has excluded the love which he most wants: a private need he is incapable of disentangling from the public responsibilities of office. This failure precipitates his downfall. Like Frankenstein's monster, he has been reduced to 'mere life', his banishment expressed in his unrequited need for love. At the conclusion of his book *Homo Sacer: Sovereign Power and Bare*

Life, Giorgio Agamben writes: 'Every attempt to rethink the political space of the West must begin with the clear awareness that we no longer know anything of the classical distinction between ... private life and political existence, between man as a simple living being at home in the house and man's political existence in the city.'[15]

Historically it has been the prerogative of men to exist in both public and private spheres, oscillating between domesticity and a manly independence in order to sustain the integrity of their selves rooted in the social contracts of civic society. With each phase of women's emancipation the distinction between public and private has become less certain, the gap diminished. In 1805 William Godwin published his three-volume novel *Fleetwood: or The New Man of Feeling*. 'The passions of men', says the hero Casimir Fleetwood, 'are temporary madnesses'. They bring misfortune to men. When women struggle for equality, the issue of men's feelings comes to the fore. Whether it be the new man of feeling of the 1790s, the New Man of the 1890s or the New Man of the 1980s, as women have pursued education, civic status and knowledge in modern society, it is the simple lived life of the body and feelings (excluded in relationships between men in the public sphere) which has proved to be the 'mere life' upon which patriarchal power operates.

ETHICS OF THE SELF

Women's struggle for equality resonates in both the public and the private spheres and confronts us with the life of our feelings, the exclusion of which has defined our maleness in the public world. In language we separate ourselves from feeling and from the simple lived life of the body. We fly in the transcendence of the word and imagine ourselves sprung free from the limitations of our corporeal selves, the flimsy, mortal, intestacy of our flesh and blood. But we will never be anything more than our bodies. We are only this beginning which can never be finished except in death. It is the nature of being male to foster a morbid nostalgia for this point of departure. In our disembodiment we continue to fear and to be fascinated by women and by the maternal in which, eventually, we will cease to exist. But another story is possible which is not about this nostalgia, nor about the sometimes desperate identification and fraught self-estrangement associated with the father.

Being male, it is necessary constantly to be present in one's self before the gaze of other men. If I am not complete in their eyes then I am diminished in my self. But the part of me that I lack is what I am supposed to lack in the rules of this game. We are hollow men. Our loss of public virtue and authority exposes our masquerade. My self-consciousness alone is not enough to overcome this experience. When we seek knowledge in order to know ourselves we grasp at words and language. To understand something we draw it in and make it our own. What is other to the self and then becomes known, is reduced to the same. Being becomes the affirmation of the same. Difference is erased. It is the principal understanding of how our identities 'work', rooted in Hegel's dialectic of recognition which structures the self and the other as a relationship of domination and struggle. Only through the domination of the other can we achieve an identity (self-knowledge, self-preservation and self-mastery). My self-consciousness, by failing to acknowledge the autonomy of the other, merely reproduces the conditions of my own existence. It changes nothing. I am, for example, aware that my experience of my self is constituted in the exclusion of certain forms of feeling. I know this, but my self awareness alone does not provide me with the words to represent these feelings and so change what I think about my self and what I want to be. These feelings which are excluded remain as something alien, threatening, disruptive, which must be dominated and controlled. This exclusion of feelings is mirrored in culture at large in the disciplining of the male body and emotions. My self-consciousness alone is not enough to alter this.

For the philosopher Emmanuel Levinas, there is an ethical dimension involved in our encounter with the other: 'One comes not into the world but into question', he writes in *Ethics as First Philosophy*. 'When one acquires language, and says "I" and comes into being, one has to respond to one's right to be.' Being in the world displaces others and usurps their space. Levinas is concerned with the effect his existence will have on others. This concern for the other originates as anterior to self-consciousness in an 'unrepresentable past.' He wants to establish an ethics which acknowledges our indefinable and yet unavoidable responsibility for the other. To do so he reaches for a metaphysical description. We are, he claims, responsible for our neighbour, ' ... for the other man, for the stranger or sojourner, to which nothing in the rigorously ontological order binds me – nothing in the order of the thing, of the something, of number or causality.'[16] Levinas insists on the sanctity of the other and on my responsibility for him or her. The ethical is the condition of our existence whatever our individual worth or worthlessness. 'It is in the laying down by the ego of its sovereignty ... that we find ethics and also probably the very spirituality of the soul, but most certainly the question of the meaning of being, that is, its appeal for justification'.[17] In his criticism of the limitations of self-consciousness, Levinas is defending 'mere life'.

The first stranger I must face, and see in him incontrovertible irreducibility, is my father. It is to him I must justify my existence. I am face to face with him. As I look into his eyes, I recognise the void where once my mother existed. For this moment we are alone. How will I behave before him? Abject, frightened, appeasing, brusque? A brittle reaction on my part which leads to my fleeing? Do I raise myself upright in defiance? Or perhaps I might experience pleasure in his presence, a sense of life's possibilities? The question of philosophy, says Levinas, is: 'Not "Why being rather than nothing?" but how being justifies itself'. It is the question sons are posed by the father's existence and it is the society's crisis that we cannot answer, but must remain caught in the life and death of his grip.

In consequence we have no male gender ethics or politics, only politics by men. There is a silence surrounded by the clamour of numerous crises: the collapse of paternal authority, the rise of absent fathers, broken families and delinquent sons; school failure; criminality, sexual immorality, suicide and violence. The apocalyptic vision of a fatherless society: 'Societies can decay from within ... Apparently civilised societies have suddenly experienced internecine and international wars, civil strife, totalitarian tyranny and genocidal massacres'.[18]

Those who attempt to defend men's traditional role of head of household, or seek to promote men's 'masculinity', call for the restoration of the father's authority over women and children. Those who oppose it have few ideas of what might take its place. There is no positive discourse of being a man. We are only what the other is not. There is no representation, and few images exist, of emotionally resilient, empathetic men rather than those who are emotionally weak and domineering. We do not know where we should be going and if we did, we could describe neither path nor destination.

There is nothing more in life than 'me, me, me.' Which is not simply me alone and unyielding to the other, but me and you and the feeling which is between us. What is between father and son if not the confrontation between love and violence, between ethics and necessity, between language and silence? We have two possible directions: the love, ethics and language we might accord to simple, lived life and another way of being, or a continuation of the violence, necessity and silence associated with its exclusion. It is in silence that this ethics of the male self begins. The word 'silence' speaks of its own end. A word which is not a word, our voice an object which is not an object. The sound of our voice connects us to the world and yet has no physical presence. It is disembodied and yet it is an expression of our bodies; it finds the dark corners of our lives and brings them into sound as the solid, corporeal noises of pleasure, grief, pain, laughter. It is necessary to follow the example of Levinas. Not just to defend 'mere life' , but to embrace it and to experience the loss of self which accompanies the sinking into the 'mere life' of feelings and the body. In the beginning is the self, and the self was made in the form of the father and, in its making, it denied the body of the mother that had given it life, and also the son's own body which is the signifier of his lack. In its ending is its search for renewal. Not in the resurrection of the father, but in the difference which separates him from me which is the mother in us both. In this ethics of my self I speak not in self effacement, nor in a lingering, nostalgic reverence for that point of departure my mother. Nor do I speak in rejection of the father. I face the two of them in one. You and me which is the three of us.

NOTES

1. S. Freud (1925), 'Some Psychical Consequences of the Anatomical Distinction Between the Sexes', *Pelican Freud Library* Vol. 7, p341.
2. S. Freud (1933 [32]), 'Femininity', *PFL* Vol. 2, p168.
3. *Ibid*.
4. S. Freud (1927), 'The Future of an Illusion', PFL Vol. 12, p212.
5. Walter Benjamin, 'Critique of Violence' in *One Way Street and Other Writing*, Verso, 1985.
6. Hannah Arendt, *The Human Condition*, University of Chicago Press, 1998, p31.
7. For a fascinating and thought-provoking analysis of the relationship between 'mere life' and political power read Giorgio Agamben, *Homo Sacer: Sovereign Power and Bare Life*, Stanford University Press, 1998, Daniel Heller-Roazen (trans).
8. Michel Foucault, *The History of Sexuality: An Introduction*, Penguin, 1985, p138.
9. Norbert Elias, 'The Changing Balance of Power between the Sexes – A Process-Sociological Study: The Example of the Ancient Roman State', in *Theory Culture and Society* Vol. 4, 1987, pp287-316.
10. Seneca 'Letter VI' in *Letters from a Stoic*, Penguin Classics, 1969, p39.
11. Michel Foucault, *The History of Sexuality: The Care of the Self*, Vol. 3, Allen Lane Penguin, 1988, p95.
12. Mary Wollstonecraft, 'Letter 10', A Short Residence in Sweden, in *Mary Wollstonecraft and William Godwin*, Penguin Classics, 1987.

13. *Ibid.*
14. See Mike Gane, *Harmless Lovers: Gender, Theory and Personal Relationships*, Routledge, 1993, p111.
15. Giorgio Agamben, *op. cit.,* p187.
16. Emmanuel Levinas, 'Ethics as First Philosophy' in *The Levinas Reader,* Seán Hand (ed), Blackwell 1996, p84.
17. *Ibid.*, p85.
18. Norman Dennis, George Erdos, *Families Without Fatherhood*, Institute of Economic Affairs 1993, p108.

The Chip and I

KEVIN WARWICK

THE SCENE

Many years ago I read, and was enthralled by, Michael Crichton's book *The Terminal* Man.[1] Roughly speaking the plot goes like this: crazy mass murderer is experimented on by doctors carrying out pioneering neurosurgery; electrodes are inserted into the mass murderer's brain and stimulated to see what reactions occur, the idea being to counter-act his murderous feelings with overpoweringly pleasant ones by stimulating appropriate areas of his brain. The fact that things went horribly wrong (the man began to have more and more murderous feelings, in order to get high on pleasure) is neither here nor there. In any case, the book had a distinct aura of Frankenstein about it.

Since that time we have witnessed numerous fictional attempts to link humans up with technology, thereby achieving either a super-powerful status for the human involved or at least a new sense of being. Indeed, television shows such as *Star Trek* and *The X-Files* have found it a useful device for a number of episodes. But this is all fiction. Where do things stand on the realistic, scientific front and what lies ahead? In particular, what does it actually mean to link humans up closely with technology? Does it change in any way what it means to be human?

WEARABLES

One line of research creates a closer link between person and technology by bringing them together in a pseudo-permanent way. The whole field of 'wearable computing' has been seen as a way of making humans smarter.[2] The approach is simple: clothes, shoes, jewellery or wrist-watches, all everyday items, are made to take on an extra role, namely that of a computer. Indeed a number of commercially available mobile phones and watches already exhibit such a function. It is claimed that wearables can improve memory, extend the senses and even help a person to stay calm.[3] Realistically, it is a way of attaching computing more permanently to an individual, so that it is readily, even constantly available.

It is, however, difficult to draw the line between portable computers and wearables, particularly where mobile phones and watches are concerned. It is also difficult to determine how serious the program is when earrings can be programmed to flash red lights in sequence or a brooch to play 'Colonel Bogie' when a similar brooch is nearby. Such intelligent ornaments have indeed been programmed to respond, when they encounter similar ornaments worn by a person of the opposite sex, when that person gives out certain indicators. Hence the tune will only play, or lights will only light, if someone exactly matching the desired criteria passes by. It is not clear what the appropriate response might be to a brooch playing 'The Stripper' when it senses another brooch emitting appropriate signals, if that brooch is worn by your Mother, an ex-spouse or someone whom you cannot stand the sight of.

Claims for the potential of wearables are manifold. Whilst with ordinary computers or portables a conscious effort must be made in order to use them, wearables can, it is claimed, be used instantly.[4] I remain to be convinced of this. Most potential wearable computer designs, for example earrings or even a wristwatch, require not only a conscious effort to be fully used, the user may also need to adopt extra-ordinary positions.

However, it does seem sensible to look into enhancing a number of everyday items with extra computing power. Medical monitoring information in a watch, a belt containing a computer or spectacles with an in-built display that only the user can see are all reasonable possibilities.

It has been noted that the way in which we humans feel about ourselves is dependent in part upon the clothes we wear and the way they look, and in this respect wearable computers in the form of 'intelligent' clothing will make us think differently about ourselves. This may well be true. However, it must be remembered that the computing 'intelligence' is external: it will not change our basic capabilities, merely our self-perception. It is also worth pointing out that changes in self-perception might be negative, just as they might be positive. If you do not have earrings bearing the latest micro-processor, will you feel behind the times and off the pace? Conversely, if your glasses have extra functions will you strut uncontrollably in front of those with last year's specs?

Some wearables, though, do appear to offer distinct advantages, for example a finger ring equipped with bar code reader and mini-display. Hence product information, consumer reviews and competitive pricing details can all be called upon merely by pointing the ring at a potential purchase.

Another device, useful to the military, contains a Global Positioning System linked to satellite communications, allowing the user to know their whereabouts, and at all times, on a global basis. To those in combat, particularly in remote locations, this is obviously of considerable benefit as a low cost navigation and communications system. With potential add-ons of a microphone system and mini-digital camera, low level military technology could take on a different form. However, as with other wearables, an immediate limiting factor is the power requirement. It is no use having an extremely sophisticated and computationally powerful device that fits snuggly into a wristwatch if it requires 40 Kg of battery power to be tugged along on a trolley.

Although wearables are generally intended to be with the user at all times, to be an integral part of their everyday life, it is not always so. In 'Wearable Intelligence' examples are given of dancing shoes which convert dance steps into music, social wearables such as necklaces which flash to communicate the wearer's name, and a video camera fixed to a baseball cap which, it is claimed, enables wearers to call themselves a 'cyborg'

However, apart from having a transitionary and potential novelty input, it is unlikely that wearable computers will have a significant impact on human existence. Importantly, because the computing power is outside the human body, albeit as close as can be achieved in the circumstances, it is still a separate entity. Human/machine interface problems, which by their nature are slow and problematic, still exist. Translating signals from human brain to machine brain, and back again, is a laborious process, involving the transfer in both directions of signals from electrical to mechanical energy and back again. This takes time, results in a loss of energy and is error-ridden. In order truly to progress fully, to question and change the whole basis for human existence, it is necessary to breach that human/machine interface. But where might this take us?

BUGS AND STUFF

Experimentation on insects and other non-human creatures is relevant as the results can give us an idea of what might happen if a similar experiment is attempted with humans. After all, non-human creatures have senses, a nervous system and a brain, even if that brain contains far fewer cells than a typical human. A bee, for example has 10,000 brain cells whereas a human has 100 billion! The principle is that if experiments are successful with non-humans, the same experiment, scaled up, will produce similar results with people.

In January 1997 a micro-processor was connected directly into the brain of a cockroach,[5] in effect replacing some of the cockroach's own motor neurons (the brain cells concerned with movement) with artificial, electronic neurons. The artificial neurons were then used to cause the cockroach to move. So, despite what the cockroach might decide, its body moved under electronic control.

In the same vein, in March 1998, the antennae from a male silk moth were connected to a little wheeled robot. When a female silk moth, gave off her attractive pheromone signal, it was received by the male antennae, resulting in the wheeled robot hurtling towards the female.

More recently, in the spring of 1999, there were reports that rats had been party to a number of successful experiments. In one, they had greatly helped in a 'terminal rat' link-up, in which a rat's movement was directed remotely by stimulating its motor neurones. Although the rat walked under its own control, its direction of travel was decided remotely.

In a second experiment, the initial arrangement was that the rats learned to pull a lever and obtain a tot of water as a reward. However, electrodes connected into the rats' brains emitted strong signals when the rats even thought about pulling the lever, before they actually did anything physically. The electrical connections were then altered so that these 'thought signals' caused the tot of water to be released. The rats quickly caught on that they did not actually need to pull the lever to get their water treat: thinking about it was enough. It is interesting to note that the same type of signals occur in human brains, just before we do *anything* physically.

SUPER HUMANS

While the experiment described above might help us to clarify the non-human/machine interface, what about the human/machine one? Machines and technology are all around us, in the Western world at least. It is inconceivable for a day to go by without coming into contact with technology in some form, but by and large technology and humans exist as separate, complementary entities. Most people's closest link with technology consists of wearing an object, such as a watch, along the lines of the wearable computers discussed earlier.

However in order to help people with physical disabilities the human body has been breached, and we now see cochlea implants to assist hearing, replacement hips and heart pacemakers. In each case technology has been readily accepted into the body because the alternative is unacceptable, a life of misery or no life at all. Essentially the recipient has no choice!

But the possibility also exists of enhancing the capabilities of all humans by linking them more closely with technology.[6] In fact most machines exist because they do things that humans cannot do alone, or perhaps because they do things in a much better way or using much more power than a human could. Machine intelligence, in terms of memory and mathematical logic, clearly out-performs humans'.[7] So why can we not consider the possibility of individuals doing things they could not otherwise achieve, by linking up directly with technology?

IMPLANT EXPERIMENT

In the fall of 1998 I had a silicon chip transponder surgically implanted into my left arm. As I entered the Cybernetics Department at the University of Reading, a radio signal across the doorway energised the transponder, causing it to issue a unique identifying signal. This signal was received by the building's computer network, allowing the central computer to recognise me individually. As a result, as I entered I was greeted with 'Hello Professor Warwick', the foyer light switched on and my own web page appeared on the foyer computer monitor. As I approached my laboratory on the other side of the building, the network tracked me and opened the door 'automatically' for me. A map of the building, updated by the computer, showed my whereabouts at all times. Whilst the interaction with the building was interesting, the potential power of such an arrangement is amazing.

Half of my implant was essentially a coil of wire, with which the radio signal in various doorways around the building reacted. The signal caused an electric current to flow in the coil, an effect originally spotted by Michael Faraday 200 years earlier. In this way the transponder does not require its own power supply as power is injected in via the radio signal. This means that the implant was relatively light and, at 23 mm long, not overly large.

The current produced in the coil was used to drive a number of silicon chips which transmitted an identifying code signal. For a joke, the researchers who worked on the project had decided to program the chips to transmit the number 666 which, according to the biblical description , gave me the 'Mark of the Beast'![8] For a reason we did not have the time to investigate, the system would not operate with this number and I became 161. Nevertheless, the experiment was a success in that we were able to transmit signals into and out of the human body, to and from a computer. In fact the transponder operated more efficiently and reliably when implanted than it had when it was external to my body.

The experiment was not without its dangers. The transponder was encapsulated in a glass tube and was not designed for the purpose of implanting in a human. There was, therefore, the distinct possibility that it might break and spill its contents, coil, chips and broken glass on a trip of adventure in my arm. The transponder was held in place with stitches, which, if they had not held firmly, could have resulted in it migrating from its original position, resulting in a lengthy search for its eventual whereabouts. The final possibility was worst of all. We had to sterilise the transponder before it was implanted and, like school kids, we attempted this by boiling our first transponder. It promptly exploded, with a loud bang, shattering and spreading its contents onto walls and ceiling. The transponder we actually used was merely heated in an oven to 80 degrees centigrade, not perhaps perfect, but it would have to do. There was always the possibility, that due to pressure and temperature, the implant might explode ... but it did not and was surgically removed several days later.

One reason for carrying out the experiment was to look at the 'Big Brother' type issues raised in George Orwell's *1984*.[9] My conclusion turned out to be the reverse of what I had expected. Perhaps because positive things happened, I felt positive about the implant, despite possible dangers described. It did things *for* me, not *against* me. I had no worries about the computer knowing where I was at all times. If it had done negative things such as closing doors and switching off lights, my feelings might have been different. Perhaps I felt the way people do about carrying credit cards. The card is convenient, flexible and easy to use, yet it gives a computer an accurate picture of an individual's buying habits. Do people worry about that? For the most part I think not.

THE FUTURE

The next step on this experimental path is to change the signals transmitted to and from human body and computer. An obvious place to connect human nervous system is in roughly the same position as my original implant, the upper arm, to transmit and receive signals from this point. Movement signals are readily available in this way. When we move our fingers or arm, electronic control signals are being transmitted from the brain and along the nervous system to extend and contract muscles. Such a connection enables the witnessing of emotional signals and these can be transmitted via an implant to a computer. When we feel angry, scared, excited or amorous, distinct signals appear on our nervous system, causing us to feel tense or to start to sweat.

Since the time of my original experiment, a group of researchers at Emory University in Atlanta implanted a similar transmitting device into the brain of a stroke victim, thereby linking up human motor neurones with silicon. The patient learned to move a cursor around on a computer screen, merely by thinking about it, in the same way as the rats had learned to obtain water. No actual physical movement was necessary. A key element is that it is not necessary for the computer to comprehend the signals it receives, but rather for the signal transmitted to be acted upon in an appropriate way. Related project work at the University of Maine has involved transmitting signals into a patient in order to control some movements and physical activity: another obvious link to the rat experiments.

We are now coming to terms with the fact that signals in the human brain and on the human nervous system can be transmitted to and from a computer. Signals in the computer and those on the nervous system are both electronic, or to be more precise electro-chemical in the latter case. Hence, by means of a radio frequency implant, a much closer link can exist between a human and technology. Before long it should be possible for humans to operate computers without the need for mechanical inputs such as keyboard or mouse, merely by thought signals alone.

Linking computer to the human brain realistically adds a sixth sense. This may mean that the human brain cannot cope with the resulting information overload, although it does offer the possibility of feeding in all sorts of otherwise unobtainable sensory input. Hence, to our present limited present set of senses we should be able to add, for example, the senses of radar, ultraviolet, ultrasonic and infrared, to name but a few. Just think of it: having a sense with which you can accurately detect heat over a very long distance (infrared). Such information could be fed directly onto a human nervous system and thereby into the brain.

In addition, by directly linking machine intelligence to a human brain, a whole new way of thinking could arise. Although it gets us by, our human brain has evolved to think in only 3, 2 or sometimes even 1-dimensions. Machines, however, can perceive and comprehend in many dimensions, where 'many' is a big number. How might we perceive a 100-dimensional world? It is difficult, perhaps impossible, for most people to understand!

TELEPHONES ARE OLD HAT

Linking the human nervous system, via an implant, to a computer, opens up other avenues. In addition to the possibility of enhancing brain capabilities – for example, why bother learning multiplication when you can get the answer merely by thinking about it or why bother watching a film when you can have the memory of it directly – we can also consider a number of people having similar implants. This would allow movement signals, emotions and ultimately thoughts, to be transmitted by means of satellite and the Internet from one person's nervous system to another, with signals flowing in the reverse direction in return. This opens up the new technology of global thought to thought communication between humans.[10]

Clearly a whole host of problems and protocols would need to be sorted out. How would you decipher signals transmitted from my nervous system onto yours? If I was angry would you feel angry too? If I thought of the colour red, would you think of red as well? We would need to learn how to transmit signals comprehensible to others to understand. It may well be possible for one person to 'read the mind' of another, to know what they want to do before they do it. But in reality this is only a small step on from the rats with their tot of water.

In the future, we will not need telephones: they will be old technology. It is also difficult to see the need for language, as we now know it, and even speech. It will be the ideas and symbols that are transmitted, not, as at present, sound signals formed by converting ideas into symbols that a number of other people understand.

This whole area of study is only just in its infancy, and is already extremely exciting. It is an area where actual implementation is the order of the day; the back-up of theory is not yet necessary and certainly it is not driving things along. Human/machine interface will have a serious impact on the field of philosophy, as it clearly questions what it means to be an individual human, if indeed such an entity will exist in the future.

Linking humans with technology, particularly when this involves the human nervous system, makes us question the way we think about ourselves. After only a few days into my own implant experiment I treated the implant as an integral part of me. Not only had my body physically accepted it, but mentally it had been accepted as well. Whilst this is, apparently, a phenomenon shared with cochlea and pacemaker implant patients, it is not, I suspect, something that is shared by those who link with technology only outside their bodies. While someone may feel very close to their car, they are not one with it!

Perhaps due to the things that happened automatically I developed an immediate affinity with the computer to which 'I' was inextricably linked. The feeling was a strong one and not one that I had expected. For my wife it was perhaps the worst part of the experiment as she felt that something had come between us!

As we look to a future in which the human nervous system will be connected, by radio, to a computer, such feelings will become much stronger. Individual identity will become more difficult to define and morals and ethics will take on a completely different frame of reference. If your senses are partly biological (original) and partly technical (new), then who are you? If your brain is partly biological (original) and partly silicon (new), then what does it mean to be by yourself? To paraphrase Descartes, 'We think, therefore, we are'. 'I' becomes 'we'!

Of even more concern is the possibility that, apart from special cases, each human (node) will be connected to a machine network, to which are connected many computers, many sensory inputs and many other humans. So 'we' does not mean one individual connected directly to one computer, but rather many individuals connected as nodes on the network. So in truth there will be an 'I' in the future, but the 'I' will be the network itself.

NOTES

1. M. Crichton. *The Terminal Man*, Vintage, 1994.
2. S. Mann, 'Wearable Computing: A First Step Toward Personal Imaging', *Computer*, 1997, Vol. 30, No. 2, pp25-32; A.P. Pentland, 'Wearable Intelligence', *Scientific American*, 1998, Vol. 9, No. 4, pp90-95.
3. A. Pentland, 1998, *op. cit.*
4. *Ibid.*
5. *Guinness Book of Records*, Guinness Publishing, 1999, p180.
6. Peter Cochrane, *Tips for Time Travellers*, McGraw-Hill, 1999.
7. Kevin Warwick, *In the Mind of the Machine*, Arrow, 1998.
8. *Holy Bible*, Book of Revelation, Chapter 13, verses 11-18.
9. George Orwell, *1984*, Penguin, 1948.
10. Jason Forsythe, 'Merging Mind and Machine', *Newsweek International*, March 1999, pp41-43; Kevin Warwick, *Cybernetics Organisms – Our Future*, Proc. IEEE, Special Guest Author, 1999, Vol. 87, No. 2, pp387-389,

Notes on Contributors

Ashok Bery is a Senior Lecturer in English at the University of North London. He has co-edited a collection of essays entitled *Comparing Postcolonial Literatures: Dislocations* (Macmillan, 2000), and has published articles on Indian literature in English.

Carolyn Burdett is Principal Lecturer in English at the School of Arts and Humanities, University of North London. Her book, *Olive Schreiner and the Progress of Feminism: Evolution, Gender, Empire* is published by Palgrave.

Paul Cilliers teaches Philosophy at the University of Stellenbosch, South Africa. His research is focused on complexity and he is the author of *Complexity and Postmodernism* (Routledge 1998). He also has a degree in Electronic Engineering.

Colin Counsell is Senior Lecturer in English Literature and Theatre at the University of North London. He is the author of *Signs of Performance*, an analysis of modernist performance practices, and has written extensively on early modern theatre.

Alan Finlayson is a Lecturer in the Department of Political Theory and Government, University of Wales, Swansea. He is the author of numerous articles and chapters on theories of nationalism and northern Irish and British politics. He is currently editing *Contemporary Political Philosophy: A Reader and Guide* for Edinburgh University Press.

Erica Fudge lectures in the School of Humanities and Cultural Studies at Middlesex University. She is the author of *Perceiving Animals: Humans and Beasts in Early Modern England* (Macmillan, 2000), and co-editor with Ruth Gilbert and Susan Wiseman of *At the Borders of the Human: Beasts, Bodies and Natural Philosophy in the Early Modern Period* (Macmillan, 1999).

Sebastian Kraemer is a Consultant Child and Family Psychiatrist at the Tavistock Clinic and at the Whittington Hospital, London. Besides clinical and training work in the NHS he has published papers and chapters on fatherhood and is the co-editor of *The Politics of Attachment: Towards a Secure Society* (Free Association Books, 1996).

Paul McSorley is a Senior Lecturer in English at the University of North London. His research and teaching interests are early modern poetry and drama, and critical theory.

Peter Middleton is a Senior Lecturer in English at the University of Southampton. He is the author, with Tim Woods, of *Literatures of Memory* (Manchester University Press, 2000), and *The Inward Gaze: Masculinity and Subjectivity in Modern Culture* (Routledge, 1992).

Stuart Murray is Senior Lecturer in Commonwealth and Postcolonial Literatures in the School of English at the University of Leeds. He is the author of *Never a Soul at Home: New Zealand Literary Nationalism and the 1930s* (University Press, Wellington, Victoria 1998) and the editor of *Not On Any Map: Essays on Postcoloniality and Cultural Nationalism* (EUP, Exeter 1997).

James Park is Director of Antidote: Campaign for Emotional Literacy, which he cofounded with psychotherapist and writer Susie Orbach. His books include *Sons, Mothers and Other Lovers*, *Shrinks: The Analysts Analyzed* and *Learning to Dream: The New British Cinema*. He is also a psychotherapist-in-training at the Centre for Attachment-based Psychoanalytic Psychotherapy.

Mary Peace is Lecturer in eighteenth-century literature at Sheffield Hallam University. She is currently completing a book on the figure of the prostitute in eighteenth century sentimental discourse.

Stephen Reicher is a Reader in Psychology at the University of St Andrews. He has published widely on the relationship between social identity and collective action.

Jonathan Rutherford is Reader in Cultural Studies at Middlesex University. He has edited and written a number of books including *Forever England: Reflections on Race, Masculinity and Empire* (1997), *Identity Community Culture Difference* (1998), *I Am No Longer*

Myself Without You: An Anatomy of Love (2000), *Art of Life: Writings on Living, Love and Death* (2000).

Jenny Bourne Taylor is a Reader in English at the University of Sussex. Recent publications include (with Sally Shuttleworth), *Embodied Selves: An Anthology of Psychological Texts 1830-1890*. She is currently working on a study of 'illegitimacy' and forms of cultural memory in nineteenth century England.

Tanya de Villiers is a postgraduate student in philosophy working on complexity and subjectivity.

Kevin Warwick is Professor of Cybernetics at the University of Reading. He lectures widely in Great Britain and overseas on artificial intelligence, robotics and cyborgs. He is presently self-experimenting with implants connected to the nervous system. He is presenter of the year 2000 Royal Institution Christmas Lectures.